for Lionel + Eva
with best wishes
Eileen

Law, Land, & Family

Studies in Legal History

Published by The University of North Carolina Press in

association with the American Society for Legal History

Eileen Spring

 Law, Land, & Family

Aristocratic Inheritance in England, 1300 to 1800

The University of North Carolina Press

Chapel Hill & London

The paper in this book meets the
guidelines for permanence and durability
of the Committee on Production
Guidelines for Book Longevity of the
Council on Library Resources.

The publication of this work was made
possible in part through a grant from the
Division of Research Programs of the
National Endowment for the Humanities,
an independent federal agency whose
mission is to award grants to support
education, scholarship, media
programming, libraries, and museums, in
order to bring the results of cultural
activities to a broad, general public.

Library of Congress
Cataloging-in-Publication Data
Spring, Eileen.

Law, land, and family : aristocratic
inheritance in England, 1300 to 1800 / by
Eileen Spring.

p.   cm. — (Studies in legal history)

Includes bibliographical references and
index.

ISBN 0-8078-2110-1 (cloth : alk. paper)

1. Inheritance and succession—Great
Britain—History.   I. Title.   II. Series.
KD1500.S68   1994
346.7305'2—dc20
[347.30652]   93-590
CIP

An earlier version of chapter 1 appeared
in the *Law and History Review* 8 (Fall
1990): 273–96. Reprinted by permission
of the Board of Trustees of the University
of Illinois Press.

97 96 95 94 93 5 4 3 2 1

To the memory of my mother, Mary Jeffries

Contents

Acknowledgments

As I hope in this work to give a new shape to a subject that has been much discussed, I necessarily take a critical stance towards much that my predecessors have written. But in turn, I could not have written without them. If in this work I succeed, then, in putting things together in a different way, it is only because of my predecessors' original thinking and investigations. My fundamental acknowledgment is accordingly to all those who have written before me on this subject, even though I must disagree with their conclusion.

Of other acknowledgments I have few, but they are to individuals whose help has been great. Thomas A. Green, editor of the series in which this book is published, has not only been a kindly and efficient editor, but his perceptive criticism has been invaluable. Anonymous readers of my manuscript have pointed to places where my ideas needed to be filled out or to be more carefully expressed, and I am grateful to them. I also wish to thank Paul M. Romney, who read the manuscript with great care, offering many detailed criticisms that have undoubtedly improved it. Finally, were it not for my husband, David Spring, I should never have produced this book. He years ago put me onto the subject of inheritance among landowners in the nineteenth century. As I ventured backward into earlier centuries, he has at every stage helped in the formation of my ideas. He has even done research for me when he has been in England and I have been in America. Above all, he has ever encouraged an amateur and a female who had developed an interest in a technical legal subject to believe she could have something to say.

Law, Land, & Family

Introduction

This small book has a large aim. With some temerity, I confess it aims to recast the story of inheritance among the English gentry and aristocracy and, in the process, to suggest that a major motive force in the development of real property law has been neglected.

Obviously, a warrant needs to be given for what must seem so reckless an aim. Warrant lies in what can only be called the confusion that surrounds the subject. It is not that there are differences of opinion on the subject. Differences of opinion exist on many historical subjects, with authorities arguing upon one ground or another for one opinion rather than another. Here the problem runs deeper. It is that basic contradictions inhere in the work of the authorities themselves.

The trouble is first noticeable about the strict settlement. In 1950, in a famous article, Sir John Habakkuk argued that portions for younger children, especially for daughters, rose with the development of the strict settlement. At the same time, however, he recognized that the strict settlement was an invention for the better preservation of landed estates.[1] The question would seem to arise how an invention that better preserved landed estates could at the same time have better provided for younger children, when younger children are natural obstacles in the way of preserving estates.

Another authority, Lawrence Stone, has made the strict settlement the legal ground for his theory that in the eighteenth century the family became more loving and egalitarian.[2] Yet he has also declared that the effect

---

1. H. J. Habakkuk, "Marriage Settlements in the Eighteenth Century," *Transactions of the Royal Historical Society*, 4th ser. 32 (1950): 15–30.

2. Lawrence Stone, *The Family, Sex and Marriage in England, 1500–1800* (New York, 1977), 242–43.

of settlement was to increase the amount of property settled on the eldest son, which is to treat settlement as having the aim of preserving estates, but must cast doubt upon its egalitarian thrust.[3] All the same, portions for daughters are said to have continued to rise throughout the eighteenth century.[4]

Lloyd Bonfield, who has studied the origin of the strict settlement, has also claimed that it increased younger children's portions. He has, however, given two diametrically opposite reasons why it did so. In one place, he has declared that it raised portions because in the previous legal situation—against which it must naturally be judged—landowners had been in full command of their property, entails having become barrable (that is, breakable at will). In another place, he has declared that settlement raised portions because in the previous legal situation landowners had not been in command of their property. On the contrary, they had previously been bound by unbarrable entails.[5]

Despite the incoherence of these various arguments, the belief has become fixed—it is an orthodoxy—that the strict settlement raised daughters' portions and that settlement is to be associated with the development of equality in the family.

Confusion goes deeper, however, than the eighteenth century and the strict settlement. It surrounds the medieval entail. A notable medieval historian, K. B. McFarlane, has argued that the entail was a threat to the integrity of landed estates. He has also argued that the entail made for the preservation of landed estates.[6] Confusion also exists around the other medieval legal instrument, the use. The historian who has written the major work on the subject, J. M. W. Bean, finds that uses were developed as a means of providing for younger children in a legal system that was based on primogeniture. Wondering in his conclusion whether uses thus posed a danger to the practice of primogeniture, he declares they would not really have done so because landowners had always been able to provide for their younger children through entails.[7]

---

3. Lawrence Stone, *The Crisis of Aristocracy, 1558–1614* (Oxford, 1965), 181. See also Stone, *Family, Sex and Marriage*, 377–78.

4. Stone, *Family, Sex and Marriage*, 380–81.

5. Lloyd Bonfield, "Marriage, Property and the 'Affective Family,'" *Law and History Review* 1 (1983): 297–312; Lloyd Bonfield, "Affective Families, Open Elites and Strict Family Settlements in Early Modern England," *Economic History Review*, 2d ser. 39 (1986): 349.

6. K. B. McFarlane, *The Nobility of Later Medieval England* (Oxford, 1973), 64, 270.

7. J. M. W. Bean, *The Decline of English Feudalism, 1250–1540* (Manchester, 1968), 304.

The bewildered reader who turns to doctrinal histories, to those awesome compendiums of the history of real property law, in hope of finding some way out of this confusion, will not find it. Doctrinal histories virtually ignore the family in laying out the development of real property law. At best, family concerns are of fleeting and peripheral interest, and when they are touched on, confusion of the kind already noted is not quite absent. For much the greater part, doctrinal histories treat real property law as a long struggle over perpetuities. Ever since Sir Edward Coke, at least, they have treated it in these terms. This treatment cannot reflect what landowners as fathers of families must have been primarily concerned with.

Since what exists on the subject of inheritance among the gentry and aristocracy is, then, a mass of confused ideas, perhaps even a nonexpert who has become aware of the fact may hope to recast the story in a more coherent shape. At any rate, that is my hope. Curiously the very existence of the confusion has hitherto largely escaped notice. Should my attempt at clarification end only in drawing attention to what is a large historiographic tangle, and thus in pointing out the necessity for major rethinking on a basic family and legal subject, it must serve a useful purpose.

My method is twofold. On the one hand, I look at the family logic inherent in various legal devices. "Law," said Maitland, "is where life and logic meet."[8] I take that suggestion seriously. I try to put myself in the shoes of landowners, considering what arrangements they could, or could not, make for their estates and families through the agency of various legal devices. The desires of gentry and aristocratic landowners were never simple, involving at all times both familial and class concerns. To what degree could the devices available from time to time have satisfied their desires? We know a great deal about the development of legal forms, but we have insufficiently looked at them with a practical eye. The process of barring entails, for example, has been carefully and admirably studied, but it has been little considered in what ways entails had fitted, and in what ways had not fitted, landowners' desires. The development of clauses of perpetuity has similarly been laid out in detail, but again it has been little considered how these clauses answered, or whether they could have answered, the complex needs of landowners.

I do not depend only on the logic of legal devices, however, but attempt to show what landowners actually did. I believe in hard facts. I do not mean, however, to attempt to authenticate my argument by filling innumerable pages with a mass of examples drawn from events in this, that, and the

---

8. Quoted in Alan Harding, *A Social History of English Law* (London, 1966), 234.

other family. This historiographic procedure often serves more to confuse than to enlighten readers, overwhelming them with detail, and it often as well effectively allows the historian to weigh the whole according to his or her personal judgment. I look rather for statistics, or quasi-statistical material.

Historical statistics, of course, are well known to have problems. There are questions as to sampling techniques, as to the fundamental design of projects, and even as to the reliability of the data. In this case, however, we have several sets of statistics. They are by different historians and based on different samples, and they all point in the same direction. Moreover, they point in that one direction decidedly. Together they are undoubtedly telling, provided they are put into the right framework. It is the right framework that has been lacking. I also bear in mind certain natural statistical facts, which modern demographers have laid out. These in effect outline the biological possibilities within which any scheme of inheritance had to work, and they thus provide a vital background for judging the meaning of other statistics. My aim, then, is to make a logically coherent argument and to show that it is supported by statistics.

The gentry and aristocracy whose inheritance practices are considered in this work were as a class the substantial landowners of England. When the word "landowner" appears in this work it means substantial landowner unless the particular context makes clear that a wider meaning is intended. It would be tedious to have to qualify the word each time it is used. This class of landowner is, of course, the one that historians have hitherto concentrated on, not only the historians already noted but the many others who have followed in their wake. It is the class that doctrinal historians have had implicitly in mind as they focused on the question of perpetuities. As a practical matter, historians could hardly have done otherwise, for gentry and aristocratic landowners are the only class about whom we have much knowledge. These are the landowners who have left elaborate estate accounts, collections of correspondence, boxes of title deeds, and copies of family trees. Yeomen and small landowners have on the contrary left few documentary traces of their existence. This work does not attempt to say anything about small landowners. But when the habits of large landowners are worked out, we may gain a good idea as to one way in which the two groups differed in their family principles.

The landowners who are the subject of this work were, of course, important as a social group. They owned the greater part of English land, and for long they owned the greater part of the nation's total wealth. They formed the ruling class, exercising great influence upon law and politics and upon social manners and ideas. Moreover, their history takes on an importance even beyond what is intrinsic to it. Gentry and aristocratic families have bulked overwhelmingly in the construction of general theories of family development. Getting their story straight is thus important in itself, and is perhaps even more important in its historiographical implications.

For statistical material I am often dependent upon data collected by scholars whose conclusions I cannot accept. Lawrence and Jeanne Stone in particular have produced a key set of statistics. Although I interpret their statistics very differently than they do themselves, all historians owe a great debt of gratitude to the Stones for their immense labor in compiling what is an amazing collection of data. An inevitable part of trying to cast things in a new light is that one must look critically at what one's predecessors have said. I wish especially to acknowledge my indebtedness to the Stones, and to several other scholars whose data I use while concluding they have put the data into a wrong framework. Though I must point to their misperceptions, I am deeply aware that I depend upon information they have provided.

The book falls into two sections, the first three and the last four chapters. Each of the first three looks at the history of a member of the family: the heiress, the widow, and the younger child. These chapters cover all the subordinate interests in the family. In doing so they cover as well the dominant interest. The male head of the family has no chapter devoted to him, because he is present throughout, being the adversarial interest in each case. Together, then, these chapters make up the history of inheritance among large landowners, and they trace in the process the interaction of landowners' ideas and changes in real property law. The last four chapters draw things together and consider implications. Chapter 4 summarizes and reflects upon the general pattern of inheritance that has become evident. Chapter 5 singles out for more technical consideration that much-discussed legal instrument, the strict settlement, and sets it into the history of real property law in a new way. Chapter 6 branches out into a wider discussion of family history. In the light of concepts that emerge from earlier chapters, it analyzes various theories of family development that historians have put forward. A final brief conclusion sums up overall.

While I hope this work will be of interest to historians of the law, that is, to pure legal historians, I am aware that it is written in terms they may often find inelegant. Among other things, my aim is to make a difficult subject clear to ordinary historians, the class in which I am myself. In recent years, as family history has become a major field of investigation, increasing numbers of historians have turned their attention to inheritance questions, but a text on English real property law is a most forbidding work. Simplifying the subject must offend against the lawyer's canon that words are to be used only with great precision. I hope I offend no more than my purpose warrants. For example, the word "landowner" itself is, strictly speaking, not applicable to the feudal lord, or to the subsequent *cestui que use*, or to the later tenant for life. The first held his land of the king; the second had, for practical reasons, nominally divested himself of land; the third was limited in his powers of ownership. I shall nevertheless speak of any or all of them as landowners, for that is surely the essence of the matter for any social historian. What is lost in legal precision it is hoped will be more than made up for by general intelligibility. Strictly speaking too, words of inheritance are not applicable to the widow. She did not come within the rules of succession to land (also known as rules of descent): she was not entitled to land in fee. She is not to be ignored on such technicality, however, in any discussion of property rights in the family. She had a large common law right at her husband's death, and thus I include her right among the rules of inheritance. Again that is the essence of the matter for any social historian.

While I aim to make the history of inheritance intelligible to readers unfamiliar with legal terminology, they should be forewarned that chapter 5, which deals with the origin and development of the strict settlement, is on a different level than other chapters. What the strict settlement meant in practice I will have already made clear in the chapters dealing with the various family interests. For many readers these chapters may tell them all they care to know about this complicated device. In chapter 5 I attempt to put settlement into the corpus of real property law in a rather different way than has previously been done, and this necessarily means entering upon doctrinal matters that almost defy simplification. My approach to settlement allows much traditional matter to be eliminated that has previously overcomplicated discussion, but it may nevertheless be that legal historians will be more aware of the simplification achieved than other historians can be. Those who find the going heavy in chapter 5 may proceed without loss of intelligibility to chapter 6.

As I completed this study I came to wonder what Alexis de Tocqueville might have thought about the story it tells. In a famous passage in *Democracy in America* he stressed the importance of the laws of inheritance to the understanding of society. "I am surprised," he wrote, "that ancient and modern jurists have not attributed to [them] a greater influence on human affairs. It is true that these laws belong to civil affairs; but they ought, nevertheless, to be placed at the head of all political institutions; for they exercise an incredible influence upon the social state of a people, while political laws show only what this state already is." After stressing the importance of laws of inheritance, however, de Tocqueville went on to stress their permanence. "Through their means," he continued, "man acquires a kind of preternatural power over the future lot of his fellow creatures. When the legislator has once regulated the law of inheritance, he may rest from his labor. The machine once put in motion will go on for ages, and advance, as if self-guided, towards a point indicated beforehand."[9]

Would de Tocqueville find that the history of inheritance in England confirmed his second statement, or contradicted it? In the year 1100 Henry I in his Coronation Charter established what we know—or until 1925 knew—as the rules of succession to land. Contrary to de Tocqueville's premise, however, law and practice came to differ. Indeed, the history of inheritance in England is largely the story of how the rules promulgated by Henry I were evaded. On the other hand, it may perhaps be said that in their evasion these rules were for centuries strengthened in their fundamental bias. Thus perhaps de Tocqueville was right in the end. As the twig was bent, so the tree grew.

9. Alexis de Tocqueville, *Democracy in America*, Borzoi ed. (New York, 1945), 47–48.

1 The Heiress-at-Law

And thou shall speak unto the children of Israel, saying,

If a man die, and have no son, then ye shall cause his

inheritance to pass unto his daughter.

—Numbers 27:8

Jane and Elizabeth attempted to explain to their mother

the nature of an entail. They had often attempted it

before, but it was a subject on which Mrs Bennet was

beyond the reach of reason, and she continued to rail

bitterly against the cruelty of settling an estate away

from a family of five daughters in favour of a man

whom nobody cared anything about.

—Jane Austen, Pride and Prejudice

By the common law rules of inheritance women in English landed society fell into two classes. Some were altogether excluded from inheriting; others were entitled to succeed to the family estate. The woman thus entitled, the heiress-at-law, is clearly a figure due historical attention, and there are good reasons to begin an account of inheritance with her.

Despite the importance of the right she possessed, the heiress-at-law has never been singled out for long-term consideration. Where she has been the focus of attention, discussion has always been chronologically limited, and her history has not been carried any distance through the course of legal changes that are relevant to it. Usually she has been discussed as but part of the family, and attention has been focused largely on eldest sons and their relations with younger children, with younger sons or with daughters who were not heiresses, as the case may be. Indeed the very words "heiress-at-law" have an unfamiliar ring.

When the heiress is concentrated on, however, when her story is separated from that of younger children and followed over the long run, broad new historical perspectives open. They open in family history. Since no property right was more significant than the right to succeed to a landed estate, no right was more symbolic of the status of women. What became of that right must mean revision in current theories of family development, particularly as those theories have been based heavily on the families that are discussed in this work. New perspectives open in the history of real property law itself. When the interests of the heiress are followed, a hitherto unrecognized pattern becomes apparent. The heiress emerges as the principal factor in the legal history of large landowners, and thus as a principal factor in the development of real property law. There are not only good, but imperative, reasons why an account of English inheritance should begin with the heiress-at-law.

1

The common law rules of inheritance by definition form the starting point for the story of the heiress. These rules were established shortly after the Norman Conquest, and they were not overridden by statute until 1925. The prime rule is well known. Land descended to the eldest son to the exclusion of his siblings. The next rule, much less well known, was that if there was no son, land descended to daughters. The common law thus gave a preference to males but a limited preference. It chose son over daughter, but daughter over collateral male. In common law, then, the daughter where there was no son was heir, not her uncle, nor her nephew, nor her male cousin. If there were several daughters, they were equally heirs. Originally only one among daughters had been heir, but about the middle of the twelfth century this rule had been changed, and daughters thereafter took equally.

What did these rules mean in practical terms? What proportion of inheritances would by common law go to women? To some degree the answer depends on the size of the family, that is, on whether population was rising, falling, or stationary. It depends less on the demographic situation, however, than may at first be thought, for as population fluctuates, it is mostly younger children whose numbers alter, but younger children do not affect the heirship calculation at issue significantly. That is to say, the chance of the heir's being male or female remains relatively stable. Two calculations by E. A. Wrigley are helpful in making this point clear. In a stationary population there is a 40 percent chance that a man will die leaving no son. When population rises at the rate experienced during the great growth of European population, that figure is not greatly changed, becoming 32 percent.[1] It is not to be concluded from these figures that 40 or 32 percent of inheritances would go to women. The figures do not immediately indicate what proportion of inheritances would go to women; they do indicate that the proportion would not vary greatly as population rose. In any case, for the preindustrial era, for the bulk of recorded time, the reasonable working hypothesis is that population was stationary, that is, stationary in size from one generation to the next. Mere reflection on a stationary population will soon suggest that a considerable proportion of inheritances must go to women by common law rules. Since each generation only reproduces itself, the average family must in the end be small. Many children may have been born, but many of them would have died in the lifetime of their father. Given families small in the end, some considerable number must consist of female children only.

Fortunately we are no longer dependent upon general reflection. Demographers have produced a formula that may be used to calculate more precisely what proportion of inheritances would in a stationary population go to women by common law rules. Wrigley has further calculated that in a stationary population 20 percent of men who married left no children, 20 percent left daughters only, and 60 percent left one or more sons.[2] If this

---

1. E. A. Wrigley, "Fertility Strategy for the Individual and the Group," in *Historical Studies in Changing Fertility*, ed. Charles Tilly (Princeton, 1978), 150–51.
    2. Ibid., 139.

calculation is put together with the common law, 20 percent of inheritances would go to women directly, going from fathers to daughters. More than 20 percent of inheritances would, however, go to women all told. The 20 percent of men who died without children did have heirs, and some of these were bound to be female. Under the further rules of common law, the heir of a man dying without children was first his brother, or if brother was deceased, any children he had left, male and female according to the rules already laid out. Failing the brother and his children, the sister or her children took. Should there be neither brother nor sister, the heir was sought further back in the male line, first among uncles and their children, and then among aunts and their children.[3] (Fathers and grandfathers were excluded as heirs. This is what is meant when it is said that land did not ascend: it did not ascend lineally. The exclusion of lineal ascendants persisted until 1834.) Precision is not possible as to the extent of collateral inheritance, but it is accurate enough to say that about one-quarter of collateral inheritances would go to women. Thus when indirect inheritance by collateral females is added to direct inheritance by daughters, 25 percent of all inheritances would at common law go to women.

What the rules meant in practical terms may be seen in another way—by considering what percentage of women would at common law be heiresses. More than one woman in a family would often be heir, for as already noted, daughters took equally, and this was but a specific example of the general rule that females of equal degree took equally. The percentage of women who would be heiresses, when coheiresses are considered, can readily be reached through Wrigley's formula. Let us assume for the sake of simplicity a population of 100 men leaving, by definition in a stationary society, 100 sons and 100 daughters. The formula indicates that the sons are not spread evenly, but that all are sons of 60 of the men. Thus it tells us that 60 of the sons are eldest son (meaning eldest or only sons) and that 40 are younger sons. The formula also indicates that there are 20 families with daughters only, where naturally there must be 20 eldest daughters (that is, eldest or only daughters). If 60 eldest sons have 40 younger brothers, then 20 eldest daughters have 13 younger sisters. Therefore 33 out of the total of 100 daughters would be directly heiresses, heirs to their fathers. Putting the conclusion in general terms, 33 percent of women in a stationary society would by common law be directly heiresses. Since a further number would be heiresses when collateral inheritance is considered, it is

3. For a full description of the rules of succession, see A. W. B. Simpson, *A History of the Land Law*, 2d ed. (Oxford, 1986), 56–63.

to be calculated that nearly 42 percent of women would be heiresses by common law.

Thus despite the well-known generalization that the common law sent estates to eldest sons, upon examination it is found that in the norm of a stationary population, the common law would send 25 percent of estates to women. Since by equal division 50 percent of estates would go to women, the common law may be looked on as cutting female inheritance in half, but only in half. Moreover, 42 percent of women would at common law be heiresses, though many of the heiresses would be required to divide estates. Fully 33 percent of women would be directly heirs of their fathers. The heiress was no rare bird by common law rules.

2

Such was the common law, but what were the hard facts? How often were women who were heiresses-at-law actually heiresses? Evidence on the down-to-earth aspect of female inheritance exists for two widely separated periods that clearly indicate the course of development.

In two important articles S. F. C. Milsom and J. C. Holt have discussed female inheritance in the twelfth and early thirteenth centuries.[4] While noting that in the period rules were not quite hard and fast, both portray women as succeeding according to common law rules. Where there was no son, the daughter was heir, her succession ensured because the principle of heritability of land had been established while the feudal system of land tenure gave no right of testamentary disposition. In other words, wills of land being then impossible, the common law heir succeeded to whatever land his—or her—father died possessed of. Neither Milsom nor Holt enters into quantitative analysis, although Holt does point out that a good number of baronies in short order went to females. In effect, both indicate that in early feudal times something like the figures laid out above for female inheritance were real, not merely theoretic.

Milsom and Holt discuss other aspects of female inheritance, and both

---

4. S. F. C. Milsom, "Inheritance by Women in the Twelfth and Early Thirteenth Centuries," in *On the Laws and Customs of England: Essays in Honor of Samuel Thorne,* ed. Morris S. Arnold, Thomas A. Green, Sally A. Scully, and Stephen D. White (Chapel Hill, 1981), 60–89; James Holt, "Feudal Society and the Family in Early Medieval England: The Heiress and the Alien," *Transactions of the Royal Historical Society,* 5th ser. 35 (1985): 1–28.

stress—it is the theme of their articles—that in early feudal times a woman's land went in fact to her husband for his life, and that the right of the heiress was less to enjoy property than to transmit it. Until she was widowed, an heiress did not enjoy the use of her property. This is an important aspect of the heiress's history. It indicates what is a long-term continuity in it. Until the end of the nineteenth century the use of a married woman's landed property in law went to her husband; and for centuries in practice it did too. Among substantial landowners it seems to have remained the norm to settle an heiress's land upon her husband for life. When that greatest of all eighteenth-century heiresses, the Percy heiress, inherited her vast estates, their use went to her husband, and he (who had been an unremarkable baronet) was duly created Duke of Northumberland. Important as this aspect of the heiress's history is, when all is said and done, it is of secondary importance. Of prime importance is the question of entitlement: Who was the heir? And this is where change took place. What Milsom and Holt make clear is that in early feudal times the daughter where there was no son was heir. She, or her husband through her, did take. She was the heir in the sense that her father's brother was not.

Thanks to extraordinary statistical work by Lawrence and Jeanne Stone we have figures for inheritance by women at a much later date. In *An Open Elite?*, a book that focuses on the relations between businessmen and landowners, the Stones have presented as thorough a study of landed inheritance as we are ever likely to have. They have analyzed the dispositions of more than two thousand owners of 362 country houses in three English counties—Hertfordshire, Northamptonshire, and Northumberland—from 1540 to 1880.[5] The study deals in country houses, but the houses are but the visible and countable hearts of landed estates. The coverage of Northumberland is less thorough than that of the other two counties. This discrepancy is a matter of significance for some historical questions, particularly for questions about the professional background of entrants into the elite, but it is not a matter of significance for discussions of inheritance. There is no reason to think that the heirship principles of English landowners differed from county to county. On matters of inheritance, the Stones' study well represents the body of English elite landowners, including both the aristocracy and the gentry.[6]

5. Lawrence Stone and Jeanne C. Fawtier Stone, *An Open Elite? England 1540–1880* (Oxford, 1984).

6. The Stones have considered what level of landowner their book deals with. They have compared the number of landowners in their samples for each county in the nine-

There is no need to consider the Stones' figures with statistical nicety, comparing them period by period, for the order of magnitude they display leaps from the page. In one table the Stones indicate what proportion of inheritances went from fathers to children, showing what proportion went to sons and what to daughters. If the average is taken over the period 1540 to 1780, 5 percent went to daughters.[7] In a second table the Stones indicate what proportion of inheritances went to women and what to men, thus considering inheritance by collateral females as well as by daughters. If a similar average is taken, 8 percent went to women.[8] These figures for female inheritance, 5 percent and 8 percent, are to be set alongside the comparable figures to be expected at common law, 20 and 25 percent respectively. Landowners had thus cut the rate of female succession dramatically, to less than one-third that by common law rules. Or to put the conclusion another way, since the common law itself when compared to equal division cut female inheritance in half, landowners had actually cut it to less than one-sixth. As for the number of women who were disherisoned, whereas 33 percent of women would have inherited from their fathers if the common law had prevailed, less than 10 percent actually did so; and whereas 42 percent would have inherited all told if the common law had prevailed, less than 13 percent actually did so.

While these figures tell a decided story of the reduction of female in-

---

teenth century with the number of landowners in the same counties as recorded in John Bateman's *The Great Landowners of Great Britain and Ireland,* which is a summary of a nineteenth-century official census. The numbers they use from Bateman—64, 67, 146—are from the fourth edition (London, 1883), appendix 6. As the definitions attached to the appendix show, these numbers are of landowners who owned estates of 1,000 acres or more. The Stones have concluded that their study generally dips lower in the social scale than Bateman's, as they have 107, 73, and 64 landowners in their samples (p. 62 and table 11.1). Since historians ordinarily define the gentry as those who owned estates of 1,000 to 3,000 acres, the Stones' study generally includes the gentry. In two counties, it includes the gentry completely. And those two counties provide the bulk of their evidence. The data from Northumberland, the statistically discrepant county, underrepresents gentry landowners; but Northumberland itself provides only 12 percent of the data before 1760. (Unfortunately the Stones have mistakenly declared that Bateman's numbers are of landowners owning estates of more than 3,000 acres.) As there is no Bateman for earlier centuries, this comparison is suggestive rather than conclusive about the level of landowner reached down to in earlier centuries. But note the discussion later in this chapter, which shows how few of the owners in the Stones' study at any time were peers.

7. Stone and Stone, *An Open Elite?,* table 3.8.

8. Ibid., table 4.2.

heritance, they do not tell quite so complete a story as it is possible to tell. How far, it may be asked, could inheritance by females be reduced? As John Knox bewailed, reviewing what he called the "monstrous regiment of women" who were heirs to Edward VI, sometimes God unaccountably leaves only women wherever one looks in the family tree. The question how far female inheritance could be reduced is not answerable in quite the form in which the question has been phrased, but an answer sufficient to the point is to be had if the rate at which patrilines die out is considered. When a patriline dies out a female has become at least unavoidable. The female thus unavoidable may succeed to the estate or she may not; but if she does not, the male who succeeds must be her son and must trace his inheritance through her. At the end of a patriline, then, inheritance need not go to a woman, but it must go either to or through a woman. From an analysis of the baronetcies created by James I, Peter Laslett has calculated that between roughly 1610 and 1760 almost one-eighth of patrilines died out at each succession.[9] That is to say, 12 percent of inheritances had by the dispensation of God or nature either to go to women or through women.

(Theoretically, it should be noted, a male heir could always have been found by searching far enough back in the family tree. We can all, as it were, be traced back to Adam. But this possibility is not of the real world. People require some sense of their connection with those they would make their heirs, and they only look within reasonably close branches of the family tree, earlier branches being beyond conscious memory.)

The Stones provide a figure that is to be compared with Laslett's, although they do not make the comparison. Their table showing what proportion of inheritances went to women also shows what proportion went either to or through women. Again taking the average, 13 percent of inheritances between 1540 and 1780 went either to or through women.[10] This is a rate little above what was biologically unavoidable. It is clear, then, not only that landowners had much reduced female inheritance, but also that they had reduced it almost as far as nature permitted.

The conclusion that female inheritance was greatly reduced differs from that reached by the Stones themselves. Because they have not considered what the common law meant numerically for female inheritance, or what amount of female inheritance was unavoidable, the Stones conclude that their figures show generosity to females. By adding together inheritance

9. Peter Laslett, *The World We Have Lost*, 3d ed. (London, 1983), 239.
10. Stone and Stone, *An Open Elite?*, table 4.2.

by women and inheritance through women they believe they have shown how "extraordinarily important" was the female role.[11] Rather, they have essentially shown the extraordinary decline of female succession.

At the outset of this chapter the point was made that population growth had limited effect upon the chance of the heir-at-law's being female, because the proportion of men who die leaving no son does not fall greatly between a stationary population and one growing at the rate appropriate to European history, falling from 40 to 32 percent as Wrigley has shown. It is worth considering the meaning of population growth a little further now that we have empirical evidence about actual female inheritance. Wrigley has calculated that 20 percent of men in a stationary population leave daughters only—half the 40 percent who leave no son. For a growing population he has not separated out men who leave daughters only from the total who leave no son. On the reasonable assumption that these men are again half the total, then 16 percent of men in a population growing at the rate appropriate for European history leave daughters only. This is to say that in a growing population 16 percent of inheritances rather than 20 percent as in a stationary population go at law to daughters from their fathers. The difference is hardly a major one. What we can now appreciate is that the percentage of inheritances that actually went from fathers to daughters (5 percent) was less than one-third of either of these figures. In other words, whether population is assumed to have been stationary or growing, the conclusion is the same: that female inheritance was reduced to less than one-third that to be expected at common law. Running a check on the Stones' figures for the period 1800 to 1880, when population was certainly growing, shows that 4 percent of inheritances then actually went from fathers to daughters.[12] In a nutshell, the fall in the rate of actual female inheritance was far too great to think that population movements had anything but marginal meaning.

The Stones' is not the only evidence to indicate the great decline of female inheritance. Two other studies also do so once the data they present are seen in relation to the common law, though again the authors fail to look at their data in this way. A study of the great landowners of East Yorkshire includes a table showing the blood relationship of each owner to his successor. If the table is scrutinized in terms of sex, it shows that out of the total of 127 successions between 1530 and 1919 only 7—about 5 percent—went to females.[13] The second study is an analysis of the terms

---

11. Ibid., 119–20.

12. Ibid., table 3.8.

13. Barbara English, *The Great Landowners of East Yorkshire* (London, 1990), 100.

of settlements themselves. All the strict settlements made before 1740 that have survived in two county record offices have been analyzed as to their heirship policy. (This collection of settlements would include some that were made by very small landowners, landowners beneath the gentry level.) As the author states his conclusion, interpreting it as an advance for women, nearly one-quarter of all the settlements in the collection allowed the succession of the daughter before the collateral male. The fact of note, of course, is that more than three-quarters (78 percent) of them rejected the daughter in favor of the collateral male.[14]

3

The question discussed so far has been whether the heiress-at-law succeeded to the estate. This is naturally not the only question that arises about her fortunes. As means were developed by which the collateral male came to dislodge her from the succession, a question arises about the division of property between heiress and collateral male. Fathers do not utterly disinherit their daughters in favor of their nephews. Some provision was always made by landowners for the lesser members of the family, for younger children and for the postponed heiress, the heiress-at-law who was not to succeed to the core of the estate. Nor was paternal affection the only factor that guaranteed the heiress a share of the property. The husbands of heiresses were interested in guaranteeing substance to their wives' rights by common law. The postponed heiress then took some part of the estate or some charge upon it. Thus the provision for the postponed heiress needs discussion.

The strict settlement is of paramount importance in this aspect of the heiress's history. Before the era of settlement, provision for the postponed heiress was generally at the discretion of her father, who had come to have power of disposition over his estate, and it was also influenced by her husband's interests. Under settlement, the father was reduced to a life tenancy of his estate by a deed that had been made at his marriage, a deed that entailed the estate in the male line and provided portions, that is sums of money raisable by mortgage, for any children to be born of the marriage who were not to succeed to the estate. What the strict settlement made possible, when fully developed, was estate planning at marriage. Estate

14. Lloyd Bonfield, "Marriage, Property and the 'Affective Family,'" *Law and History Review* 1 (1983): 305.

planning at marriage was planning undertaken when the integrity of the estate and the aristocratic imperative that demanded descent in the patriline had fullest sway. It was a means of limiting in advance charges for a family, limiting them more strictly in proportion to estate value.

It aimed first and foremost at limiting the interest of the heiress-at-law. That she was the principal object of attack is proved by a fact that has long gone unnoticed: The strict settlements of Orlando Bridgman concern themselves only with her among children. Not until later were younger children a concern of settlement, although until they too were put under it, settlement's usefulness for reducing the heiress was circumscribed by the impossibility of employing the device comprehensively on estates. In short, limiting in advance the claims of the heiress-at-law and sending the estate as little reduced as possible to the collateral male is what the strict settlement was primarily about.

Unfortunately it is difficult to compare directly the property the postponed heiress received before and after the invention of the strict settlement. The problem is that before settlement she usually received land whose value is unstated and which must be nearly impossible to determine in any statistically valid way. Comparison before and after settlement of the heiress's interest has thus never been undertaken. It will be shown in chapter 3, however, that portions for daughters who were not heiresses-at-law, which portions were long normally in cash, fell under the strict settlement. (Daughters who were not heiresses-at-law, that is, daughters who had brothers, will hereafter be called, to give them a simple appellation, ordinary daughters.) Portions for ordinary daughters thus moved as logic suggests they would have done, logic suggesting that children are better provided for by fathers who possess power over their property than by fathers who have arranged matters at their marriage. In the first case, a father provides freely for children who stand before him in flesh and blood; in the second, a man provides for children unborn, children hypothetical. The logical argument is the more telling in the case of the heiress. Thus though the sums cannot be pointed to, the direction of movement is not to be doubted.

Clearly the history of the heiress in gentry and aristocratic families is of a great downward slide. From once succeeding according to common law rules, she came to succeed about as seldom as possible. With the strict settlement of the eighteenth century she reached her nadir. She was not to succeed except as a last resort; inheritance would not be traced through her except as a last resort; and her portion, calculated before her birth, was calculated at a time when the interests of the patriline were uppermost. In short, English landowners had moved from lineal to patrilineal principles.

4

There is a change of attitude to women as heirs in this story that cries out for attention. The prejudice against women as heirs is often passed off as the result of military obligations that were attached to land in feudal times. Possibly the roots of the prejudice lie there, although they may lie far deeper; but military considerations will not take us far in accounting for the facts laid out above. Why should the exclusion of women have become more rigorous as the feudal levy lumbered its way out of history? There is a change of attitude to women as heirs above and beyond any military justification.

Holt has described the early attitude thus: "In the absence of male heirs in the same generation, [the daughter] was the only means of continuing the lineage, the only legitimate route whereby her father's blood could be transmitted. Her children were his grandchildren just as her brother's might have been. This determined the woman's position as heir."[15] In a word, it was natural for daughters to succeed if there was no son. For contrast, Dr Johnson's sentiments may be cited: "An ancient estate should always go to a male. It is mighty foolish to let a stranger have it because he married your daughter."[16] There is a change of attitude to blood here, nothing less indeed than a flying in the face of nature. It is, after all, one thing for a father to favor one child out of a brood of children, and another thing for him to favor his nephew over his daughter. The succession of a female came to be held not the natural means of continuing the family, but the end of the family, its very dying out, as terminology can even currently testify. Surely a curious idea when a female continues the blood of her father actually more certainly than a son ever can.

Although this change of attitude cannot be traced in detail here, the major signposts that must mark its growth can be suggested. To begin with, there was the twelfth-century change in the rules of succession, by which all daughters, not just one of them, came to inherit when sons were lacking. Holt has suggested that the aim of the change was to better the younger

15. Holt, "Feudal Society," 3.
16. *Boswell's Life of Johnson*, Oxford ed. (London, 1904), 2:520.

son's chance of marrying an heiress.[17] Very likely it was, but it is hard to imagine that such a change would not at the same time have caused misgivings. The prospect of a divided estate, perhaps divided even three or four ways, must have rendered the prospect of female heirs newly disagreeable.

Later, when the Crown began to create baronies by letters patent, the heiress was bound to lose. Whereas early baronies, baronies in fee, had been attached to the land and were inheritable by females, from the fourteenth century onward the Crown when creating baronies virtually always specified that the honor was to go in tail male, that is, was to be inheritable only by males. As the higher ranks of the peerage came to be established, individual creations were virtually always in tail male too. Titled landowners thus came to face the possibility, as they had not with baronies in fee—nor with that intermediate species of barony, the barony by writ[18]— that land would go to daughter while title went to collateral male. Titles were unthinkable without land to support them. Thus the Crown had made the common law a problem for peers—if it had not already become that. Peers would inevitably have begun to apply Salic principles to parts of their estates. Presumably the nobles who went off with Henry V warring to France on behalf of his claim through the female line to the throne of that country never reflected on their or the English monarchy's inconsistency about Salic principles. James I even diverted the descent of some historic baronies from their traditional course in fee to tail male. (When in the nineteenth century, however, Queen Victoria wanted to convert some peerages the other way round, she was persuaded that the Crown had not the power to alter the form of descent that had been designated.)[19] The genealogist J. H. Round has observed that as a result of the adoption of patrilineal principles, "the three most famous ducal castles in England, Alnwick, Arundel, and Belvoir [passed] away from the heirs of their feudal

17. Holt, "Feudal Society," 20.

18. Baronies by writ are inheritable by heirs female, but if there are more daughters than one, the barony falls into abeyance between them until one of the daughters, or the sole heir of one of the daughters, only survives. With a plurality of females the title disappears temporarily, but land and title still go together essentially according to common law. The rule is different for baronies by writ that are of Scottish creation. These do not go into abeyance upon a plurality of female heirs but descend to the eldest daughter.

19. J. Horace Round, *Studies in Peerage and Family History* (London, 1901), 466–67.

lords to the families of Smithson, Howard, and Manners, who are not their present representatives."[20]

Titles cannot, however, account for the whole story, or for anything but a minor part of it. England's landowners, titled and untitled, moved to patrilineal principles. The Stones' study has demonstrated the strength of patrilineal principles among landowners, yet few of the landowners in their sample were titled. Only 7 percent possessed peerage titles in the sixteenth century, 11 percent in the seventeenth, and 15 percent in the eighteenth. After the creation of baronetcies in the early seventeenth century, those who possessed inheritable titles, peerage and baronetage together, rose to 23 percent in the seventeenth century and to 27 percent in the eighteenth. Thus at all times untitled landowners made up by far the greater part of the Stones' sample, though it solidly demonstrates the rejection of the female heir.[21] Moreover, the bare fact that a comprehensive collection of strict settlements—a collection not limited even to gentry and aristocratic owners—shows that more than three-quarters of the settlors chose the collateral male as heir, rather than the daughter, testifies to a general development.[22]

Although English landowners, titled and untitled, moved towards patrilineal principles, the Crown itself, despite some early hesitations, did not. "What's in a Name?" Holt has asked, discussing the gradual adoption of surnames in medieval England.[23] A great deal, it would seem.

In 1594 Chief Justice Popham of Common Pleas opined that it was "utterly contrary to the providence of God" to try to keep land "always in the same sex."[24] Plowden, however, thought it quite in accord with the Almighty's wishes, "for the males are more worthy than the females, man being the most precious creature that God made on earth, and far exceeding women."[25] Popham might protest, but Plowden's lengthy discourse in a leading case of 1565 told of the way things were going:

By the continuance in the name of the Baynton's [Andrew Baynton] intended to exclude all females from inheriting this land and to place it

---

20. Ibid., 466.

21. Stone and Stone, *An Open Elite?*, table 8.2.

22. Bonfield, "Marriage, Property and the 'Affective Family,'" 305.

23. The words form the title of Holt's Stenton Lecture of 1981, published by the University of Reading (1982).

24. J. H. Baker and S. F. C. Milsom, *Sources of English Legal History: Private Law to 1750* (London, 1986), 156. The words were uttered in *Chudleigh's Case* (1594).

25. *Clere v. Brook* (1573), 2 Plowden 443.

in the heirs male; for a female by marriage changes her surname into her husband's name and loses her father's name, whereas the male continues his first name. Sir, various good reasons might move him to do that. For God has divided reasonable creatures into two sexes, namely male and female. The male is superior (*soveraigne*), the female inferior (*plus base*). Aristotle in his *Politics* says, *Mas est praestantior; deterior femina.* Also men are for the most part more reasonable than women, and have more discretion in guiding things than women have; for men are more apt than women in all government and direction . . . and perhaps Andrew Baynton was thinking of this and felt that the profits of his inheritance would not be so well spent or employed by females as they would by males, nor the lands so well ordered by woman as by man, nor hospitality so well kept by one as by the other, nor that there would be so great a stay or comfort to his race or class, his allies or friends or acquaintances, or the country generally where he and his parents have lived, if this inheritance should come to females; which is something a man cannot think without grief. . . . Also by establishing the inheritance in the heirs male having the name of Baynton, Andrew would thereby obtain fame and memory with his posterity; and every man has an appetite for fame after his death, and this appetite urges many to perform notable acts or things in their lifetimes which shall be monuments to them long after their death; which appetite is laudable. And to establish a great inheritance (as this is) in one name is a feat which begets great fame with his posterity, and he deserves to be called founder of the family.[26]

5

The scale of the movement against the heiress could not be appreciated before the figures that have been assembled and analyzed above had become available. The outline of the heiress's history has, however, always been perceptible from legal considerations. A comparison of either an entail in tail male or a few strict settlements with the common law rules of inheritance would suggest it. Moreover, reflection on a stationary population would suggest that heiresses-at-law were not uncommon, and thus that they deserved consideration. How then, it might be asked, has the heiress been perceived in historical works on landownership?

26. *Sharington v. Strotton* (1565). Quoted from abstract of the case in Baker and Milsom, *Sources of English Legal History*, 488.

Given the perceptible importance of the heiress, it is surprising to find that two out of the three major works on medieval landownership virtually ignore her. G. A. Holmes, in his study of the estates of the higher nobility in the fourteenth century, briefly notes the importance that women then had as property holders, but he says nothing about the lessening of that importance, and in his conclusion the heiress is quite forgotten. The medieval landowner desired "rather to defeat than to promote the operation of primogeniture, to buy lands for his younger sons, husbands for his daughters and masses for his soul."[27] The heiress has disappeared in a conclusion that considers only the division of property between eldest son and younger children. The question who the heir was if there was no son has not been faced, though it was a question to which the common law gave one answer and to which landowners were coming to give another. It is the same in J. M. W. Bean's *The Decline of English Feudalism*. Landowners were intent on evading "a system of landed inheritance which was based on primogeniture"; they desired "to provide for younger sons and daughters."[28] Again the only question considered is the division of property between eldest son and younger children; again daughters are held to have been benefited with no notice taken of the fact that daughters fell at law into two classes, not one; again the heiress is invisible.

The heiress surfaces in K. B. McFarlane's *Nobility of Later Medieval England*. She is separated out from ordinary daughters, and the decline of her fortunes is pointed to. McFarlane, however, simply takes it for granted she should be put down. It is a "sad prospect" for an estate "to go out of the family's possession" with a female heir. "It is not surprising that means were sought to enable those threatened to avoid such a disaster."[29] Apparently little more need be said. The entail is noted, but beyond that there is no discussion. Virtually nothing is said about the provision for postponed heiresses. It is a major theme of the book, however, that medieval landowners made large provision out of their estates for their younger sons.[30] Logically this implies a limited use of the entail, for landowners could not have made large provision out of their estates for their younger sons if they themselves were strictly bound by entail. McFarlane clearly recognizes the

27. G. A. Holmes, *The Estates of the Higher Nobility in Fourteenth-Century England* (Cambridge, 1957), 57.

28. J. M. W. Bean, *The Decline of English Feudalism, 1250–1540* (Manchester, 1968), 148.

29. K. B. McFarlane, *The English Nobility in the Later Middle Ages* (Oxford, 1973), 270.

30. Ibid., 62–72, 276–78.

problem that the common law came to pose for landowners, but the heiress is summarily dismissed from the scene rather than considered in any detail.

Historians who deal with landownership in the seventeenth and eighteenth centuries have on the other hand devoted much attention to female inheritance, recognizing it as a significant matter in estate and family history. Unfortunately two interconnected misperceptions mark the influential literature they have produced.

First, the legal instrument that was developed in the period, the strict settlement, is very often confusedly treated. While its aim is generally recognized to have been that of preserving estates, it is nevertheless also treated as if its aim were the contrary, that of increasing daughters' portions. The association of the strict settlement with rising portions was made by H. J. Habakkuk, who put forward the theory that in the eighteenth century daughters had to be better endowed than they had been earlier if they were to make satisfactory marriages, because marriage had become increasingly a matter of commercial and dynastic advancement.[31] Habakkuk offered several arguments in support of this theory, but his intrinsic evidence came from Orlando Bridgman's precedents. These precedents easily suggest the idea of a new and special concern for the endowment of daughters. Marginal notations conspicuously indicate "portions for daughters" where there are no notations indicating portions for younger sons. Only Bridgman's very technical text makes it clear that the portions were for daughters in default of sons, that is, for daughters who were heiresses-at-law, and who in the logic of their rights were not being better endowed, but limited. Following Habakkuk's article, a series of works on landed estates in the seventeenth and eighteenth century appeared in which interest concentrated heavily on portions for daughters, portions whose movement was ever deemed to be upward. Little attention in these works is ordinarily directed to the heiress-at-law. There is much emphasis upon the pursuit of "heiresses" in marriage—the word "heiress" left ill-defined—but the heiress-at-law is actually again lost sight of, this time among "well-portioned daughters." The implication of this literature, however, is that female inheritance was on the rise. (An annotated settlement by Bridgman is reproduced in Appendix A.)

Second, the common law sometimes suffers actual misinterpretation in the literature of this period. If the collateral male is held to be heir-at-law rather than the daughter, judgments will inevitably be made within a legal

---

31. H. J. Habakkuk, "Marriage Settlements in the Eighteenth Century," *Transactions of the Royal Historical Society*, 4th ser. 32 (1950): 15–30.

framework that is unreal. Unfortunately the two principal works that discuss landed inheritance over the span from late medieval times to the era
of the strict settlement are based on the belief that the collateral male was
heir-at-law, although the works otherwise have considerable differences.

This belief underlies J. P. Cooper's long and well-known article—almost
a small book in length—that runs from the fifteenth century to the eighteenth. Curiously, Cooper begins by attempting to set out the true facts
about the right of females to inherit land, disarmingly confessing that he—
along, he thought, with others—had once held mistaken ideas on the subject. Alas, though he emphasizes that females were not totally excluded at
common law, he lays it down that "males of remoter degree took priority
over females."[32] In other words, the collateral male is heir before the
daughter.

An empirical account then follows that tells of a running conflict between
daughters and collateral males, who are respectively called heirs general
and heirs male. The terminology is to be remarked. Had Cooper realized
that the words "heirs general" mean heirs by common law, he would have
had to revise his statement of the common law, and would have seen deeper
into the conflict that he perceptively senses. Instead his usage indicates that
he believed that the words "heirs general" applied to daughters who had
no brothers, and that they were words meant to signify that although such
daughters had, or might lay claim to have, a natural right to be their fathers'
heirs, they had no right in common law. It is upside down, of course.
Cooper is not the only historian to use the words "heirs general" in this
way, and to speak of daughters as heirs general while holding the collateral
male to be heir-at-law.

It is a merit of Cooper's work that he perceives the conflict between
daughters and collateral males and that he discusses it at length, but under
the circumstances, he can see it only in a half-light. His first statement
about his "heirs general" is that fathers in making settlements "would
want provision for female issue when male was lacking."[33] The suggestion
is of a fatherly act of caring; but as the females concerned were heirs-at-
law, what landowners were busy engineering in their settlements was the
lowering of the provision for female issue when male was lacking. Later,
discussing the extent of the provision, Cooper has this to say: "Despite the

32. J. P. Cooper, "Patterns of Inheritance and Settlement by Great Landowners from
the Fifteenth to the Eighteenth Centuries," in *Family and Inheritance*, ed. Jack Goody,
Joan Thirsk, and E. P. Thompson (London, 1976), 199.

33. Ibid., 200.

widespread desire of peers to settle major parts of their estates in tail male with perpetuities, no clear trend to the disadvantage of heirs general emerges in the second half of the sixteenth century. The Statute of Wills made it seem that at least a third was what the heirs general might expect."[34] It is impossible for Cooper to see the import of that third. Though he later speaks of "the process of limiting the heir general," thus perceiving that she suffered loss in the conflict—and perceiving this against the prevailing belief—he cannot appreciate the extent of her loss, because he does not perceive her initial position.[35] Nor can he properly assess protests by her or on her behalf. These are dismissed as "providential arguments" about "the divine right of heirs general."[36]

The common law is also misunderstood in Lloyd Bonfield's *Marriage Settlements*, a book that traces the transformation of the medieval marriage settlement into the strict settlement and attempts to assess the social meaning of the latter. While Bonfield never lays out the common law rules, he clearly believes that the collateral male was heir rather than the daughter. Making the point that a settlement could set aside common law rules, he gives as example a settlement in which a father granted remainders (in effect, the right of succession) to his daughters before collateral males.[37] This settlement, however, did not set aside common law rules; it followed them. There then ensues the general statement that settlements could be used "to disinherit the collateral heir male by [granting] remainders to female children in default of male issue."[38] What settlements could do was, of course, the opposite: they could disinherit female heirs by granting remainders to collateral males.

Having in fact reversed common law rights, Bonfield is naturally handicapped in assessing the social meaning of the developments he traces. A crucial part of his book revolves around portions in early strict settlements. He is aware that these settlements provided only for some children—only for "daughters if no son survived" in his terminology—and the question he sets out to answer is, When did settlements come to provide for all children? The discussion is most valuable in showing when settlements came to encompass younger children, but it cannot but miss the fundamental point.[39] There is no insight possible into why settlors should have

34. Ibid., 210.
35. Ibid., 232.
36. Ibid., 206, 209.
37. Lloyd Bonfield, *Marriage Settlements, 1601–1740* (Cambridge, 1983), 47–48.
38. Ibid., 50.
39. Ibid., 104–20.

begun making such limited, such apparently odd, family arrangements; no insight possible into the main reason for settlement. Indeed an inverted conclusion is inevitable. Portions granted to daughters, which cannot be recognized as being in lieu of their right to inherit the family estate, become the very proof that landowners "were far more concerned with their daughters and granddaughters than with their collateral heirs."[40] The strict settlement, it is concluded, "indicates that the notion of patrilineal descent . . . was on the wane."[41]

The treatment of the heiress in works of history, it might perhaps be said, has been almost as unfortunate as her treatment at the hands of history itself.

6

It is clear that the heiress suffered a great decline between the system of feudal tenures in the thirteenth century and that of the strict settlement in the eighteenth. Between these centuries, major developments in English real property law took place, and in all of them the heiress had an interest or was a factor being conjured with. She was a factor in the development of the entail and in its destruction; she was a factor in the development of uses and in the consequent Statute of Uses and Statute of Wills; she was a factor in the antecedent form of the strict settlement and in the invention of the trust to preserve contingent remainders by which this form was converted into the strict settlement. When these developments are considered from her point of view, not only is the thread of her interests traced over time, but a new strand in the history of real property law becomes apparent.

THE ENTAIL

The entail, which in its common form of tail male represents a conspicuous move against the heiress, is the first instrument for consideration. In practice it had different potentiality at different times, and it can only be discussed as a changing phenomenon.

The tenurial system, as has been seen, guaranteed that the common law heir would succeed to whatever land his—or her—father died possessed of. It was not impossible, however, for a father to dispose of land in his lifetime. The entail arose from this fact, and it arose out of a natural human

40. Ibid., 119.
41. Ibid., 122.

desire. Fathers wanted some of their land to go to younger sons and to daughters who were not heiresses. The original entail was thus a grant of land to a younger child upon his or her marriage, the *maritagium*. It was a grant conditional upon the marriage producing heirs, heirs as defined by the deed, heirs male if so desired. The purpose of such a grant was double-sided. On the one hand, it aimed to allow the establishment of a junior branch of the family. On the other hand, it aimed to ensure that should the junior branch fail to become established, then the land granted, which in the interim was inalienable by the donee, would return to the senior branch. As long as the entail was used as provision for younger children, it was no more a threat to heirs female than to heirs male. Land departed the main branch of the family from time to time, and sometimes later returned to it, but these movements did not alter inheritance rights in the main estate.

The entail, however, introduced the idea of greater discrimination against females than that embodied in the common law. Because the entail could specify the sex of those to take under it, females could be cut out so long as the entail lasted. By the statute *De donis* (1285), at least as that rather enigmatic statute came to be interpreted, an entail, which had earlier been of limited duration, became perpetual. It could direct land from male to male so long as there were males anywhere among the settlor's descendants, regardless of females who by common law were heirs. The entail had thus come to embody the concept of land descending indefinitely by a mode of succession different from that of the common law. The possibility arose that land might be entailed on eldest sons, thus keeping females out of succession to the main estate for so long as that was biologically possible.

Clearly entails could be used for two different purposes. On the one hand, they could be used to distribute land to younger children. On the other hand, they could be used to keep land indefinitely—that is, so long as was biologically possible—in the hands of the male descendants of the settlor. Not only were these different purposes—distributing land to younger children and entailing it upon eldest sons—but they were mutually exclusive purposes.

There is no statistical evidence as to how entails were used, but the increasing hostility to female heirs must have meant some use of such a weapon against them. Nevertheless there are grounds for hesitating before ascribing large importance to entails used in this way. A "juridical monster," Milsom has called the entail.[42] In using these words he would seem

42. S. F. C. Milsom, *Historical Foundations of the Common Law* (London, 1969), 147.

to have had only the entail's presumptuous duration in mind, but the words are applicable to its family principle as well. The landowner who entailed his estate on his eldest son no doubt provided for his younger children beforehand, but he inevitably rendered future generations unable in their turn to provide for their children, either younger children or heiresses-at-law. The landowner might, of course, entail only a part of his land on his eldest son and allow part to descend in fee simple. Such a landowner would be acknowledging tacitly the inherent problem of the entail. Even so, he would likely only postpone the problem of younger children and heiresses. Some future heir under the entail could well find that entailed land was all that he possessed. European entails were not of this uncompromising sort, and the very origin of the English entail as a provision for younger children suffices to indicate that utterly disinheriting younger children was never acceptable. If younger children were not to be disinherited, much less were daughters who were heiresses-at-law. The logic of the entail was such that it solved one inheritance problem only by creating another.

It would be surprising only if entails had not become barrable. The subject of barring is, however, a complex one. It would seem that almost from the beginning means were sought by which entails might be brought to an end, although what general results were achieved remains unclear. Indeed Milsom has declared categorically that we know little of the entail between the fourteenth and the sixteenth century: "We do not know in point of law how secure it was, or was thought to be; nor do we know in point of fact what use was made of it, or how long individual entails actually lasted."[43] What is clear is that efficient means of barring were developed by the end of the fifteenth century and that they were soon in common use. The entail had thus become, to all intents and purposes, as freely alienable as an estate in fee simple.

This was not to be quite the end of the story of the entail. Some landowners responded by adding to their deeds of entail clauses designed to prevent barring, clauses of perpetuity. Thus a final question about entails arises: How commonly were clauses of perpetuity employed? It has traditionally been held that these clauses were ephemeral, unusual expedients dubious in law. From the account of Sir John Dalrymple in the mid-eighteenth century to that of Sir Frederick Pollock in the late nineteenth, it has been held that the period from the end of the fifteenth century to the end of the seventeenth, when the strict settlement became common, was

---

43. Ibid., 146.

one of general freedom of alienation.[44] Fortunately, in this case there is at least some empirical evidence, and it goes to support the traditional view.

Mary Finch has studied the estates of five families from 1540 to 1640. This is a small sample, to be sure, but it is more than an impression from haphazard sources, or from sources bound to be biased, such as law cases or private acts of Parliament. In her five families Finch finds three perpetuities, but they amount to little. One was not on the principal estate of the family, but on an estate that accrued to it through marriage to the heiress of a legal family. One hardly deserves the name perpetuity, for it was designed to limit the power of a particular eldest son, and it allowed the settlor's grandson to succeed freely as tenant in tail. It lasted from 1534 to 1552. Significantly, both these perpetuities proved nuisances. In short order, each had to be twice altered by act of Parliament, three at least of the four acts being to allow provision for younger children. The third perpetuity was established by a settlement made in 1583, a settlement over which the settlor and his brother, who was his successor, maintained power to alter the uses. Since both men were dead by 1587, this perpetuity may have lasted until 1614, when perpetuities were finally struck down. In sum, on the five principal estates from 1540 to 1614—through roughly four hundred estate years—perpetuities existed for forty-five years at most.[45] Generally Finch portrays landowners in possession of their estates disposing of them by deed or will as they chose.

THE USE

The entail was not, however, the only instrument available against the heiress. There was—or came to be—the use, which is to say the will, for to make a will was the common purpose of the use. Feudal tenures, as earlier noted, had precluded wills of land, and strictly speaking, wills of land remained forbidden until 1540. Well before that, however, they came to be effected by subterfuge. Landowners granted their estates to feoffees (in modern terms, to trustees), continuing to enjoy the beneficial use of their estates but not dying possessed of land. Through instructions to their feoffees, who corporately survived, they were able to devise interests to their children, or to others, as they chose. Paradoxically, landowners divested themselves of their land in order to deal freely with it.

---

44. John Dalrymple, *An Essay towards a General History of Feudal Property in Great Britain*, 3d ed. (London, 1758), 165–68; Frederick Pollock, *The Land Laws*, 3d ed. (London, 1896), 88.

45. Mary Finch, *The Wealth of Five Northamptonshire Families, 1540–1640* (Oxford, 1956), 53, 103, 144.

G. A. Holmes and J. M. W. Bean have both found that estates were commonly held to uses by the end of the fourteenth century, and both have stressed the landowner's desire to effect dispositions through uses that would provide for their younger children, who by common law rules inherited nothing.[46] Through uses, landowners are portrayed as providing for their families. What needs to be stressed is that providing for their families according to their wishes meant two things, not one: better provision for younger children than what the common law afforded, and worse provision for the heiress. The heiress could, however, be flexibly treated through wills, the rigidities of the entail avoided. Once the heiress-at-law is recognized, the significance of uses in her history becomes obvious. Conversely, so does her significance in the history of uses.

Uses were to lead to a well-known conflict with the Crown and to the promulgation of the Statute of Uses and the Statute of Wills. In this conflict the heiress had much interest, but like her interest in uses themselves, it has tended to escape notice.

The Crown's objection to uses was that it lost the feudal dues to which it was entitled on successions to land, the most valuable of these dues being the wardship of heirs who were minors. Since military obligations attached to land, and since a minor could not see to their performance, at law the land of a minor fell during his minority into the hands of the Crown for administration. By Henry VIII's day wardship had become in practice a form of death duty, but through uses landowners had found a means of dodging it. Minors did not come into legal possession of estates that were held by feoffees. Given the great benefit that uses conferred upon landowners by allowing them to do what they wished about estates and families, it is much to be doubted that tax evasion was their primary motive as they took to uses. Be that as it may, the Crown found its tax base eroding, and Henry VIII set out to restore it. By the Statute of Uses of 1536 he boldly put a stop to the fiction that the man in enjoyment of the land was not its legal owner. Wills again became impossible, and the common law heir was restored. Land could not be devised away from the heir male, a fact everywhere recognized; nor could it be devised away from the heir female either, which fact goes unnoticed, crucial though she was in landowners' thinking.

Landowners in their lifetime could still entail land away from females, although the entails would by this time have been barrable unless reinforced by a clause of perpetuity. The existence of the entail, however, is not good reason to ignore the interest of the heiress in the statute, if indeed her interest has been ignored for this reason, and not for the common rea-

46. Holmes, *Estates of the Higher Nobility*, 55; Bean, *Decline of English Feudalism*, 126.

son that females have tended to be ignored in history. Landowners in their lifetime could still also entail land on younger children. In other words, the entail remained as much available for one of its purposes as for the other, and if it is to be remembered in the one case, so it is in the other. The significant point is that entails had already been found unsatisfactory as a method of directing inheritances—which is why they had become barrable. Leaving landowners a choice between entails and the common law, as the statute did, put them back on the horns of their old dilemma: neither could meet their needs as they perceived them. Wills had become essential to them, and wills had been commonly employed by them for over a century.

Inevitably the statute aroused opposition. The king had forced it through an unwilling Parliament, and he was soon to recognize that he had over-reached himself. It is clear that he had gone to the extreme of the Statute of Uses in order to teach landowners a lesson in law and power, for Parliament had refused to ratify a much more modest reform he had proposed seven years earlier, and to which the peers had then agreed. Four years after the statute, with landowners chastened and the king relenting, much the compromise he had originally proposed became law. By the Statute of Wills all land held by socage tenure became disposable by will, and two-thirds of that held by knight service, which was the tenure normal among large landowners. Landowners thus gained an undisputed right to dispose of most land by will. The king, for his part, while giving up claim to two-thirds of his feudal dues, made the remaining one-third inescapable.

The Statute of Wills did no more than recognize reality, and thus it represents no veering from the trend of the preceding several centuries. It marks, however, a great transition from early feudal times. It has been seen as signaling the victory of younger children. By the same token, it signals the defeat of the heiress. Both classes were involved in what the Statute of Wills recognized.

With the Statute of Wills the common law rules of succession, long evaded in practice, were officially on the way to becoming default rules, rules that would apply only upon intestacy. They did not wholly become default rules until the time of the Commonwealth, when all feudal dues were abolished and full power of devise was granted.

THE STRICT SETTLEMENT

A terminological matter might first be got out of the way. The strict settlement is often spoken of as an entail. When land was settled strictly, it was commonly said to be entailed. There is good reason for this usage, for a deed of settlement was technically built around a life estate and an entail; and the purpose of settlement as a system was to keep land in the male line. There can be confusion on account of the usage, however. The two instruments were in fundamental ways different, and an entail itself, as we have seen, had in any case not the same meaning in one century as in another. The entail that Mrs Bennet never ceased to rail bitterly against was a strict settlement. By the date of Jane Austen's story, had it been a simple entail, Mr Bennet could have brought it to an end at any time. That he could not do so is the starting point for the story.

To return to the chronological story, the Statute of Wills had officially conceded to landowners substantial freedom to arrange their estate and family matters as they chose. Though landowners had themselves sought this freedom through their barring of entails and through uses, freedom to arrange matters as they chose could only be a negative virtue in their eyes. Freedom of alienation was a boon compared to the common law, but it was far from ideal. Freedom of alienation naturally offers no real means of preserving estates. Wills are essentially the opposite of entails, allowing scope for whims and passions of all sorts, particularly allowing large scope for paternal affection. Compared to the common law, wills would cut the heiress down, but not reliably, nor possibly substantially. A positive restraining device was what aristocratic landowners required, some device to restrain parental generosity. Aristocratic landowners in many countries developed a legal device of this sort. It was to be arrived at in England through the marriage settlement, specifically through the strict settlement.

Marriage settlements were not new in English landed society. The maritagium existed in early feudal times, and no doubt marriage settlements in some form go back far beyond that. The strict settlement was a marriage settlement with a difference. It was not, like the maritagium, a provision for a particular child. It was the means by which estate and family affairs could be arranged in all details at the marriage of the heir male. Estate planning at marriage is what it amounted to; and estate planning at marriage in gentry and aristocratic families was estate planning undertaken with the claims of the patriline uppermost in mind as opposed to the claims of unborn younger children and heiresses-at-law.

The form of settlement that immediately preceded the strict is of particular interest. This is not because of its practical importance, for it could have had little (except perhaps politically as protection against forfeiture, a subject that will be considered in chapter 5). It is of interest as a faulty prototype is of interest in pointing up what makes for the working machine. In the early seventeenth century a form of marriage settlement is commonly found in which the groom took a life interest only and the remainder in tail went to his unborn son. That is to say, the entail, instead of going to the groom as it would earlier have done, was projected forward onto his unborn son, the groom being reduced to a life tenancy. (In this way, the strict settlement was, as noted above, built upon a life estate and an entail.) The fault of this device, according to the usual explanation, was that the land was not certain to descend to the unborn son, because the entail upon him was contingent until he was born; and while it was contingent it was destructible by the tenant for life. No son might ever be born, and the law, quite reasonably, for long declined to protect estates that only might come into existence. Thus though he was nominally a tenant for life, the groom could alienate before he had a son. Indeed, because of a further legal principle, he would usually have been free to alienate even after the birth of his son, free throughout his life to alienate.[47] The trustees to preserve contingent remainders, whose invention turned this device into the strict settlement, are thus declared in the usual explanation to have been necessary to make secure the contingent remainder on the unborn son.

To be sure, so they were; but that is not the real story. A strict settlement dealt with more than fathers and sons, being concerned above all to lay out the succession in case there should be no son. Compared to the strict settlement the fault of the prototype was that any remainders to collateral males were insecure. The man who never had a son, but who did have daughters, was not only free to destroy any remainders to collateral males but would inherently have a motive for doing so. The prototype then was not up to ensuring the patriline; and ensuring the patriline was the object. In other words, the trustees to preserve contingent remainders are not realistically to be seen as guaranteeing the descent to the unborn son, although they did that. (He was after all the heir-at-law.) What the trustees are realistically to be seen as doing is guaranteeing the descent to collateral males.

Provision was necessary for the postponed heiress, of course, or the scheme could not work. Without such provision the scheme would have had the faults of the unbarrable entail. Under a strict settlement provision could be made securely for the heiress—and subsequently for younger children—because the trustees to preserve contingent remainders, in preventing the destruction of the settlement, in effect prevented as well the

---

47. As the law held that a living man could have no heir, heirs being determinable only at death, the remainder in tail was held to be contingent, and therefore destructible, throughout the life of the tenant for life. While means had been developed by which the destructibility of the settlement might be limited to the period before the tenant for life had a son, little advantage was gained by settling in this way. The real danger to the settlement lay before the son was born. For further discussion see chapter 5.

destruction of trusts to raise portions. The provision would not only be secure, but also—what is most important—it would be prospectively determined. By those "portions for daughters" at one and the same time the scheme was made humanly acceptable and the heiress was fobbed off with a portion determined at her father's marriage rather than by his will.

Thus with the strict settlement a workable restraining device had come into existence, one that made comprehensive estate settlements possible. The heiress was granted a portion determined before her birth and accordingly limited, while the trustees to preserve contingent remainders guaranteed the descent of the estate in the patriline. This is the essence of Orlando Bridgman's work, although it has not been clearly perceived.

From beginning to end, then, landowner's legal history is much to be seen as the effort to overcome the common law rights of daughters. It was heiresses who threatened to divide estates. It was heiresses whose rights threatened to leave titles bare of land. It was heiresses who would alter the name tags associated with estates. And heiresses were no remote possibility. From the entail, to the use, to the strict settlement, what landowners were above all seeking was a means of dealing with the problem that female inheritance posed. While heiresses clearly were not the only factor in landowners' minds, they must have been the dominant one in the minds of all who were out to preserve their estates. Younger sons and ordinary daughters were less a threat, less a problem. "Putting down the heiress-at-law" would be a not inappropriate subtitle for landowners' legal history.

7

In considering the heiress-at-law we have thus come upon the principal character in landowners' legal history.

We have come as well upon a method of treating the development of real property law, which if not totally new, has not hitherto been carried out with any consistency. In considering the heiress we have been considering legal developments against a common law rule of succession. This is a process that naturally invites extension to other common law rules and other members of the family. It can already be perceived that landowners' history was also an effort to overcome the common law rule that completely disinherited younger children. It will ultimately be perceived that their history was also an effort to overcome the common law rule on widows' dower. Landowners had their rules, and the common law had its, and they differed in every major respect. Landowners' legal history is a long, multi-faceted struggle against the common law rules of inheritance.

Histories of real property law are not organized around this perception. They find their organizing principle in the problem of perpetuities. As they present it, landowners' legal history runs from *De donis* and the development of perpetual entails in the thirteenth century, on through the cases several hundred years later that established the barrability of entails, *Taltarum's Case* and *Mary Portington's*, then on to the strict settlement of the eighteenth century, which is described as a roundabout form of entail. When uses are mentioned, there is some reference to younger children, but then always follows a discussion, bewildering in its complexity, of how uses might be employed in the search for enduring settlements. The story is of a running battle between landowners and the common law judges over facilities for tying up land. This view is imbedded in the structure of legal histories, from Frederick Pollock's in the nineteenth century, through William Holdsworth's and Theodore Plucknett's in the early half of this century, to those that have been written since. "The desire of great landowners," said Pollock in words that have often been quoted, "has constantly been to make the strictest settlements which the law would allow."[48]

There are good grounds for telling the story this way. It is true that large landowners were dynastically oriented and wanted their estates preserved. It is also true that their peculiar institution, the strict settlement, had an element of entail about it, despite the fact that it had to operate within the rule against perpetuities. In a complicated way, as has necessarily to be explained, one deed of settlement tended to lead to another, and thus to long-term restrictions over estates through a chain of settlement and re-settlement, forged anew between father and son each generation, that is to be likened to a form of entail. It is also true that in the nineteenth century battle waged around settlement as social thinkers inspired by the doctrines of Adam Smith assailed it as a device unbefitting an industrial and commercial nation. Not until 1882, when the Settled Land Act passed, were tenants for life granted power of alienation, or in other words, not until then were commercial principles at last fully established with regard to land. The story of the land law told in this way is part of a larger story of how English law gradually adapted itself to, or laid the basis for, the liberal capitalism of our own age.

This time-honored way of treating the development of law—which has been called "evolutionary functionalism"—has recently come under critical scrutiny. Questions have been raised about the philosophical pre-

---

48. Pollock, *Land Laws*, 117.

sumptions underlying it, and about the presumed fit between legal and social development. The variety of objections that may be raised against it have been discussed at some length in the work of Robert Gordon and in that of G. R. Rubin and David Sugarman.[49] I do not wish, nor am I able, to enter in any general way into what is a profound legal-philosophical debate. It is evident, however, that there are difficulties about the particular story told of landowners; and the question must arise whether concentrating on perpetuities is the most realistic way of treating the history of real property law.

How can a hankering after perpetuities explain the fourteenth-century landowner, busy developing uses? Cooper pointed to the problem here when he noted the paradox of the simultaneous growth of freedom of alienation and perpetual entails.[50] And was it the judges who barred entails? Or was it landowners themselves who devised—or had ingenious conveyancers devise for them—the fantastic collusive action by which barring was effected? Moreover, the strict settlement, when judged strictly as entail, was in practice notably inefficient—not so inefficient as two investigations have suggested (one of them my own), but notably inefficient all the same.[51] As a chain, it depended in practice upon fathers' living to the marriage of eldest sons. They quite often did not do so, and landowners must have perceived that the system of settlement and resettlement was by no means certain to run uninterruptedly for long. Nevertheless settlement became and remained a ritual in aristocratic society, a ceremony normally accompanying the marriage of eldest sons whether father lived or not.

49. Robert W. Gordon, "Critical Legal Histories," *Stanford Law Review* 36 (1984): 57–125; David Sugarman and G. R. Rubin, "Towards a New History of Law and Material Society in England, 1750–1914," in *Law, Economy and Society, 1750–1914: Essays in the History of English Law*, ed. G. R. Rubin and David Sugarman (Abingdon, Eng., 1984), 1–123.

50. Cooper, "Patterns of Inheritance," 201.

51. Eileen Spring, "The Settlement of Land in NineteenthCentury England," *American Journal of Legal History* 8 (1964): 209–23; Lloyd Bonfield, "Marriage Settlements and the Rise of Great Estates: The Demographic Aspect," *Economic History Review*, 2d ser. 32 (1979): 483–93. The point made by these articles—that settlement often failed as entail—is undeniable. Both articles exaggerate its failure, though for different reasons. My own does so because its sample is untypical, two out of its three families being ones who worked their own coal mines and who would thus have put an unusual premium on freedom of action. Bonfield's makes demographic calculations based on a misperception of the form of a strict settlement. It is not recognized that collateral members of the family were reduced to life tenancies so far as possible, and thus that in collateral successions a percentage of settlements could be renewed.

While it would thus appear that landowners themselves had reservations about perpetuities, it is on the other hand to be noted that long-term restrictions were not actually essential to the aim of preserving estates. The strict settlement, the culmination of landowners' interaction with the common law, had a short-term content that itself made for estate preservation. A deed of settlement certainly laid out affairs for one generation. It restricted the son on his succession to a life tenancy with a limited power of providing for his unborn children and his widow; and it determined who his heir was to be. These are the decisions on which estate preservation depends in the next instance, and they deal with the nitty-gritty of estate preservation, heirship and the division of property.

All this is to suggest that if social reality is the issue, then the content of landowners' devices would seem to need consideration as much as their duration. In landowners' eyes long-term restrictions were probably as icing on cake, a desirable extra, but not what was essential. We really may be sure that landowners had their eyes fixed less on misty generations in the future than on what the common law proposed for their estates in the foreseeable future unless they took care to determine otherwise. A more realistic way of treating their legal history would make these immediate matters primary. Landowners' legal history is thus most realistically to be seen not against the background of perpetuities, but against the common law rules of inheritance.

To take this point of view is to make the family, in its complex of interests, central to landowners' legal history. Landowners' minds were not bent on perpetuities at all costs. It might even be wondered, as some anthropologist has wondered—unfortunately I forget who—whether human concern has ever extended further than grandchildren. Even dynastic interests doubtfully extended very far into the future, no matter what the psalmist might say about men wishing that their houses shall continue forever. Rather, perhaps, sufficient unto the day was the evil thereof. Nor were landowners' minds mainly determined by a desire to evade feudal dues, although they no doubt found it agreeable to evade taxes in the pursuit of more important ends. Because perpetuities, and to some extent feudal dues, have been the points concentrated upon in legal texts, the human wellspring of landowners' actions has not been well appreciated.

Thus in looking at the heiress-at-law we have found that the mainspring of landowners' actions lay in their objection to the common law rules of succession; and in view of the importance of great landowners in English history we have as well found a strand in the history of real property law that has not had the attention that it deserves.

2 The Widow

I think you must e'en do as other widows—buy yourself

weeds, and be cheerful.

—*John Gay*, The Beggar's Opera

The history of the heiress has suggested the general idea that the history of inheritance in gentry and aristocratic families is much to be seen as an effort to overcome the common law rules of inheritance. If this idea is to be pursued with respect to other members of the family, the widow is naturally the next member due consideration. Like the heiress she was a female with a large common law right. By her right of dower, she was entitled to one-third of her husband's land for life. What became of her right is again a story important in both legal and family history.

Parts of the widow's story have been considered in works by Susan Staves and by myself. We have both independently been interested in the undermining of the widow's right by the Statute of Uses. We have each focused on different aspects of the story, however. In several articles I have discussed, among other economic trends in landed families, the practical question what happened to the income of widows.[1] In an admirable book

---

1. Eileen Spring, "The Family, Strict Settlement and Historians," *Canadian Journal of History* 18 (1983): 388–90; idem, "Law and the Theory of the Affective Family," *Albion* 16 (1984): 8–10. The first of these articles also appears in *Law, Economy and Society, 1750–1914: Essays in the History of English Law*, ed. G. R. Rubin and David Sugarman (Abingdon, Eng., 1984).

Staves has more recently dissected the case law around dower in the eighteenth century.[2] This chapter looks at the history of the widow in the round. It considers both legal changes and their economic consequences, considering the latter in much more detail than I have previously done. It also extends the widow's history back before the Statute of Uses, covering the same time span for the widow as the previous chapter covered for the heiress.

1

The common law right of dower was established about the end of the thirteenth century, but dower as an institution was of ancient origin. Before the Conquest, to quote Maitland, "very generally the widow [had obtained] a right to enjoy for her life some aliquot share, a fourth, a third, a half of her husband's property." For a time, feudalism had "made against dower" because it conflicted with the lord's right of wardship.[3] Wardship was the profitable right a lord had to administer the land of a tenant who died leaving an heir who was a minor. The amount of land that could fall into wardship, however, was reduced by the amount that fell to the widow. Thus in the twelfth and early thirteenth centuries, legal dower was one-third, but a husband might endow his wife with less by specifying at the time of his marriage what dower she was to receive. There were at this period, then, two forms of dower: dower by the common law, that is, the third; and dower specified, as the phrase went, at the church door. From the frequency with which Maitland found that dower had been specified at the church door he concluded that "many widows of high station had to be content with less [than a third]."[4] The widow's right was gradually strengthened—reasserted is probably the better word—and by the time of Edward I dower had become an irreducible third. Moreover, while the husband could no longer specify less, he might now specify more, although it was possible for the heir to object if he did so.

The widow's right to her third was well protected. It extended over any land her husband had ever held during her marriage, not only over land

2. Susan Staves, *Married Women's Separate Property in England, 1660–1883* (Cambridge, Mass., 1990), 27–131.

3. F. Pollock and F. W. Maitland, *The History of English Law before the Time of Edward I*, 2d ed. (Cambridge, 1898), 2:425–26.

4. Ibid., 2:421.

he died possessed of. If a husband during marriage wished to alienate land, his wife's consent was required. Should he alienate without her consent, she could claim dower against the purchaser. Dower was not to be evaded by entailing land, for the widow's right extended over land held in fee, whether in fee tail or in fee simple. To be more precise, her right extended over land held in fee tail provided the entail granted any issue of hers the right of succession, but this it would normally have done. The widow did not have to have issue who in fact succeeded; it was enough that issue by her might have succeeded. Finally, a woman could not contract herself out of dower. As Britton, a late thirteenth-century authority, put it, "dower was ordered by the common constitution of the people, and cannot be undone by a single person. For if by one then by another, and so the constitution would be destroyed."[5] Holdsworth made the point more forthrightly: "To allow a woman to contract herself out of her rights would put her rights at the mercy of the unscrupulous."[6]

Social historians have testified to the importance of dower in practice. In his analysis of fourteenth-century landownership G. A. Holmes declared that "one prominent fact, which cannot be neglected . . . is the importance of the dowager." Emphasizing that wives tended to outlive husbands, he noted that "it was not unusual for a widow to control one third of the inheritance for much of her son's lifetime."[7] In his most conspicuous pronouncement on the subject K. B. McFarlane found widows even better endowed, declaring that they "did not enjoy merely a dower right in the traditional third of their late husband's landed property: they often held it all in jointure, or if not all, at any rate a greater part of it."[8] This is undoubtedly an exaggeration, one of McFarlane's unbalanced remarks on the subject of women, and to accept it would be to exaggerate the widow's subsequent fall, which needs no exaggeration. As proof of his statement McFarlane went on to give an impressive list of powerful medieval dowagers, making the point that their survival—called "obstinate"—inconvenienced their heirs, who were kept waiting for land until their mothers died. The list is skewed by the fact that most of the dowagers on it, probably all of them, had been heiresses, who as widows would have resumed their own property, as well as taking jointure or dower in the lands that had

---

5. W. S. Holdsworth, *A History of English Law* (London, 1922–66), 3:194–95.

6. Ibid.

7. G. A. Holmes, *The Estates of the Higher Nobility in Fourteenth-Century England* (Oxford, 1957), 35.

8. K. B. McFarlane, *The Nobility of Later Medieval England* (Oxford, 1973), 65.

belonged to their husbands. Such women held a good deal of property, but part was their own inheritance, and it cannot be held an inconvenience to their heirs to have to wait for that. McFarlane later modified his position, as was plainly necessary. The idea is not tenable that the feudal lord had generally to wait until his mother's death to come into possession of the main part of his father's land. Saying only that it was "not uncommon in the case of the heiress" for a woman to have jointure of all her husband's land, McFarlane then found with Holmes that "the normal dower" was one-third.[9] There is agreement on the fundamental fact that the common law right of the widow to one-third of her husband's land was once a real right.

Medieval histories often tell of active and forceful widows. The importance of medieval widows as property holders may still perhaps be glimpsed in their benefactions to the universities of Oxford and Cambridge. Five colleges owe their foundation to medieval widows, or widows-cum-heiresses. At Oxford, Balliol was founded by Dervorguila, widow of John Balliol. At Cambridge, Christ's and St John's were both founded by Margaret Beaufort; Pembroke by Mary de Valence; and Clare by Elizabeth de Burgh, who substantially reendowed an earlier small foundation. Benefactions by women were not quite foreclosed until after the time of Elizabeth, for in 1588 Sidney Sussex was founded at Cambridge by Frances Sidney.

2

The widow's importance would have remained real so long as land was held by husbands in fee, whether in fee simple or in fee tail. Uses were to break in upon the relative simplicity of the early land law, however, and they were to make for a complicated situation for widows in the fifteenth and early sixteenth centuries.

Inherently uses presented a problem for the widow. The man whose land was held by feoffees to his use technically held no real property. In modern terms we should say he had but a life interest in a trust. Since it was real property that dower adhered to, the widow of a man whose land was held by feoffees had nothing against which to assert her right. "No dower out of a use" was a legal maxim. When a man's land was held by feoffees and he wished to marry, he would naturally have desired at that time to make some provision for his widow, since upon his death she would be precluded

9. Ibid., 137.

from dower. At his instructions his feoffees would convey some land to himself and his wife for their joint lives, she to have use of it for her life should she survive him, the land ultimately to go to the heirs of the marriage. This is jointure in its original form, an enfeoffment of land to the joint use of husband and wife, with survivor rights to the widow for her life. Later a jointure was to be but a rent charge granted the widow, and it is probably most familiar in this later form. The amount of land the husband ordered his feoffees to settle in jointure could clearly be whatever was agreed upon by husband and wife at the time of their marriage. The rest of the husband's land remained in the hands of his feoffees, where it was not subject to dower, and the husband was in practice free to do with it as he pleased. The way would seem to have been opened to the lowering of the widow's provision through the substitution of jointures that were of less value than dower.

The traditional view is that this is indeed what happened with the appearance of uses. Holdsworth emphasized that uses allowed dower to be evaded.[10] Early legal authorities often took the same view. Thomas Audley, later Lord Chancellor, did so in his "Reading on Uses."[11] So did Francis Bacon in his reading on the subject, and so too did Christopher St German in his *Doctor and Student*.[12] Such was as well the view of Henry VIII, if we are to judge by the preamble to the Statute of Uses, where among the evils ascribed to uses is the defrauding of widows. That Henry was more concerned that uses defrauded himself does not make him wrong about the widow.

This view of the effect of uses has not been universal, however. It has been challenged especially by J. M. W. Bean in his *Decline of English Feudalism*, which is a study of the origin and development of uses. If Bean's arguments are analyzed it may be possible to effect some interweaving of apparently irreconcilable views and to make a very rough and tentative assessment of what the arrival of uses meant for the widow.

Emphasizing that a widow had the right to seek redress in the courts, Bean finds it impossible that jointures could have been less than dower. "A widow had an absolute right," he writes, "to one-third of the lands which

---

10. Holdsworth, *History of English Law*, 3:196–97.

11. Audley's "Reading on Uses" is printed in J. H. Baker and S. F. C. Milsom, *Sources of English Legal History: Private Law to 1750* (London, 1986), 105.

12. *The Works of Lord Bacon*, ed. J. Spedding (London, 1857), 7:418–21; *St German's Doctor and Student*, ed. T. F. T. Plucknett and J. Barton, Selden Society, vol. 91 (London, 1974), 224.

were solely held by her husband during her marriage and to which any issue she had by him might succeed. Even if part had been alienated by him before his death, she nevertheless had the right at common law to obtain the original dower from the alienees, a right which could if necessary, be prosecuted in the courts. . . . There is evidence to show that several widows in the fourteenth and fifteenth centuries successfully sued for their dowers against their husband's feoffees."[13] So far as it goes, this is an unexceptionable statement of the widow's right and of what must follow from it. That feoffees fully recognized this right can be seen in the case of a trust described by Holmes. The feoffees are noted to have granted the widow dower out of a complicated trust because it had been established during her marriage, and thus her husband had at some time during the marriage held the land.[14]

Unfortunately, however, Bean's argument does not take into account all the possibilities. What if the husband had never in his marriage held any land? What if he had granted it to feoffees before he married? In such a case the widow would have had a jointure made upon her in the manner outlined at the beginning of this discussion, for speaking to human rule, men have never wished to leave their widows penniless; but there was then nothing to prevent the jointure determined on being less than dower. In an unusual case where a husband had failed to provide his widow with a jointure, the court spoke to public morality when it declared that "a man ought in common decency to provide a jointure for his wife when she is excluded from dower"; and it sanctioned the feoffees' granting the widow a jointure, but it clearly took it for granted (this in 1535) that a wife could be excluded from dower.[15]

Despite the unfortunate conclusion that uses could not be employed to reduce the widow's provision, Bean's argument draws attention to a crucial factor in the history of dower. Unless it is recognized, an oversimplified story will be told, one in which major change comes too early in the history of the widow. The argument brings forcibly into the context of uses the fact that the widow's right to dower extended over land her husband had ever solely held during her marriage. If this fact is kept in mind while different inheritance situations are considered, it will become evident that evading dower had its complications. It will further become evident that a very unstable state of affairs had been brought about.

13. J. M. W. Bean, *The Decline of English Feudalism, 1250–1540* (Manchester, 1968), 136, 287n.

14. Holmes, *Estates of the Higher Nobility*, 45.

15. Holdsworth, *History of English Law*, 4:442n.

For the landowner out to evade dower there would seem to have been a simple rule: do not marry without first raising a use over your land; that way you may substitute less valuable jointure for dower. A good number of men would have been able to follow this rule. Given the mortality of the age, many men inherited while they were young and still single. They would have been able to put their lands into uses before they married, thus depriving their widows of any claim to dower and limiting them to jointures that were agreed on at marriage. On the other hand, many men would not have been able to follow the rule, having married as eldest sons in the lifetime of their fathers, their inheritance thus coming to them when they were already married. When a son married in the lifetime of his father, the father would have settled some fraction of the estate on him, probably in the form of an entail, but such settlement could not foreclose the dower right that would inhere in any land that son subsequently came into under his father's will or came into by inheritance. Nor could the wife be barred from dower in such land, no matter that her husband later granted his land to feoffees, as he undoubtedly would do, in whole or in part, making a will to endow the patriline, to provide for younger children, and to defeat the king's right of wardship.

It was thus by no means certain that a man could reduce his widow's provision. It depended much upon demographic chances, upon whether he inherited before or after marriage. The chances would seem to have been about fifty-fifty in late feudal times, if data for the early sixteenth century are applicable. In the early sixteenth century, age of marriage was apparently close to age of inheritance.[16]

A further complication could arise in the attempt to defeat dower. Though a man had put his land into the hands of feoffees before he married and had reduced his wife's right by providing a jointure smaller than dower, should he subsequently inherit further land through some demographic accident in the branches of his extended family, which accidents were not uncommon, he would find that his wife had dower right in that land. Historians have suggested that there was something improper about a widow's taking both jointure and dower. The widow who did so has more than once been declared to be unscrupulous. Her jointure would have been out of some land, however, and her dower out of other land; and it is hard to see why the wife should not have partaken of her husband's unexpected good fortune. Normally she would still have received less from the jointure and

16. Lawrence Stone, *The Family, Sex and Marriage in England, 1500–1800* (New York, 1977), graphs on 49, 53.

dower together than she would have received from dower on all the property. From the husband's point of view, however, dower had not been successfully eliminated. There is no reason for historians to see things as he did.

In a further argument Bean emphasizes that the widow's provision could be increased through uses, and he declares that in practice it often was.[17] Questions as to class would seem to arise in considering this view. There is undoubtedly reason to think that the widow's provision was often increased by small landowners. Bean's aim, as he makes clear, is to give an exhaustive account of uses, one paying attention to all levels of landed society—to the great lords who were tenants-in-chief of the Crown, to the lesser or mesne lords, and even to "the lowest reaches of the feudal hierarchy." Among his conclusions is the finding that uses spread "to the lowest ranks of the peasantry," even to bondmen.[18] Small landowners, however, had ideas about family that differed from those of substantial landowners. Even if their ideas had not differed, small landowners had little room for maneuver. Their family arrangements must have been largely a matter of natural necessity. Where property was small, widows required, in order to live, proportionately greater rights than widows where property was large. Before dower had been established at one-third, the widow whose husband held by socage tenure had succeeded to half her husband's land. The widow of a villein—villeins not, of course, being owners in fee simple—succeeded to the whole of her husband's holding, at least on some manors; and historians have found the mark of villein status to lie in the existence of the right of the widow to succeed to the whole.[19] A study of medieval peasant wills has shown that a majority of husbands in the class left their widows more than one-third.[20] Drawing a distinction between men whose landed possessions were large and those whose possessions were small would go a good way towards reconciling contradictory claims.

There can be no doubt, however, that substantial landowners desired to reduce the provision that the common law mandated for their widows. This is proved by the fall in jointures that followed hard on the heels of the Statute of Uses, a fall that will shortly be described. The statute could not have altered

17. Bean, *Decline of English Feudalism*, 136–37.

18. Ibid., 20, 179.

19. T. F. T. Plucknett, *A Concise History of the Common Law*, 5th ed. (Boston, 1956), 567.

20. Cicely Howell, "Peasant Inheritance Customs in the Midlands, 1280–1700," in *Family and Inheritance*, ed. Jack Goody, Joan Thirsk, and E. P. Thompson (London, 1976), 142–43.

family attitudes in a twinkling. Rather it is to be seen as giving free rein to attitudes that had been developing, but which had been kept in check.

To sum up, great landowners desired to reduce the provision mandated by the common law for their widows, but the coming of uses can have had but an uncertain effect in forwarding their desire, here effective and there not. How far provision was reduced on those occasions when it could legally be reduced is impossible to say. Estate accounts, which alone could provide the answer, do not exist in any quantity for the period. Possibly the widow's provision did not fall greatly, for there could well have been some stickiness about the third, some limit to a fall that was possible only for one group of women but not for another when the groups were rather equal in number. On the other hand, in view of later developments, it is more likely that uses had effect in reducing widows' provision. With movement against them, women may have come to fear repercussions if they attempted to enforce a right that was obviously growing tenuous. The coming of uses then was an ominous development for the aristocratic widow, but it cannot be seen as reducing her right with general success.

3

It is the Statute of Uses that is the husband's charter, undoubtedly the major event in the history of the widow. The main provision of the statute was forthright and simple. It declared that though a man had transferred his land to feoffees he remained its legal owner. At a stroke it became impossible for landowners to escape wardship through the fiction that their undying feoffees were the owners of their land and not their mortal selves. Henry VIII thus regained his fiscal rights, putting an end to wills of land, though he had shortly to compromise with landowners in the Statute of Wills. Since the Statute of Uses made her husband the legal owner of his land, any use notwithstanding, it might be supposed that the widow was restored to her rights along with King Henry. But this was not to be; was never intended to be. The very statute whose preamble speaks of the wrongs done widows proceeds to give statutory embodiment to those wrongs. Henry had shed crocodile tears for the widow. The statute gave its blessing to the evasion of dower by providing that any jointure made before marriage acted forever as a bar to dower.

After the statute things stood thus: If a man married without granting his wife a jointure, then his land was subject to her dower. If he granted his wife a jointure after marriage, she was free as widow to refuse it and

to elect her dower instead. But so long as a man made a settlement of jointure on his bride before marriage, she was forever barred from dower, no
matter that he later inherited half a county. The widow's provision thus
became a matter of contract pure and simple between bride and groom, or
in view of an early time perhaps it should be said it again became that.

The Statute of Uses was in most respects soon set at nought. Maitland
spoke of it as "that marvellous monument of legislative futility . . . the
statute through which not mere coaches and four, but whole judicial pro-
cessions with javelin-men and trumpeters have passed and repassed in
triumph."[21] But it was not so with the statute in respect of dower. The
settlement in bar of dower became an invariable accompaniment of aristocratic marriage, the permanent effect of the statute upon landowners'
family arrangements.

According to Blackstone the dower provisions of the Statute of Uses were
necessary to prevent widows who had had jointures made upon them claiming their dower as well; and the story has been standardly repeated. Following the statute, as Blackstone explained, "all wives would have become
dowable of such lands as were held to the uses of their husbands, and also
entitled at the same time to any special lands that might be settled in jointure."[22] Certainly had the statute been silent on the subject of dower that
would have been the result. Nevertheless Blackstone's reasoning cannot
bear scrutiny. The problem he pointed to was a temporary one, affecting
only women who had already had jointures made on them; and it was
solved by clauses of the statute concerning such jointures. Women who
had had jointures made upon them before the statute were precluded from
claiming dower, except for women who were already widowed, who were
allowed to enjoy both dower and jointure if that was what they had been
entitled to. The problem Blackstone pointed to was solved simply by ensuring that the statute did not act retroactively. But the statute did not stop
there. Had it done so, dower for the future would have been restored, because husbands would no longer have been able to disguise ownership
behind a use. Blackstone's reasoning obscures the essence of what was
done. Parliament did not want dower restored. Quite the contrary. It went
on to provide a sure and general way of barring dower for the future.

Both Coke and Blackstone praised the dower provisions of the Statute of
Uses. Dower was "a great clog to alienations," Blackstone declared, "and

---

21. F. W. Maitland, "The Law of Real Property," in *The Collected Papers of F. W.
Maitland,* ed. H. A. L. Fisher (Cambridge, 1911), 1:191.

22. William Blackstone, *Commentaries on the Laws of England,* 2:137.

was otherwise inconvenient to families."[23] Dower must, of course, have hindered free dealings in land, because the wife's consent had been necessary in alienations by married men. Not only must this have hampered alienations by husbands, but also incautious purchasers ran the risk of finding unexpectedly that someone's widow had a charge on land they had bought. Under the statute, if the husband created a jointure before marriage he could deal freely with the part of his land that was not affected by it.

Dower had, it must be recognized, given the wife a power over her husband's land during marriage that is at odds with later concepts of the right of individuals to control their own property, her consent being necessary to any alienations he might want to make of his own lands during his lifetime. This aspect of dower would sooner or later have been abolished, but so radical an attack as was made upon dower is not explicable in these terms. Dower in copyhold land (normally called freebench) did not circumscribe the husband's power to deal with his holding during his life. A model for reform thus existed if the effect of dower upon alienations was the problem. The widow's right of dower could have been limited to land the husband died possessed of. The extent of the attack on dower must lead to the suspicion that the real objection to it is to be found in Blackstone's vague charge, that it "was otherwise inconvenient to families."

Coke and Blackstone also attempted to paint jointure as more advantageous than dower not only to the national economy but to widows themselves. To claim her dower a widow had had to sue out a writ and had had to wait, perhaps as much as forty days, until the heir assigned her the lands that were to constitute her dower. With a jointure she was automatically provided for at her husband's death. Moreover, the widow of a man who had been attainted as a traitor and had lost his head on Tower Hill lost her dower, but not her jointure. Jointure was thus, in Coke's words, "more sure and safe for the wife."[24] His words have often been repeated approvingly even to this day. The real question for the widow's story is what happened to the sum she received.

4

The Statute of Uses has had a magical effect upon the way the widow's provision is calculated. In medieval times her provision was judged in re-

23. Ibid., 2:136.

24. Edward Coke, *The First Part of the Institutes of the Laws of England, or a Commentary on Littleton*, 36.

lation to her husband's land, and medieval historians discuss it in those terms. After the statute the relationship followed became that of jointure to portion, and this has been the relationship followed by modern historians. After the statute, in other words, the jointure a husband provided for his widow is judged against the portion that she as bride had brought him from her natal family. This is an amazing shift in the method of accounting. Whereas the widow's right in earlier periods is calculated as a right over her husband's land, in later periods it is calculated as a return on her own fortune. The husband's land, the very item that dower was all about, has dropped off the balance sheet.

While the new method of accounting hides from view the husband's land, it nevertheless speaks of changes in the relationship between husband and wife. Changes in the ratio of jointure to portion indicate changes in the bargaining power of husband and wife as they negotiated at their marriage how much he promised in the future for what she gave in the present. Changes in the ratio, then, at least tell of the direction of movement, which is of interest in itself; and if the trend is followed to the end, it so happens that it will be possible to put the husband's land back onto the balance sheet.

Until jointures were paid in cash rather than land, it is difficult to establish their value with any precision. Only under the strict settlement do we thus have a firm figure for the relation of jointure to portion. For the sixteenth and seventeenth centuries, we have figures that their compiler, Lawrence Stone, has cautioned are tentative, for the reason just noted, but they are figures that must accurately enough reflect the trend. They show that in the mid-sixteenth century the ratio of jointure to portion stood about one to five; that is, for one pound of jointure the wife paid five pounds in portion. The ratio apparently fell to about one to six or seven by 1600; and by the latter half of the seventeenth century it had further fallen to one in ten. The ratio then steadily fell in the century after the Statute of Uses, clearly indicating a significant decline in the bargaining power of wives. For the same amount of jointure in 1700 the wife had to give twice as much in portion as she had in 1550.[25]

The final ratio of 10 percent is common in Orlando Bridgman's precedents. These precedents are actual settlements printed apparently unchanged except for clients' names being replaced by initials. The 10 percent ratio thus clearly established before the end of the seventeenth century was to remain the norm all through the eighteenth century. Other ratios are to be found, as low as 5 percent and as high as 20 percent, but 10 percent

25. Lawrence Stone, *The Crisis of Aristocracy, 1558–1601* (Oxford, 1965), 643–45.

is by far the commonest. This is the norm that is to be extracted from the book of precedents published by Gilbert Horsman about the middle of the eighteenth century, where the ratio of jointure to portion ranges between 7 and 12 percent.[26] Ten percent is also the norm that has been found in a collection of over fifty strict settlements made by eighteenth-century peers.[27] Indeed the 10 percent ratio was to prevail right through the nineteenth century. F. M. L. Thompson in his study of landownership in that century has found that 10 percent was the relationship settlors expected, and the examples he has given range from 5 to 15 percent.[28]

People came to speak of 10 percent as the customary ratio, as family papers and estate accounts testify. "The lady's portion is proposed to be £15,000," the Marquis of Rockingham's solicitor reported, adding, "To follow the usual method of making jointure, it would be proposed to settle for that portion 1500 a year in lands."[29] One father of a bride writing to the father of her groom made a gesture of protest: "The proposed jointure is what is very common in settlements, being ten percent on the lady's portion, yet [my solicitor] does not think it enough." Feebly, if realistically, he went on, "but [my wife] and I are content to leave this to you to provide for in your will."[30] Sir Ralph Vyvyan, reporting on a friend's settlement, wrote that the lady's fortune was £8,000, "for which in accord with ordinary custom she had the jointure of 10 percent."[31] There is no doubt then that dower had been replaced by a jointure that was 10 percent of portion.

The husband's land can now be brought back onto the balance sheet. With jointure at 10 percent of portion, an elementary calculation will suggest that the widow's claim on her husband's land had been reduced even to vanishing point. A widow would have to outlive her husband for ten years before she would consume her portion. Only after that would she become a charge upon her husband's land, and even then, in what must in normal circumstances be her last few years, she would be a charge far short

26. Gilbert Horsman, *Precedents in Conveyancing*, 2d ed. (London, 1757). Horsman printed twenty-two marriage settlements. Not all of them allow calculation of the jointure/portion ratio; and some families were clearly merchant families with little land, and I have eliminated these from my calculation.

27. Randolph Trumbach, *The Rise of the Egalitarian Family* (New York, 1978), 82.

28. F. M. L. Thompson, *English Landed Society in the Nineteenth Century* (London, 1963), 100–103.

29. Trumbach, *Rise of the Egalitarian Family*, 82n.

30. Thompson, *English Landed Society*, 101.

31. Sir Ralph Vyvyan to C. W. Popham, 3 February 1858, Vyvyan Manuscripts, Cornish Record Office.

of dower, for speaking to averages, 10 percent upon her relatively small portion would be far short of one-third of his income. Blackstone himself printed a settlement that tells of the relation between jointure and portion.[32] In that settlement land was granted the widow for her jointure. Settlements of land do not normally state the value of the land settled, but this one happens to allow it to be roughly calculated. (Blackstone used this settlement of jointure land simply to exemplify a grant of land.) Farmland of 540 acres was settled in return for a portion of £5,000. Allowing one pound an acre as the rental value of the land, which would be reasonable for the time, the ratio of jointure to portion is about 10 percent. If Blackstone ever drew the conclusion that is to be drawn from such a ratio he did not see fit to mention it.

A more systematic calculation is possible. It will only strengthen the rough and ready conclusion already reached, but it will allow further arrangements to be discussed that affect, or might be thought to affect, the balance sheet between husband and wife.

From data in the *Complete Peerage* it has been calculated that between the years 1601 and 1740 widows outlived their husbands by twelve years in Kent and by sixteen years in Northamptonshire.[33] If we assume the median longevity of the widow, and further assume, for ease of calculation, a portion of £1,000 and a jointure of £100, then an initial calculation is that the husband received £1,000 and paid, or rather his estate paid, £1,400. Throughout the marriage, however, the husband held the portion, or its equivalent in land, and he must be accounted as receiving income from it over the years of the marriage. If in fact he did not hold the portion because he had spent it rather than investing it, that was his imprudence, and is irrelevant to the balance sheet between husband and wife. When interest at 4 percent during the years of marriage is added to the husband's account, then he received a further £800, for the average marriage lasted about twenty years.[34] Furthermore, as the widow did not receive a lump sum upon her husband's death, even after his death the husband's estate continued to receive interest on the declining balance of her portion. This would add a further £180 to the husband's credit. Thus on second calculation the husband or his estate received £1,980 and paid £1,400. The widow has taken not a nibble at her husband's land. Indeed her husband has made a profit on the transaction involving jointure and portion—on top of the fact that he has escaped dower through it.

32. Blackstone, *Commentaries*, appendix 2 to book 2.
33. Lloyd Bonfield, *Marriage Settlements, 1601–1740* (Cambridge, 1983), 118.
34. Stone, *Family, Sex and Marriage*, 55, 57.

These calculations may be thought to overstate the case, and admittedly they do. Landowners contracted to pay pin money to their wives during marriage, and this would seem to mean that some, or even all, the interest during marriage accrued to their wives. Pin money was naturally much less than jointure. It has never been investigated from family accounts, but from precedent books it would seem not to have been more than half jointure. It could be much less, but with some frequency it seems to have approached one-half. It may be that pin money came gradually to be calculated so that it would consume the interest on the portion, and thus in effect give the wife the interest on her portion during her marriage. If landowners calculated at 5 percent, pin money would consume the interest if it were half the jointure. If they calculated at 4 percent, pin money would consume the interest if it were rather less than half the jointure. Thus it would seem that the £800 that has been treated above as going to the husband may well have gone to the wife, she in effect taking the interest on her portion during marriage.

How pin money is to be taken into account is, however, a difficult question. It was a peculiar form of property, as an analysis of the legal decisions concerning it has shown. Its peculiarity is to be sensed in the principle that a wife could not claim arrears of pin money beyond one year. Arrears on contract debts could be claimed much beyond that. The wife could not claim arrears because she had during her marriage been maintained by her husband. Pin money and the ordinary maintenance of wife by husband were thus connected. Despite the wording of settlements, which declared it to be for "the sole and separate use of the wife," pin money had strings attached to it. It was understood to be for the wife's clothes, for tips to her servants, and for her charities. Since a husband had in common law the duty to maintain his wife according to his station in life, pin money was on this view a contract by which a man bound himself to do what he was legally bound to do anyway. Pin money operated really to relieve the wife of the humiliation of asking for money each time she required it. This was certainly a great benefit to wives psychologically, giving them a sense of independence, but it was doubtfully a real transfer of property.[35]

Legally there is thus ground for treating pin money as no real transfer of resources from husband to wife, but as merely a mutually convenient way of running their household. In practice, however, this is undoubtedly too strict a way of treating it. Most husbands would not have thought they were making a contract that had no substance when they agreed to pay pin

---

35. Staves, *Married Women's Separate Property*, 131–61.

money; nor would most fathers have thought they were accomplishing nothing when they demanded pin money for their daughters. In many families, probably in nearly all, some part of pin money must have gone on things a husband would not otherwise have consented to, husbands interpreting the words "to the sole and separate use of the wife" with more generosity of spirit and more in accordance with their commonsense meaning than the courts would do in cases of family conflict. In gentry and aristocratic families, moreover, pin money was inconsequential to the family's finances, and so long as husbands were not troubled by requests for things they held covered by it, and so long as their wives kept up appearances, they were probably indifferent how it was spent. Pin money was less valuable to wives than it appears on the surface, but to the degree that it allowed them in practice to have or to do things that there would otherwise have been opposition to, it was a real transfer of property to them. All that can be said is that the profit to husbands of their marital negotiations was rather less than has been suggested in the calculations above. But husbands can hardly have lost on the transaction involving jointure, pin money, and portion when it is judged on its own, while escaping dower rights over one-third of their land.

Let us suppose, however, that the bride's portion had been settled to her own use, a form of settlement that avoided the legal ambiguities of pin money. Such settlements seem to have come late to landed families, where pin money was normally the provision for the wife during marriage, at least through the eighteenth century; and it is possible that settling the bride's portion to her own use was never common practice in landed families. But it was sometimes done, and the separate estate might well be considered, representing as it does the extreme of husbandly generosity. In this case the husband, or his estate, paid out £1,400 in jointure without any recompense, and the question becomes simply, What did he escape in dower? This can be calculated at least in a rough and ready way. On the assumption that the wife's portion was one year's income of her father's estate (which was about the norm, as will appear later), then her father's estate was on the order of £1,000 a year. On the further assumption that her father's estate and her husband's were equal, then her husband also had an estate on the order of £1,000 a year. The two estates in any one marriage might in fact not have been equal, and either that of the wife's father or that of her husband might have been the larger. Rough equality is to be calculated upon, however, for in an intermarrying group the disparities that were possible in individual cases would tend for the group to cancel out. Dower on an estate worth £1,000 per annum would have

claimed one-third of that sum for fourteen years, or £4,662. Since by jointure the husband paid only £1,400, the widow's provision was reduced by
about two-thirds under the most liberal of marital transactions.

A certain class of strict settlements gives further evidence about the mea-
gerness of jointures. A marriage agreement was sometimes negotiated under the umbrella of a family settlement that had been made earlier. This
happened when the family estate had been settled at the coming of age of
the heir, or when it had been settled by a will. In these cases the family
settlement laid out the terms upon which the tenant for life could arrange
for his marriage, including the terms upon which he could raise jointure
on the estate. These settlements sometimes dealt with jointures by determining the ratio that was to be observed between jointure and portion,
usually determining on 10 percent. Sometimes they stated in money terms
the amount of jointure that could at most be charged upon the estate. In
settlements of the latter form, the relation of jointure to land value is directly evident if the latter can be determined. In one example where the
land value can be determined, the fourth Duke of Marlborough under the
will of the third was allowed to charge by way of jointure £4,000 at most
on an estate whose gross rental in 1731, or about the time, was between
£50,000 and £60,000.[36] In 1847 Sir Tatton Sykes was allowed to raise £4,000
at most on an estate worth a clear £30,000 per annum.[37] Whatever the
arrangements, the story of jointure is essentially the same.

The foregoing calculations, except for the last, are actuarial in nature.
Some landowners would, of course, have been less lucky than average and
would have been saddled with long-lived widows whose cost, even at 10
percent of their portions, might be considerable. Complaints about jointure
thus continued to be voiced, but they obviously need to be taken with a
grain of salt. The sixth Lord Monson complained of a jointure he was
obliged to pay to the widow of his predecessor in the title. After seventeen
years, we find him writing to his son, "I have just heard an account of the
Dowager Lady Monson. She flourishes about the country with a sister (unmarried) a maid and a nephew and a groom, a Dog cart and two saddle
horses. She rides until tired then puts the groom on her horse and drives
the Dog cart and thus makes her way about the Lakes and Scotland. I see

36. Blenheim Papers, British Library, 61446 f. 8.

37. Barbara English, "The Family Settlements of the Sykes of Sledmere," in *Law,
Economy and Society, 1750–1914: Essays in the History of English Law*, ed. G. R.
Rubin and David Sugarman (Abingdon, Eng., 1984), 234.

and envy. She will live for ever."[38] She was in fact to outlive the writer by nearly thirty years and almost to outlive his son, all the while taking a jointure that, so far as their calculations went, simply ate up nearly 20 percent of their income. The sixth lord and his son are hardly to be sympathized with, however. They had had the unexpected good fortune to inherit their estate from a cousin who had left the widow complained of when he died at the age of thirty-two.

Such is human nature, that even in more normal situations, it was easy for complaints about the cost of widows to arise, for when the jointure came to be paid, the portion was likely to have been forgotten, long spent or mentally merged in the estate's capital account. Families that produced few widows or produced short-lived ones never wrote about their good fortune. Historians' literary sources are thus naturally biased on the subject of widows.

By any actuarial calculation, then, the widow's right to one-third of her husband's land had, in the run of cases, virtually disappeared. Effectively the cost of the aristocratic widow had been transferred to her own family, which paid the portion, which paid the jointure.

Not only had the amount of the jointure declined, but its form had also changed. It had once been an enfeoffment of land to the use of the husband and wife for their joint lives and after the husband's decease to the use of the widow. The widow had then held land, whether equal to dower or not. Under the strict settlement the jointure became merely a rent charge, the land itself on the husband's death going directly to the heir. This happened despite the legal requirement that a jointure be "a competent estate of freehold for the widow." A cash payment was not a good jointure in common law, being no freehold; but the court of equity, when it came to review the practice, maintained that since a woman was competent to bar her dower, she was competent to bar it on any terms she thought fitting. Thus money replaced land in law as in practice.[39] Given the mystique attached to land, this decision was a further demotion for the widow, who ceased to hold even jointure land, let alone land in dower.

It might well be asked how all this could have happened. After all, a jointure was a bargain struck between bride and groom, and usually a bargain in which their respective families played a major part. Why was the

38. Lord Monson to his eldest son, 24 April 1858, Monson manuscripts, Lincolnshire Record Office.

39. Holdsworth, *History of English Law*, 3:197 n. 7.

woman not better protected by her family? Answers are not far to seek. In the first place, the families were not of equal bargaining power in these negotiations. Far from it. On the one side was an eldest son with a landed estate; on the other side was a daughter with a small portion. Economically the power of the one to the other was about as one hundred is to five. The groom and his family inevitably called the tune. Furthermore, this very imbalance made the marriage far more desirable to the bride's family than it was to the groom's, and the former thus came to the bargaining table with a stronger desire that the marriage take place. The daughter's fate might have been a younger son and downward social mobility. Her father pressed his luck no further than attempting to ensure some equivalency between what he turned over with his daughter and what she received in jointure and pin money. Dower went by the board.

In the second place, while the families were not of equal bargaining power, they were normally social equals. Both of them understood the aristocratic ethos. Both were imbued with primogenitive and patrilineal ideas. The bride's family in its turn would normally have an eldest son to make marriage arrangements for, and it would not then have high ideas about the rights of daughters. Looked at in the round, the bride's family understood very well what preserving an estate meant for various family members. In the negotiations between the families, provisions were being laid out that would preserve for the next generation the power and prestige of an aristocratic family, something understood and pressed for on both sides. Bargaining there was, but on the outlines of the agreement there was fundamental accord from the beginning. What it comes to is this: dower and aristocratic power were essentially antithetical.

It has been common for historians to portray settlement as of advantage to women. It did offer them one advantage that needs to be noticed, the importance of which should not, however, be exaggerated. Willy-nilly, settlement protected a wife and her children from a husband who was so irresponsible that if his property were left unsettled he might waste it, might possibly even destroy it completely, thus destroying the base of the family's livelihood. This advantage of settlement to women is not to be utterly forgotten, and it must have counted for something with fathers of brides as they entered into negotiations with fathers of grooms. But landowners did not often utterly destroy their family estates, and with regularity they provided for their families. The main force making for the diminution of estates actually lay in the family itself, lay in leaving a man free to do as he chose about his daughters and younger children. The insurance a woman received against the possibility that her husband would turn out a wastrel was a side effect of a deed that on balance decidedly favored males, insuring patrilineal and primogenitive principles.

The final step in the putting down of the widow was taken by the Dower Act of 1833. Dower was not formally abolished. A widow continued to have a right to it; her right was even extended to trust property; but at the same time her husband was given absolute power by deed or will to bar her dower. The "right" of dower had become purely and simply conditional upon the husband's allowing it. So far as the Dower Act affected prenuptial contracts, it was to make them—such as they were—protection a bride had better seek or possibly do worse. The act stands as evidence that through those prenuptial contracts dower had become an anachronism. That was the point made by the Real Property Commissioners in 1829, when they had proposed giving husbands power to bar dower at their pleasure. Dower, they said, was of little value because it was never calculated upon as a provision for widows.[40] The Dower Act thus completed what the Statute of Uses may not quite have begun but what it certainly gave free license to. A legal witticism runs that the great Statute of Uses, by the time lawyers had finished with it, had no other effect than to add three words to a conveyance—a calculation clearly made without regard to the widow.

To be sure, in the end some widows received more from their husbands than the above discussion would suggest. Their husbands left them bequests in their wills out of personal property, or granted them charges out of unsettled land; or their sons agreed at resettlement to increase their jointures. One dowager Duchess of Devonshire simply had her jointure doubled when she complained that it was not equal to that of her Russell counterpart.[41] ("Our old duchess is as good as yours.") But these additions were gifts; they were not rights. They depended on the will of others and were uncertain. They cannot logically be held to compensate for the loss of a right; nor could they in practice in the great majority of cases have come close to dower in value.

5

With the transfer of dower into jointure, an invariable right in law had become a matter of private contract. Contracts for their validity normally

---

40. Parliamentary Papers 1829, *First Report of the Real Property Commission,* 16.
41. D. M. Stuart, *Dearest Bess* (London, 1955), 182.

require two consenting adult parties. Sometimes, however, women married before they were of age. We now know that age of marriage in England was higher than we had imagined, and that most women were of age when they married.[42] Still some were not, and their history, raising as it does a striking question of principle, needs to be added to the larger story.

The question whether a bride who was a minor could contract to bar herself of dower ought to have arisen, or so it would seem, immediately after the Statute of Uses. Given the care that the courts have normally taken to protect minors, laying upon those who deal with them special responsibility to deal fairly, one would expect the question would soon have developed a body of law about it. That the marriage of minors raised legal problems was well recognized in certain cases. When male heirs married under age, the precaution was usually taken of seeking a private act of Parliament to facilitate the settlement of the estate. Such acts are also found facilitating settlements on the marriage of minor females who had actually inherited land, although such acts are rare because females who actually inherited land were rare. Most women, including even most women who were heiresses-at-law, possessed only portions. Minors who had inherited land were apparently one thing in the eyes of settlors, however, and minor females possessed only of portions another. While it was understood that binding settlements could not be made by the one class, it was apparently taken for granted that they could be by the other, for when a woman who was possessed only of a portion married under age, settlors regularly proceeded in indifference to the question whether she had the capacity to bar herself of dower. Parliament could not reasonably have been expected to pass a private act each time a portioned woman married under age; but utter silence on the question of the minor female's capacity to deal with dower is surprising. It was to surprise Lord Chancellor Northington, who in *Drury v. Drury* was to comment on "the want of curiosity" of conveyancers who confessed never to inquire whether a woman was a minor when drawing up a settlement, "a point which, unless we have much misspent our time, was certainly worth inquiring about."[43]

It was in *Drury v. Drury* (1760), more than two hundred years after the Statute of Uses, that the question was finally aired. In this case, a woman who had married before the age of twenty-one sought to have her settlement overturned exactly on the ground that as a minor she had been prevailed upon to accept a jointure that was less than dower. Possibly the

---

42. See discussion in chapter 6.
43. *Drury v. Drury* (1760), 2 Eden 59.

Marriage Act of 1753 had something to do with the filing of the case. That act had determined that twenty-one was the age at which either males or females became fully capable of contracting marriage, and it had swept aside lingering ecclesiastical ideas about the age at which marriage was permissible, ideas that might earlier have complicated legal arguments. On the other hand, it had long been the rule that a woman, like a man, had to be twenty-one before she could alienate lands or chattels.[44] Lord Northington found in the plaintiff's favor, allowing her to elect her dower instead of her jointure. In the process he had some sport at the expense of aristocratic heirs whose necessities prevented them making "the law's reasonable provision for their mothers." "The law has been much arraigned as being too liberal in its provisions to the wife," he observed, "and it was asked what man of £15,000 per annum would marry, if the wife was to take a third, when the heir was to be cramped to £10,000 per annum and stinted in luxury, expense, and diversion for the sake of his mother?"[45]

Upon appeal to the House of Lords—almost to a man aristocratic heirs who were not making the law's reasonable provision for their mothers—Lord Northington was overruled. In *Earl of Buckinghamshire v. Drury*, (the case upon appeal) it was thus indubitably determined that a female, though she was a minor, could contract to bar herself forever of dower.

The dominant reasoning of the age is most thoroughly laid out in a lengthy opinion by Justice Wilmot. Wilmot, who was later to be Lord Chief Justice, had been one of the judges in *Drury*, and this opinion was his submission to the appeals court. It was published by his son in filial tribute along with others of his father's opinions. It is a signal document in the history of the widow and worth extensive consideration.

Wilmot appropriately began his discussion by considering whether the Statute of Uses in its dower provisions intended to make a difference between infant and adult females, and he concluded that it did not. He then turned to consider practice, for if a statute might be in doubt, long usage was the way to judge of its intent. In practice, he declared, "every great family in the Kingdom" was in possession of settlements made on minor females, and yet there was "not one single instance where they have been disputed," clear evidence of "the sense of two Centuries on the Question."[46] Furthermore, it was to the advantage of females who married under

44. Pollock and Maitland, *History of English Law*, 2:439.

45. *Drury v. Drury* (1760), 2 Eden 52.

46. John Eardley Wilmot, *Notes of Opinions and Judgements*, edited by his son (London, 1802), 218–19.

age to have the capacity to bar dower at the time of their marriage, and not to have their jointures contended about when they came of age. Otherwise, "it would check the most advantageous Marriages they could make."[47]

Nevertheless, the question of fraud by husbands could not be quite ignored; and here Wilmot is at his most interesting. He denied that fraud had ever been practiced. Before the statute it could not be practiced, because "dower could not be fraudulently barred when it could not be barred at all."[48] This is legally nice, but socially evasive. The reasoning runs thus: A husband could not bar dower after marriage; therefore he could not bar his wife of dower. By making an arrangement about dower before marriage, he did not bar his wife of anything she was entitled to, because she was not then his wife and no dower right was in existence at the time. Wilmot had, however, just shown exactly how dower was, if not technically barred before the statute, then prevented from arising; and he had emphasized that the principle of the statute was that women who had already had jointures made upon them in lieu of dower were to accept those jointures "whether they be great or small, adequate or inadequate, whether they have been made by the agreement of themselves, or have been the mere spontaneous act of the husband." Still he roundly contended that "a Jointure before the Act could not have the least shade of Fraud in it."[49]

After the statute, he conceded, fraud might have become possible, for a jointure had come to be defined as a competent livelihood of freehold for the widow; and he acknowledged that what would constitute a competent livelihood might be difficult to determine. The difficulty the court had faced in *Drury* in attempting to determine what jointure was suitable to the plaintiff's fortune and status had been a major factor in Lord Northington's decision to allow her the right to elect her dower. Nevertheless for Wilmot it showed little faith in the capacity of a British jury to think that it would be incapable of determining what was a suitable provision and what was not.

Finally, Wilmot faced up to the issue. He was well aware that jointures might be far less than dower; and with the air of a man reaching at last the substance of the case and delivering what must be the knockout argument, he showed why this gave no cause of complaint to the minor female. A man of his own day, he observed, might have all his estate in trust—the Statute of Uses not long preventing uses under a different name—and as

47. Ibid., 225.
48. Ibid., 202–3.
49. Ibid., 209.

there had been no dower out of a use, so there was none out of a trust. Thus a man need not pay his widow anything. "All the Objection of prejudice to Infants, as the Law now stands, vanishes in a moment; for what detriment can it be to Infants to preclude them from Dower by a small Estate, when they may equally be precluded from it without giving them any Estate at all?"[50]

Lord Mansfield agreed with the *Buckinghamshire* decision, as Wilmot's son pointed out.[51] Mansfield based his argument simply on the belief that marriage was a desirable state for women. As he put it, the jointure agreement was one "to the Infant's advancement: Marriage is so." And he went on to calculate in the manner of the day. Before her marriage the infant Drury had had "only £2,000 for her fortune: it was an advantageous bargain for her at the time." Lord Mansfield perhaps held that marriage was an aspect of the uniform commercial code.

One can only wonder what Britton would have thought of it all. In the thirteenth century he had emphasized that dower, being "ordered by the common constitution of the people," could not be negotiated about by individuals, "for if by one then by another, and so the constitution would be destroyed."

6

Widows also lost their right to a mandatory share of their husbands' personal property. Logically this was a development of less importance to widows in landed society than to those in the middle class, where many a family's entire worth consisted of goods and chattels, that is, of personal property. The development was not without considerable meaning for landed families, however. On the one hand, the widow's early and complete loss of her right to personal property was a legal precedent for the Dower Act. On the other hand, English landowners often owned substantial property that fell into the legal category of personal property. Something then needs to be said of the history of a widow's right to personal property.

According to early authorities, a widow had a right to a "reasonable part" of her husband's personal estate, which reasonable part was defined as one-third. The right was to one-third absolutely, not merely for life as in the case of dower. Blackstone could not trace when the alteration began, but

50. Ibid., 213.
51. Ibid., 226.

he cited authority to the effect that the right to one-third remained general law until the time of Charles I. Between that time and 1725—when the "custom of London," the last of several local ordinances, was abolished—he described the law as having been "altered by imperceptible degrees" until a man became free to bequeath the whole of his personal property as he chose. Englishmen (but not Scotsmen, he noted) could, if they were so minded, dispose of all their personal estate by will, and the claims of the widow would be totally barred.[52]

Allowing a widow to be freely cut off at her husband's pleasure was surely an extraordinary legal development. It is one difficult to account for except as a patriarchal development, and even in that light it remains astonishing. The course of development would seem to have been circular, although connections have not been traced. In the sixteenth century the Statute of Uses reduced the widow's right to landed property. In the seventeenth century that precedent must have exerted a powerful influence when her right to personal property was eliminated. In the nineteenth century, the policy established relative to personal property was applied back again to landed property. Blackstone did not even attempt to say why the widow's right to personal property became barrable. "Thirds," unlike dower, were not a clog on alienations. Indeed for once Blackstone failed to deliver an encomium on a law of England, and reading between the lines, he seemed uncomfortable with what he had to relate. Maitland no more than Blackstone was able to say when or how the widow lost her right. The law seemed, as he put it, to have slipped "unconsciously into the decision of a very important and debatable question."[53]

It is not to be suggested that in practice widows of business and professional men ever suffered loss of property to the same degree as did the widows of landowners. Their husbands had not the primogenitive impulse of landowners, at least not unless they were socially aspiring of becoming gentry, which may be a significant proviso. Nor had they often so great wealth that their widows could live on less than one-third of their property. A leading nineteenth-century authority found that wills in the middle class generally followed the Statute of Distribution of 1670, which determined distributions in cases of intestacy and gave the widow the traditional third.[54] No matter how testamentary freedom translated into action in the middle class, of course, the power it gave to husbands, and the fear it must some-

---

52. Blackstone, *Commentaries*, 2:493.
53. Pollock and Maitland, *History of English Law*, 2:355.
54. George Brodrick, *English Land and English Landlords* (London, 1881), 97.

times have occasioned among wives, and the injustice it must from time to time have inflicted, meant that an increase in patriarchal power occurred even in the middle class. Utter testamentary freedom has since been questioned, and the twentieth century has seen the widow gain a right of appeal against her husband's will.[55]

In considering what the husband's power to dispose of personal property at will meant for widows in landed families, we have no statistics to go on, nor have we any authoritative opinions. In view of landowners' general attitude to women's holding property, which has become evident, it is very likely that they would again have taken the opportunity to cut down the widow's right. All that can be surely said is that the landowner who enlarged his widow's provision through his personal property may well have given her, all the same, less than the common law would have mandated. Historians, alas, must look gift horses in the mouth.

7

In sum, the history of the widow in landed society is the story of how a real right to one-third of her husband's property was transformed into a provision specified through negotiations before her marriage. These negotiations took place in such unequal circumstances in primogenitive families that they left the widow without any right over her husband's land, and with her only certain right the return of her own property. Theoretically the Statute of Uses could be defended as fair on the ground that a woman (provided she was not a minor) might be assumed to act in full knowledge of what she was doing as she negotiated for jointure in place of dower and that she ought to have been able to protect her own interests. It did not work out that way, could not work out that way, given the difference in power between the parties to the contract in gentry and aristocratic families.

As a result of those prenuptial contracts the widow ceased to be of consequence in landholding. As long as the common law had prevailed, widows at any one moment would have held a significant proportion of the land of the country. Wives, being younger than their husbands, were often the survivors, and surviving as they did a considerable number of years, inev-

---

55. Inheritance (Family Provision) Act, 1 & 2 Geo. 6, c. 45. Extended by the Family Provision Act of 1966 and the Inheritance (Provision for Family and Dependants) Act of 1975.

itably a good proportion of the estates of the country would have had widows enjoying dower upon them. Empirical investigation has shown that in the sixteenth century landed estates had widows upon them more than half the time.[56] A calculation for the eighteenth century has shown much the same thing. In the year 1783, 70 percent of Irish peers either were or had been paying jointure.[57] Thus, had the common law prevailed, a dowager as often as not would have been in possession of one-third of a family's land, which is to say that dowagers would at any one time have been in possession of one-sixth of aristocratic lands. With the disappearance of dower, then, a position of social and economic power that women had at one time enjoyed disappeared. The aristocratic widow faded into insignificance, an annuitant, that well-named relict, comfortable enough no doubt, but not of the account she had been.

Sarah Duchess of Marlborough might seem to counter this conclusion, for she certainly never faded into insignificance; and she has more than once been cited as an example of the aristocratic widow, forceful and rich. Though it is to puncture a colorful stereotype, it has to be noted that Duchess Sarah was in a legal position that few aristocratic widows were in, or ever had been in. Through an act of Parliament, passed at the behest of her personal friend Queen Anne, she had dower of the whole Woodstock estate should there be no male heir to the dukedom, which in fact happened with the early death of her son.[58] She had as well under the will of the duke a highly unusual jointure of £20,000 out of his private estate.[59] "In England," Sarah's grandson once reminded her, "£3,500 a year is counted a great . . . jointure."[60] Probably the scale of her jointure also owed much to Queen Anne, although indirectly. By another act of Parliament the queen had made the Marlborough title inheritable by Sarah's eldest daughter; and the choice before the duke in making his will was thus between two females each holding estates. That Duchess Sarah did not fade into insignificance but lived to be the bane of architects and of her sons-in-law was exactly due to her powerful legal and financial position, a position that was quite different from that of most aristocratic widows.

56. Stone, *Crisis of Aristocracy*, 172.

57. David Large, "The Wealth of the Greater Irish Landowners, 1750–1815," *Irish Historical Studies* 15 (1966): 38.

58. Statutes, 5 Anne, c. 3.

59. Blenheim Papers, British Library, 61451 f. 172.

60. Ibid., 61446 ff. 128–29.

3 Younger Children

We have always considered the talents of younger

brothers as an unanswerable argument in favour

of Providence.

—*Benjamin Disraeli*, The Young Duke

The third, and final, rule of the common law that landowners sought to evade was the rule that younger children took no part of
their father's land. This was really the obverse of the basic rule that land
went, where there was an eldest son, to him entirely. The histories of the
widow and the heiress are tales of how a large common law right was more
or less eliminated. The history of younger children is both more complex
and less dramatic because landowners wholeheartedly believed in the primacy of the eldest son. When in the nineteenth century primogeniture
came under attack by philosophical radicals, landowners time and again rose
in its defense. Primogeniture was in their minds some essential virtue at
the heart of the nation's life. The well-being of agriculture, the stability
and good sense of English political life, the very British constitution, were
claimed to depend upon it. Thus in the case of younger children landowners
merely wanted some modification of a rule that was basically congenial to
them, wanting some provision for younger children but also decidedly
wanting the eldest son guaranteed most of the estate. The resulting history
is not unidirectional throughout but is one of up and down for younger

children—a story of how they came to be provided for, but also of how their provision was later on limited.

1

It would be surprising only if landowners had not objected to the common law on the score of their younger children. England's was a uniquely harsh rule of primogeniture. Maitland spoke of it as "our amazing law of inheritance."[1] It stood in contrast to continental laws, which mandated some form of partition, at least among sons. In Normandy, for example, there was parage, a system whereby sons shared the inheritance, the younger holding in feudal dependence upon the elder. The common law rule seems also to have stood in contrast to Anglo-Saxon habits. All indications are that land in Anglo-Saxon England had been divided upon sons. That continued to be the rule of law in Kent.

So abnormal a rule as became fixed invites speculation as to its cause. Maitland suggested that the cause lay in the centralization of government brought about by the Conqueror and his immediate successors. England's "absolute and uncompromising form of primogeniture . . . belongs not to feudalism in general, but to a highly centralized feudalism in which the king has not much to fear from his mightiest vassals, and is strong enough to impose a law that in his eyes has many merits, above all the great merit of simplicity."[2] J. C. Holt has suggested, tongue in cheek perhaps, that the rule derived from the fact that England was a conquered country. It was a colony, on the receiving end of colonial exploitation. The younger son of an Anglo-Norman baron had plenty of opportunity to gain land and satisfy his ambitions without impinging on his elder brother's inheritance.[3]

However the English rule is to be explained, its peculiarity was later much commented on. In the sixteenth century primogeniture came under discussion in several European countries, its merits being debated and the forms of inheritance that had developed in various countries being compared. England's rule caused much unfavorable comment, not to say simple

1. F. Pollock and F. W. Maitland, *The History of English Law before the Time of Edward I*, 2d ed. (Cambridge, 1898), 2:266.

2. Ibid., 2:265.

3. J. C. Holt, "Feudal Society and the Family in Early Medieval England: The Revolution of 1066," *Transactions of the Royal Historical Society*, 5th ser. 32 (1982): 205–6.

surprise.[4] Continental countries seem always to have had some concept of the right of each child, certainly of each male child, to some part of the family inheritance, but the concept is not to be found in the English law of real property. It is to be found in the law of chattels, but chattels were for long a relatively insignificant form of property, and even in regard to chattels it was to die out.

Though the English law of real property had thus no concept of the legitime, that concept may be said to be written in the human heart. Common law and common practice soon parted company in this case, a fact not sufficiently recognized in the sixteenth-century literature on primogeniture. Younger children in England were not long cut out of their father's land. Maitland, though speaking of the nineteenth century, might have spoken of almost any time when he stressed that this common law rule was one that fathers virtually never allowed to take effect.[5]

The legal instruments that feature in the history of younger children are the same as those that have been discussed in relation to the heiress, that is to say, the maritagium, the entail, the use, and the strict settlement. As legal devices, they need brief reconsideration to set them into the changed family context.

In the twelfth and thirteenth centuries there was the maritagium, the gift made at the marriage of a younger child. It seems that the feudal landowner had always possessed the power to make such a gift on the marriage of a daughter; indeed it seems that the daughter had the right to demand the gift. If the landowner wished to make such a gift on a younger son, however, it seems that originally the consent of his eldest son, the heir, had been required. By the thirteenth century this consent was no longer required, and the landowner was free to make inter vivos grants on his younger children, male or female.[6] The maritagium, earlier noted because it could ominously specify the sex of the heirs who were to take under it, and thus is to be seen as instituting the attack on the heiress, is now noteworthy because it indicates the natural ambivalence of aristocratic landowners towards younger children. The gift to the younger child was conditional; it became absolute only when the marriage had produced heirs

4. Joan Thirsk, "The European Debate on Customs of Inheritance," in *Family and Inheritance*, ed. Jack Goody, Joan Thirsk, and E. P. Thompson (London, 1976), 185–89.

5. F. W. Maitland, "The Law of Real Property," in *The Collected Papers of F. W. Maitland*, ed. H. A. L. Fisher (Cambridge, 1911), 1:193.

6. Pollock and Maitland, *History of English Law*, 2:308–9; W. S. Holdsworth, *History of English Law* (London, 1922–66), 3:75.

for several generations. If heirs failed within that time, the land returned to the senior branch of the family. The junior branch had to prove its viability before the senior would release land to it absolutely. Thus on the one hand, the maritagium indicates a desire on the part of landowners to keep land intact in the main branch of the family. On the other hand, it also indicates their determination to make some provision for younger children.

By the fourteenth century the maritagium had developed into the entail. The statute *De donis,* alleging in its preamble that donees in receipt of conditional grants had frequently alienated the land against the will of the donor, declared that henceforth the will of the donor was to be observed. As the statute was to be interpreted, conditional grants, which had earlier become absolute after several generations, became conditional forever. The maritagium had developed into a new kind of fee, a perpetual estate that in comparison with a fee simple was limited, giving its possessors, one after another, what was in effect only a life interest. Whenever the heirs of the donee died out, no matter how far in the future, the land returned intact to the donor, or to his right heirs. The donee and his heirs could never, in words that are now appropriate, bar the entail. Like its forebear, the entail was useful for providing for younger children, and medieval historians note its employment in this way.

The entail, however, was no answer to the desires landowners had for their estates. Indeed the entail was a more problematic device for landowners than has generally been recognized. Landowners' desires did not center upon younger children; the heiress was also to be put down. The entail could certainly cut the heiress down. If a man entailed his land on his eldest son in tail male, he cut out females from the succession for so long as that was biologically possible. But though the entail could cut out heiresses, and though it could provide for younger children, it could not do both these things together. The man who entailed parts of his land on his younger sons left future heirs, even female heirs, to succeed to the bulk of the estate. The man who entailed his land on his eldest son, thus preventing females from succeeding to the estate, prevented any provision for the future heiresses who were postponed and as well prevented any provision for future younger children. The two uses that are to be ascribed to the entail were in principle opposed to one another.

Inevitably the entail caused trouble for landowners. It has also caused trouble for historians. Charles Neate, a professor of political economy at Oxford in the nineteenth century, wrote in one work that medieval landowners were so anxious to perpetuate their families that virtually all aristocratic land was entailed, and in another work, taking notice of the "very simple and common form of entail," by which landowners provided for their younger children, declared that medieval landowners were unlikely to have entailed all their land on their eldest sons and that "a very large part of the land of the country was free from the restriction of entail."[7] The entail has caused trouble for later historians as well. K. B. McFarlane emphasized through most of his work that the entail was one of the causes of a great weakening of primogeniture among medieval landowners, who through it took to dispersing large parts of their estates among their sons. Meanness to cadets, he declared, was not a principle that medieval landowners subscribed to. He ended with the conclusion, however, that the entail preserved primogeniture by maintaining the unity of the inheritance against the perils of female heirs, who would have caused division where there was a plurality of them and who would, even when there was but a single one of them, have carried the inheritance to strangers.[8] In the one case he assumed that entails were used to provide for younger children, and in the other that they were used to keep estates in the hands of eldest sons. A legal historian of the highest caliber, J. H. Baker, speaking of the contention between Crown and landowners over the Statute of Uses, has stressed that landowners rejected thoroughgoing primogeniture.[9] Turning to discuss family settlements, he declares that "it is not unlikely that entails were effective in most families at least to exclude females and collaterals."[10] But entails could not be effective in excluding females without enforcing primogeniture.

Baker's comment about entails' being effective to exclude collaterals needs brief notice in view of the idea, emphasized in this book, that landowners aimed not to exclude collaterals but to postpone direct females in favor of collateral males. Of course, an entail excluded collaterals in the sense that it was initially made upon one man and "the heirs of his body" or "the heirs male of his body" (depending upon whether it was in tail general or in tail male). In this elementary sense an entail made upon an

---

7. Neate's difficulties were pointed out in P. M. Lawrence, *The Law and Custom of Primogeniture* (Cambridge, 1878), 54n. Lawrence quoted from two works by Neate: *Two Lectures on the History and Conditions of Landed Property* (London, 1860) and *The History and Uses of the Law of Entail and Settlement* (London, 1865). I have not been able to consult the former directly.

8. K. B. McFarlane, *The Nobility of Later Medieval England* (Oxford, 1973), 64–68, 270–74.

9. *Spelman's Reports*, ed. J. H. Baker, Selden Society, vol. 94 (London, 1977), 203.

10. Ibid., 206.

eldest son excluded the younger; and one made upon a younger son excluded the elder. The "exclusion of collaterals" in this sense simply means, however, that a landowner had to begin by deciding whether to use the entail to limit succession to the line of his eldest son, or whether to use it to disperse land upon a younger son. (If he "rejected primogeniture," he could not really do the former.) In operation, an entail in tail male, whomever it was initially made on, proceeded by favoring collateral males over direct females; and this is undoubtedly the main point to be emphasized about collaterals.

The problematical nature of the entail cannot be too much stressed. It has seldom been clearly pointed to, let alone sufficiently emphasized; and yet it is fundamental in understanding the development of real property law. Discussions of entails have skirted around problems that need to be confronted, and the device has not been seen whole. Logically, the unbarrable entail could never have satisfied landowners' desires. A summary of it would be that where it was used to settle estates on eldest sons it must prove an intolerable nuisance, disinheriting all other family members in the future; and where it was used to provide for younger sons it was simply inadequate to the range of desires that landowners entertained. Landowners might, of course, attempt something of a juggling feat. They might attempt to juggle land in fee (for younger sons and daughters), land in tail male (for eldest sons), and land in tail general (in case there should be heiress daughters); but it is hard to see that they could succeed. The attempt to match family needs to available resources by such unsystematic arrangements would have required marital and demographic luck that was unlikely to continue for long, or it would have required a substantial amount of land out of entail. But it was the problems that afflicted land held in fee simple that had led to the very development of entails. It is not surprising that on the one hand entails became barrable, and that on the other hand landowners generally turned to a different way of handling inheritances.

They turned, of course, to uses. By granting his land to feoffees who were to hold it to his use a man was able to make a will leaving instructions how the land was to be disposed of after his death. Under uses each landowner was thus free to take stock of his actual family situation and to act as it dictated. He who had more children than an eldest son could provide for his younger children. He who had daughters only could distribute some land to a male collateral. Through uses landowners as a class could both provide for younger children and cut down heiresses without utterly disinheriting them. In legal terminology, through uses landowners gained full freedom of alienation, freedom not only inter vivos but by will.

The words "freedom of alienation" need to be understood in their medieval setting. Through later association they have come to have about them the sense of "freedom to sell" and are associated with the growth of a commercial attitude to land. A commercial attitude to land was unlikely to have existed to any significant degree among large landowners in medieval times. Selling for commercial reasons was probably not a common desire among large landowners until late in the nineteenth century. Until then the social and political advantages conferred by the ownership of land remained too great. A study of land law reform in the nineteenth century shows that throughout that century most large landowners resisted selling so far as possible.[11] Freedom of alienation was primarily sought and valued by medieval landowners because it gave freedom to alienate against the heir-at-law. A provision for younger children was an alienation against the heir male; a provision for a collateral male was an alienation against the heir female. Freedom of alienation meant freedom from the common law rules of succession. The king lost his feudal dues as uses proliferated, but it is much to be doubted whether escaping medieval death duties was the object landowners had principally in mind as they took to uses.

Though the use had the dual capacity landowners desired, it could never have wholly satisfied them even so. Aristocracies in principle are opposed to wills as the means of conveying estates. They have regularly sought legal means of limiting the power of the landowner in possession to distribute his estate among his children quite as he chose. That English landowners at a point in their history turned to wills, seeking full freedom of alienation, was the result of common law rules that had first of all to be escaped. Indeed that the English law of real property is of abnormal complexity is due to landowners' distaste for the common law rules coupled with the fact that they could not find any ultimate solution to their problems in freedom of alienation. Landowners have always had two-sided desires for their younger children. Such children were to be provided for, but their provision was to be limited in the interests of estate continuity. The use in no way restrained provision for younger children. Neither had the entail before it, when employed as a provision for younger children. What landowners wanted was a workable system of primogeniture—one that would make some compromise with family feeling but would at the same time actively limit family charges in the interests of the male head of the family.

They found what they desired—so far as they ever found it—in the strict

11. Eileen Spring, "Landowners, Lawyers, and Land Law Reform in Nineteenth-Century England," *American Journal of Legal History* 21 (1977): 41–59.

settlement. Portions for younger children were naturally subjected to limitation by the development of a system that laid them out at their parents' marriage rather than leaving them to be determined by their father's will. Portions were laid out before the children were born, before they were beings entwined in their parents' affection, and a total sum was established for portions before the number of children could even be known.

To be sure, providing for younger children at their parents' marriage was of some advantage to younger children. It protected them against the possibility of intestacy on the part of their father and the consequent application of the common law rule of primogeniture. (It offered no equivalent protection to the heiress, of course, for whom her father's intestacy would have been an advantage.) The advantage of settlement to younger children is not to be wholly ignored; but it would be a matter of significance in the history of the family only if it could be shown that fathers earlier had neglected to declare their will, had in fact left their younger children unprovided for. Historical investigation has decidedly shown the opposite. Medieval historians emphasize that despite the absolute primogeniture of the common law, such was never practiced. Thus the conspicuous provision for younger children in strict settlements does not imply that younger children had earlier gone unprovided for or that their lot was being improved. The strict settlement provided for younger children in a different way. Realistically the change it brought about was that whereas younger children had earlier been provided for by their father's will, they were now provided for under his marriage settlement.

An analogy may serve to sum up the meaning of the strict settlement for younger children. Any benefits that younger children seem to have received from that form of settlement are akin to the benefits that consumers receive from the limited warranty. Just as the limited warranty conspicuously grants consumers certain rights but aims fundamentally to limit rights they would otherwise enjoy, so the strict settlement conspicuously granted younger children portions but fundamentally aimed to limit their share of the inheritance. Younger children would have been better off if the deed that ostensibly protected them had never been devised.

2

The inherent meaning of the strict settlement was pointed out by Lord Chancellor Nottingham soon after the device appeared. No authority was greater than Nottingham's on the subject of future estates, his name being indelibly associated with the development of that branch of law. It was his decision in the *Duke of Norfolk's Case* in 1681 that established the general principle under which all future interests were thereafter to be governed. Future interests had earlier been governed by a complex body of rules, and Nottingham unified them under a single rule that depended upon remoteness of vesting, that is, under a rule that limited the length of time that could run before someone had to come into possession as owner in fee simple. Although he did not spell out exactly how long vesting could be postponed, he foreshadowed what was later formally enunciated as the rule against perpetuities. Nottingham had not only well considered future interests in this public and general way, however, but seven years earlier, as Baron Finch, he had considered the strict settlement in a personal way.

In 1674, in negotiating the marriage of his eldest son, he was pressed by the bride's family to settle his estate on his son strictly. He refused to do so, evidently being generally averse to the rigidity that the strict settlement imposed. Land sales might be necessary, and the strict settlement would prevent them. (Lord Nottingham had fourteen children.) He objected also to the absolute security that a strict settlement conferred on the eldest son to be born of the marriage. That settlement made the eldest son absolutely secure of the inheritance was an objection raised against it from time to time, an objection that had been voiced occasionally as well against earlier conveyances that had had the same effect. "This manner of conveyance," Chief Justice Popham had declared of an Elizabethan example, "breaks asunder the law of nature so that when the disobedient and sensual son considers to himself that his father cannot dispose of his land at his good pleasure but must leave the heritage to him willy-nilly . . . he becomes undutiful in demeanour against his parents, in manner and conversation dissolute, and in the end subject and made as prey to all brokers and usurers . . . an impregnable grief to his parents and friends."[12] Or as Lord Nottingham more briefly and less affectingly put it, such a conveyance made the father subject to the son. Nottingham's first objection, however, was that if his son were made a tenant for life, he (the son) would find himself limited in what he could do for his future family. He would be unable to add "a shilling to [his wife's] jointure or to his daughters' portions."[13] That

12. J. H. Baker and S. F. C. Milsom, *Sources of English Legal History: Private Law to 1750* (London, 1986), 157. The words were uttered in *Chudleigh's Case* (1594).

13. Lloyd Bonfield, "Marriage Settlement, 1660–1740: The Adoption of the Strict Settlement in Kent and Northamptonshire," in *Marriage and Society: Studies in the Social History of Marriage,* ed. R. B. Outhwaite (London, 1981), 109.

a strict settlement limited provision for younger children is what Lord Nottingham pointed out.

Blackstone, however, gives a contrary interpretation of the strict settlement—or at least he appears to do so. What Blackstone said needs scrutiny, for his words have had far more influence among historians than Nottingham's. Nottingham's have been dismissed as self-interested, while Blackstone's have been held the meaningful ones.[14] The purpose of the strict settlement, Blackstone declared, was "to secure in family settlements a provision for the future children of an intended marriage who before were usually left at the mercy of the particular tenant for life."[15] This would seem to mean that settlement improved younger children's inheritances, and that is what Blackstone has been held to mean. It is to be remembered, though, that Blackstone was an apologist for English law. For him everything, or almost everything, moved for the best in English law. He managed to hold that jointure was better for widows than dower, emphasizing a benefit that was minor while ignoring a loss that was major. In the light of his assessment of jointure, his words on younger children might be taken with some reservation from the start

It is true that compared to the antecedent form of settlement—or compared to an entail—the strict settlement differed in making provision *within it* for younger children. It is furthermore true to say that its success depended on this fact. As has been emphasized here, any device of primogeniture and entail that does not provide for younger children is of very limited usefulness. Thus far there can be no quarreling with Blackstone's words. Nevertheless it would be misleading to say that the purpose pure and simple of the strict settlement was to provide for younger children. But does Blackstone quite say this? When his words are drawn out, they are notably ambiguous. He goes on to say that the invention made by Orlando Bridgman and Geoffrey Palmer had to be "restrained within proper limits."[16] Why should an invention so humane, one that aimed to provide for younger children, have had to be restrained? The reference is obviously to the fact that the strict settlement removed the power of the landowner over his estate and thus had to be restrained within the rule against per-

---

14. H. J. Habakkuk, "Daniel Finch, 2nd Earl of Nottingham: His House and Estate," in *Studies in Social History*, ed. J. H. Plumb (London, 1955), 155; H. J. Habakkuk, "Marriage Settlements in the Eighteenth Century," *Transactions of the Royal Historical Society*, 4th ser. 32 (1950), 20.

15. William Blackstone, *Commentaries on the Laws of England*, 2:172.

16. Ibid.

petuities. Blackstone had just finished showing how, before the invention of the strict form, settlements had been easily broken. Men who were nominally tenants for life had not really been in the position of tenants for life but had been able to do as they pleased. The strict settlement, he thus emphasized, had been necessary to make settlements secure. A proper comparison for judging the fate of younger children would then have been a comparison between landowners who were in practice free to provide for their children as they chose and landowners who were bound by settlements that had been made at their marriage—the comparison that Lord Nottingham recognized had to be made.

Blackstone's words are thus less straightforward than they seem. Their apparent meaning and their contextual meaning conflict. The words declare that the strict settlement provided for children; the context shows that it did so within a scheme designed to limit the father's powers. All in all, Blackstone apparently saw no need in speaking of children to look beyond forms: strict settlements contained portions for younger children, entails did not. That was analysis enough for him. No more in this case than in that of the widow did he consider the real thrust of legal change.

3

Thus far the discussion has been legal and theoretical. Is the history of younger children arrived at in this way borne out by empirical evidence as to the movement of portions?

In turning to the actual movement of portions, there can be no need to show that medieval landowners soon came, despite the uncompromising attitude of the common law, to provide for their younger children. That they did so is the burden of the work of Holmes, McFarlane, Bean, and Cooper. What is required is empirical evidence about later movements, and especially about movement under the strict settlement. There is an almost unchallenged belief running through the social and economic history of landed estates and landed families that the strict settlement made portions rise, especially for daughters. This belief, as has been seen, is to be associated with a legal misunderstanding: the portions for daughters so conspicuous in Orlando Bridgman's precedents and in early settlements were not understood to be portions limiting the interests of daughters who were heiresses, but instead were taken as evidence of a new concern for daughters in general and ultimately for younger children as a group. That the origin of the belief lies in a misunderstanding is a serious count against it, but in view of the persistence of the belief and of its wide spread, empirical evidence as to the movement of portions is called for.

The first fact that might be noted is the form of paying portions under the strict settlement. Portions were normally paid on a sliding scale according to the number of children, and had a top limit set to them. A typical settlement by Orlando Bridgman runs: If there should be only one daughter, she was to have £10,000; if there should be two or more daughters, they were to divide £12,000 between them.[17] Bridgman's settlements normally provide only for daughters where there was no son. Gilbert Horsman's precedents take the same basic form although, as they are later than Bridgman's, they provide for all children. A typical settlement by Horsman allows £4,000 for one younger child; £3,500 each for two younger children, £3,000 each for three of them; and for four or more £10,000 to be divided among them.[18] A settlement recited in a private act of Parliament concerning the Marquis of Grandison's estates lays down the total allowable for portions thus: "in case there shall be one child of the marriage other than an eldest son, £12,000; in case two or more such children £15,000."[19] The form itself suggests the desire to limit charges for a family. At the least it suggests the determination to prevent a large family from burdening an estate.

What the combination of large family and father free to do as he pleased could on occasion mean for estates has not escaped historians' notice. In the fourteenth century there was Sir John Archdeacon who, having eight sons, divided his estates eight ways; and William Lord Lovell in the fifteenth century who, having four sons, divided his four ways.[20] In 1683 one of the heirs of Lord Burghley, who had divided his estates upon his two sons, charged £78,000 for seven younger children on an estate worth £12,000 annually. The Earl of Westmorland in 1650 left £5,000 to each of his six daughters, charged on an estate worth £5,500 annually, and he had as well a younger son to provide for.[21]

Large families are not common in stationary populations. In stationary populations the cycle of births and deaths involves what might be called the "wandering" of estates from family to family, rather than their dis-

17. Orlando Bridgman, *Conveyances,* 2d ed. (London, 1689), 256. For another example see the Bridgman settlement reprinted here in Appendix A.

18. Gilbert Horsman, *Precedents in Conveyancing,* 2d ed. (London, 1757), marriage settlement no. 3.

19. Private Acts of Parliament, 2 Geo. 2, c. 8.

20. McFarlane, *Nobility of Later Medieval England,* 71.

21. Lawrence Stone, *The Crisis of Aristocracy, 1558–1641* (Oxford, 1965), 175–76.

integration through a superfluity of children, for there are the same number of persons in each generation to share the land. It is only in growing populations, when each generation exceeds in number its predecessor, that there is a general problem of estate disintegration. Such reflection would be small consolation, however, to the individual landowner concerned to preserve his particular estate and to whom nature had given a large family. Even in stationary populations there are always some large families, and inevitably as population rose there would have been more of them. It was to be among the many good fortunes that befell the English landed aristocracy that the strict settlement was devised at a most opportune time, being in place before population began its long secular rise. Had the strict settlement done nothing but contain charges for large families, this was always a useful function, and one for which there was to be increasing need.

While the form in which portions were laid out suggests the desire to limit provision for younger children, it is not conclusive evidence that provision was limited, for even without settlement men with large families would often have tended to curtail the provision they made for their younger children. The effect of settlement is only to be certainly assessed by more careful calculations over time. Before such comparison can be attempted, the conditions for valid comparison require consideration. Since younger children always received portions in some form or by some method, the question has at the outset to be decided: When is settlement to be held the force that generally determined portions? In other words, what base period is to be used in making comparisons? Obviously settlement cannot be held to determine portions before it was fully formed or before it had become the vehicle commonly used to convey younger children's portions. The strict settlement was invented about 1650, if one judges by the invention of trustees to preserve contingent remainders. Early settlements, however, did not convey younger children's portions, but only portions for daughters where there was no son, only for daughters who were heiresses-at-law. Younger sons and ordinary daughters continued for some time to be provided for by separate deed or by will, which is to say that settlements had for some time of necessity to be limited to parts of estates. Fortunately we now have evidence as to when settlement came generally to provide for younger children. From an analysis of the settlements made in two counties from 1601 to 1740 it has been shown that few settlements provided for younger children before 1680, but that almost all did so by 1700 or by 1710 at the latest.[22] What is necessary for assessing

22. Lloyd Bonfield, *Marriage Settlements, 1601–1740* (Cambridge, 1983), 114.

portions, then, is a figure for about 1700 and one for a considerably later time—a considerably later time because developments in family history, being by their nature very gradual, are impossible to measure over short periods.

Meaningful measurement of portions requires, moreover, that the figures found in settlements—which are simple sums of money—be related to estate value. It is only thus that portions tell of the division of property in the family between eldest son and younger children, only thus that they tell of changes in family principles. Unfortunately settlements do not normally state the value of the land they encompass. They no more do this than wills state the total value of the assets they convey. Settlements of jointure lands may sometimes state the value of the land encompassed, as did the jointure settlement, earlier mentioned, that was printed by Blackstone.[23] This was a guarantee that enough land was in the settlement to bear the jointure charge. But settlements of jointure land were inherently minor settlements. In a full-scale, or substantial, settlement of family land no guarantee was ordinarily necessary that the land could bear the charges being put upon it, for jointure and portion were then small in relation to the whole. A normal settlement describes the land it encompasses by delimiting parcels, by mentioning manors or parishes, or by referring to an earlier deed.

There are various ways of relating portions to land values. Settlements may be put together with estate accounts, or with land values known through family correspondence, or, at a late period, with land values ascertained from Bateman's *Great Landowners*, which is a summary of an official census of landownership.[24] The opinions of knowledgeable contemporaries as to norms may provide guidelines, as of course will any evidence to be found in legislation. Whichever way it is to be done, establishing the relationship of portion to land value depends on information extraneous to settlements themselves. A collection of settlements will leave one in the dark about the fundamental matter, the division of property being made in the family, and it may even mislead. Altogether, then, what is wanted in order to weigh the effect of settlement on inheritance is a figure for portions about the year 1700 and one for a considerably later time, both figures in terms of estate income.

23. Blackstone, *Commentaries*, appendix 2 to book 2. Discussed above in chapter 2, section 4.

24. John Bateman, *The Great Landowners of Great Britain and Ireland*. The definitive edition is the fourth (London, 1883), which has been reprinted with an introduction by David Spring (Leicester, 1971).

4

The firmest evidence would come from legislation. At first sight there would seem to be none. Parliament never passed any public general act establishing or altering portions under English settlements. It passed numerous acts dealing with other matters under settlements—with powers of leasing, borrowing for improvements, and selling to pay off encumbrances or to exchange lands—but it never sought to interfere in any public general act with the heirship strategy of English settlements. Nor did it do so in the private acts that it was prepared to grant to tenants for life. Hundreds of private acts were granted whose purpose was to improve the tenant for life's capacity to manage his land, but private acts are not found that alter the portions that had been laid out in a settlement, or that alter the series of heirs that had been designated. Parliament had been willing in the sixteenth century to break entails in the interests of younger children where the entail was unbarrable because of a clause of perpetuity. Both Mary Finch and J. P. Cooper have pointed to such acts.[25] This is evidence of the decided objection to unbarrability, and as well, of course, evidence that it was never held proper to leave younger children unprovided for. But strict settlements were not open to objection on either score, and Parliament never interfered with the family principles embodied in them.

Nevertheless there exists a public general act that gives key information about the practice of settlement. Parliament passed an act dealing with the settlement of land in Scotland. In this act the strict settlement was, as it were, being imported by the Scots, and the act gives a vital insight into practice in the land of settlement's origin. As it gives the firmest figures for portions that we have, providing a clear benchmark, discussion might well begin with it, despite its not being for the base period but for the early nineteenth century.[26]

Parliament came to legislate about the settlement of land in Scotland because of the peculiarities of Scottish land law. Entails had been established in Scotland only in 1685. The date is significant, being about the time that England was taking to the strict settlement, clearly suggesting the affinities of the devices. Scottish entails were, however, unbarrable.

25. Mary Finch, *The Wealth of Five Northamptonshire Families, 1540–1640* (London, 1956), 53n., 103n.; J. P. Cooper, "Patterns of Inheritance and Settlement by Great Landowners from the Fifteenth to the Eighteenth Centuries," in *Family and Inheritance,* ed. Jack Goody, Joan Thirsk, and E. P. Thompson (London, 1978), 206–7.

26. Statutes, 5 Geo. 4, c. 87.

Unbarrable entails had gone in England, but Scottish property law hailed from a different legal tradition. Because of the difficulties that unbarrability inevitably caused, Scottish entails came to Parliament's attention more than once in the eighteenth and nineteenth centuries. Ultimately they were assimilated to the English, by Scottish desire, being made barrable about the middle of the nineteenth century. The movement of assimilation had centered in the early years of the century on protests about portions under Scottish entails. Unlike English unbarrable entails, Scottish entails could actually set out portions for younger children. It was the fact that English entails could not do this that had made them inherently unworkable. Scottish entails need not set out portions, however, and apparently some did not do so. That was one cause of complaint by Scottish landowners. More generally their complaint was, as the preamble to the act explains, that portions that had been set out in early deeds had in the course of time become inadequate through the increase of prices and rents. Thus in 1824 Parliament was prevailed upon to pass an act giving Scottish entailed proprietors statutory power to charge their estates with portions for younger children. A permissible scale of portions had to be set out.

It is clear that in every act about Scottish entail English practice under the strict settlement was the model. Sir John Dalrymple, in his history of feudal property, which was written in the middle of the eighteenth century and which compared and contrasted the history of entails in England and Scotland, held then that Scottish entails ought to be reformed on the English model, and held indeed that this reformation was already under way. He cited an act of Queen Anne's in which Scottish entails were made subject to the English law on forfeiture. He believed that as he wrote a bill was being drafted that would allow Scottish tenants in tail "to provide wives and children with moderation." (If such a bill was introduced to Parliament at this time, nothing came of it.) "Surely one who was a lawyer would foresee," he wrote, "that [Scottish entails] will either be abolished altogether, or exchanged for those of the English."[27] The evidence of parliamentary inquiries indicates clearly that it was English experts who were regularly turned to for practical advice in overcoming Scottish difficulties. Among the principal witnesses before such inquiries was, for example, James Loch, one of the most important of nineteenth-century land agents, a Scot by birth but chief advisor to the Dukes of Sutherland and to other

27. John Dalrymple, *An Essay towards a General History of Feudal Property in Great Britain*, 3d ed. (London, 1758), 193–94.

great English families.[28] Notable also were William Vizard, a London conveyancing barrister, and James Hurrle Fisher, solicitor to the Dukes of Bedford. Thus the portions set out in the Scottish act of 1824 undoubtedly represent the level of portions normal in England at the time. And as family principles do not change quickly, they may be presumed to represent a level that had prevailed for some time.

Scottish landowners were allowed to charge up to one year's income for one younger child, up to two years' income for two younger children, and up to three years' income for three younger children or for any number more. Income was defined as income net of charges already on the estate. In capital terms this scale meant that a generation of younger children inherited at most a charge equal to 15 percent of the family's landed wealth, and in no case did a single younger child receive more than 5 percent. These calculations assume land was worth twenty years' purchase—a low estimate for the nineteenth century. On a more realistic assumption as to the value of land, younger children would have received an even lower proportion of the capital value of the paternal land.

Evidence directly from English settlements coordinates with the scale in the Scottish statute. A small empirical study that I made before I knew of the Scottish statute found that out of a sample of nineteen settlements sixteen established a top limit for a generation of younger children at two years' income of the estate or less. All but one limited portions to less than three years' income, and that one limited them to less than four years' income. While my figures suggest an even lower level of portions than the Scottish legislation, suggesting a top limit of two years' income rather than three, they are based on gross rental rather than net income.[29]

Further corroborating evidence is to be found in the opinions of qualified nineteenth-century observers. In 1854 William Twopeny, a London barrister, analyzed the consequences for estates of paying portions by raising mortgages. He made the point that portions tended to accumulate on estates as the generations passed, thus subjecting English land to an increasing burden of mortgage debt. It was a point coming to be used frequently by the critics of the landed aristocracy, who argued that the burden of mort-

28. David Spring, *The English Landed Estate in the Nineteenth Century: Its Administration* (Baltimore, 1963), 89–96.

29. Eileen Spring, "The Family, Strict Settlement and Historians," *Canadian Journal of History* 18 (1983): 386; also published in *Law, Economy and Society, 1750–1914: Essays in the History of English Law*, ed. G. R. Rubin and David Sugarman (Abingdon, Eng., 1984), 191n.

gages prevented the improvement of land. Twopeny suggested that land-owners should take to insuring their lives, thereby accumulating a fund that could be designated for their younger children and thus eliminating the need for mortgaging. He began with a portrayal of the current method of providing portions. For an estate of £10,000 per year he held the normal jointure was £1,200. Portions for younger children on such an estate he held to be the following: £10,000 for one younger child, £15,000 for two younger children, £25,000 for three, and £35,000 for four or more.[30]

George Brodrick also made an estimate of the level of portions. And he was well placed to do so. He was a journalist, a lawyer, and an Oxford notability; and he was as well the younger son of a viscount. In his *English Land and English Landlords* he produced what is the best known of nineteenth-century works on the land system. Emphasizing the "prodigious" difference between the amount of property going to the eldest son and that going to a younger child, Brodrick calculated that the average younger child was unlikely to receive one year's income of its father's estate: "Even if there were but one such younger child, his [share of] the property would probably not be more than one-twentieth or one-thirtieth of his elder brother's." And where there was more than one younger child, he went on, the provision for each would turn out to be less because of the principle of reducing the portion payable to each child as the number of children rose.[31] "As for the daughters, their rank is apt to be reckoned as a substantive part of their fortunes; and not only are their marriage portions infinitely smaller than would be considered proper in families of equal affluence in the mercantile class, but it is not unfrequently provided that unless they have children, their property shall ultimately revert to their oldest brother." English landowners, Brodrick thought, ought to have been ashamed of the portions they gave their daughters.[32] Brodrick's attitude to the system of landholding was conspicuously hostile—he was one of the nineteenth-century land law reformers—but Twopeny's attitude was the reverse, and the economic calculations of the two men are much the same.

5

A figure has been established for the early nineteenth century: a top limit of three years' income for a generation of younger children. What is

30. William Twopeny, *Observations on the Result of the Present Mode of Providing Portions for Younger Children by a Charge on Landed Estates* (London, 1854).

31. George Brodrick, *English Land and English Landlords* (London, 1881), 100.

32. Ibid., 102, 341.

to be said of the base period? If the strict settlement operated in a primogenitive way, portions about 1700 should have been higher, thus falling
over time.

Looking first for legislation, there is an Irish act of Parliament, which
being of the date 1704 could hardly be more chronologically appropriate
for comparison.[33] The purpose of this act, however, was very different from
the Scottish act, and the provisions it contained for portions were not its
main feature; it must be treated with considerable reservation. There was
identity of interest between Scottish and English landowners. The Irish act
was a discriminatory act of the English Parliament directed against Irish
Catholic landowners. Its aim was to diminish the power of Catholic landowners, and to that end it altered the law of descent for Catholics. Land
held by a Catholic, "notwithstanding any will or settlement," was to descend by gavelkind, that is to say, it was to be divided upon sons and not
to descend to the eldest son only. Moreover, Catholic fathers were allowed
to give any portions they desired to their daughters, thus further fracturing
estates. Thus both by altering the law of descent from primogeniture to
equal division upon males and by preventing settlements, the Irish Catholic
estate was to be broken up.

These provisions, had they been the only ones of the act, would indicate
at least that Parliament held that the effect of settlement was to concentrate
property in the hands of the eldest son. Catholic estates were to be broken
up in part by preventing settlements and by allowing Catholic fathers to
give what portions they chose to their daughters. Parliament thus is on
record as agreeing with Lord Nottingham about the meaning of settlement
for younger children, rather than with Blackstone—if indeed Blackstone
really intended what his words have been taken to mean.

These were not the only provisions of the act, however. Not content with
attempting to break up Catholic estates, the act went on to favor the eldest
son of a Catholic landowner where the son had turned Protestant. In this
case Parliament was anxious to do the opposite of what it did in regard to
Catholic sons, being anxious to ensure primogeniture; and it was particularly concerned to see that this eldest son could not be defeated by any
inter vivos act of his father, who could be assumed to be hostile to him.
Thus in this case Parliament in effect settled the estate. The Catholic father
of a Protestant eldest son was to be but a tenant for life of his estate, which
was to descend intact to the son, subject to portions of one-third of estate
value for any younger children. Portions were to be paid to younger chil-

33. Irish Statutes, 2 Anne, c. 6.

dren without regard to their religion, so the one-third was not determined on religious grounds.

This is a rate for portions at least twice as high as in the early nineteenth century. If land is assumed to be worth twenty years' purchase, this rate amounts to six years' income of the family estate, compared to three—at most—in the early nineteenth century. Given its unusual provenance, the act of 1704 might well be dismissed if it were the only evidence that indicated a higher level of portions in 1700 than in 1800, but it accords, as we shall see, with other evidence, and it is thus worth notice. Quite possibly the figure of one-third for portions was a traditional one that Parliament spent little time in deciding upon. Few can have expected there would be many Catholic eldest sons turning Protestant—whatever they might have hoped—and thus few would have thought this aspect of the legislation would ever have much application. The third may have harked back to the Statute of Wills, for that statute implies that one-third of the estate would go to the younger children. As the Statute of Wills was a compromise between landowners and the Crown, the third may well have represented the practice of its day. The third of the Irish act may not have closely represented contemporary practice, but it is not an irrelevant figure for assessing trends.

Other evidence showing that portions were higher in the earlier period than the later is to be found when the extensive statistical work done by Lawrence Stone and J. P. Cooper on portions for daughters in the sixteenth and seventeenth centuries is viewed against the nineteenth-century data. Both Stone and Cooper indicate that the portions they trace were those for ordinary daughters, and thus that they were for the same class of daughter as in the nineteenth-century data. Cooper prefaces his analysis with the remark that it refers to daughters "where there was no problem of arbitration between heirs male and heirs general." Stone notes that all his tables of portions and jointures "exclude all heiresses and heirs general."[34] All the data, in other words, are for daughters not heiresses.

Only one figure for the sixteenth and seventeenth centuries, however, is for portions in relation to estate value. Stone has calculated that in the early seventeenth century the average portion for a daughter was about one year's income of her father's estate.[35] Nevertheless this one figure gives us the essence of the story. Since that was the level in the early nineteenth century, it is clear that daughters received about the same proportionate

34. Cooper, "Patterns of Inheritance," 212; Stone, *Crisis of Aristocracy*, 787.
35. Stone, *Crisis of Aristocracy*, 642.

charge on the family estate in 1650 as in 1800. Since both Stone and Cooper show that portions rose throughout the seventeenth century, it is clear that portions fell under the strict settlement. Having risen to a peak about 1700, they fell thereafter.

The detailed figures given by Stone and Cooper indicate the range of movement of portions. Cooper finds that the average portion for a peer's daughter rose from £3,500 in 1600–25 to £5,050 in 1625–49; then to £6,250 in 1650–74; and to £9,350 in 1675–1724.[36] Stone's sample, also for peers' daughters, indicates a rise from £3,800 to £5,400 to £7,800 and to £9,700 in the same periods.[37] If portions for daughters about 1650 were one year's estate income, it would seem that by 1700 they were very roughly one and one-half year's estate income, a figure that the Stones in their *An Open Elite?* have used.[38] While portions for daughters fell under the strict settlement, it cannot be said they did so dramatically, falling back to one year's estate income from one and one-half year's income.

These figures for the seventeenth century, however, ignore younger sons. Younger sons before the strict settlement are more difficult than daughters to obtain information about, because they then usually received not a cash payment but land, the value of which is difficult, and probably impossible, to establish. One thing is certain. Before the strict settlement younger sons did at least as well as daughters, and would seem often to have done considerably better. Cooper prints in an appendix more than two hundred examples of arrangements for younger children, and though he does not analyze them in detail, summary statements he makes throughout his article indicate his general conclusion that sons were better endowed than daughters. A calculation based on the minority of his presettlement examples where the provision for both sexes was in cash confirms this judgment.[39] Since under the strict settlement sons were usually treated equally with daughters, their provision must generally have fallen from a greater height as settlement took over. Thus when younger sons are entered into the calculation, the fall in portions must be greater than when daughters alone are considered.

Indeed it is to be suggested that limiting the younger son was a greater concern of landowners than limiting the ordinary daughter. It was the for-

36. Cooper, "Patterns of Inheritance," table on 307.

37. Stone, *Crisis of Aristocracy*, table on 790.

38. Lawrence Stone and Jeanne C. Fawtier Stone, *An Open Elite? England 1540–1880* (Oxford, 1984), 98.

39. Spring, "The Family," 384.

mer who presented the greater temptation to heavy endowment. Historical sources, however, have allowed much more evidence to be gathered about ordinary daughters than about younger sons.

To the point, empirical evidence goes with the logic of the device to indicate that portions fell with the strict settlement.

6

The foregoing analysis has established the outline of younger children's history. Their history begins differently from that of heiresses and widows, for the common law gave younger children no rights, and thus landowners' objections in this case were to the harshness of the common law rather than, as in the other cases, to its generosity. Power to make grants on younger children was very soon gained, however, and thereafter the problem for landowners became the same in respect of younger children as it was for widows and heiresses: how to effect their limitation. Limitation was effected through the strict settlement, which allowed children's portions to be coolly calculated in the abstract at their parents' marriage instead of being determined as their fathers chose by grant or will. Younger children's portions thus tended, if looked at over the very long run, to move first upward and then downward.

The most significant conclusion about younger children's portions, however, becomes apparent only when they are viewed in a comparative framework. The significant conclusion is that their movement was always relatively restrained. Even the rise of daughters' portions in the seventeenth century, which seems dramatic when viewed in crude numbers, becomes moderate when viewed in terms of estate income, and becomes even small if considered against the loss of dower, with which it was certainly connected. The history of younger children has none of the drama that marks that of the heiress and the widow. The claims of younger children were always recognized, and they were as a general rule never held to be great. Landowners as a rule knew within fairly narrow bounds what was the correct division of property between eldest son and younger children. They never had serious doubt that the bulk of the estate should go to the eldest son.

Their devotion to primogeniture is a matter of political record in the nineteenth century. Time and again they and their supporters struck down bills that would have made equal division the rule upon intestacy. The Real Property Commission had early in the century dismissed the possibility of such a change, declaring that primogeniture was the principle that best expressed the spirit of the country.[40] When bills for change came to be introduced, these aroused excessive fears for the future and extravagant praise of the status quo. Lord Arundell of Wardour, a peer of very ancient lineage, warned in the House of Lords that the abandonment of primogeniture would "be tantamount to a sentence of death and extinction for many ancient families."[41] Lord Westbury declared in opposing one bill that he did not know anything "more important to preserve in this country than the great rule by which the landed property of the father passes to the eldest son."[42] J. R. McCulloch, though one of the classical economists and thus a member of a group generally hostile to the claims of aristocratic landowners, took up the cudgels for them on social grounds. Primogeniture was necessary to great estates, great estates were necessary to aristocracy, and aristocracy in turn was necessary to the British constitution. Waxing lyrical, he declared as well that primogeniture made for a leisured wealthy class and in doing so made "for the cultivation of all that is most elevated in our literature, and in science, of everything in fine that gives splendour and enduring celebrity to nations."[43] The *Times* gravely declared that "we English do not understand rank as separated from landed wealth. . . . England could not exist as England now is without large estates. Our Constitution, our agriculture, our power as a people, and our stability as a nation rest upon this very principle of primogeniture."[44] The spectacle of men thus fulsomely defending a rule that they knew landowners were careful to see never actually took effect in their families affords some amusement—as it did to Maitland—especially as the rule was additionally defended exactly on the ground that it never did take effect. "You cannot show that a law is good," Maitland scoffed, "by showing that all sensible men contrive to evade it."[45] But landowners' heated defense of primogeniture underscores the fact that their quarrel with the common law over their younger children was not great.

It was on the large rights that the common law gave to females that landowners had their eyes fixed, and against which their conveyancing stratagems were fundamentally designed. When the histories of the var-

40. Parliamentary Papers 1829, *First Report of the Real Property Commission*, 7.

41. *Hansard*, 3d ser., vol. 313 (1887), col. 1759.

42. From entry in the *Dictionary of National Biography*.

43. J. R. McCulloch, *Treatise on Succession to Property Vacant by Death* (London, 1848), 35.

44. *The Times*, 21 February 1859.

45. Maitland, "Law of Real Property," 193–94.

ious family interests are weighed against one another, one principal conclusion must be that landowners' legal history did not center on younger children.

7

The conclusion that younger children were relatively unimportant in estate affairs is an unconventional one with considerable implications, for the history of estates has often been written in terms of eldest son versus younger children, male or female as the case may be. It may be well to end this discussion with some simple demographic reflections that reinforce the conclusion from a different perspective.

In a stationary population there can be no general problem of younger children, for there are the same number of estates to be rearranged among a like number of people from generation to generation. A general problem exists only when population rises. Calculations made by E. A. Wrigley show the degree to which a general problem developed as population rose.[46] When population rose at the rate experienced during the period of great European growth, there came to be in each generation 136 sons instead of 100. There came to be, then, from one generation to the next 136 sons for every 100 estates, or 36 who were in excess of the number of estates. And of course there came also to be 36 daughters who were in excess of the number of estates. The rise that took place meant, then, that in each generation there were 72 younger children for every 100 estates who were necessarily a net cost to the society, children whose portions could not be looked upon as a transfer within the society. This, however, is less than one excess younger child per estate per generation.

It is to be stressed that this calculation is highly theoretical. The individual landowner, out to preserve his particular estate, could never calculate in this way. At any time in history, the individual landowner could turn out to have a great number of children. If he were determined to preserve his estate he could not be indifferent to the problem of younger children, and had to be interested in legal means of countering it. Rational calculation could not be the same for him as for society as a whole. It is also to be stressed that sustained population growth has meant a crucial change in the world's history, a long-term cumulative change of horrendous proportions.

46. E. A. Wrigley, "Fertility Strategy for the Individual and the Group," in *Historical Studies in Changing Fertility*, ed. Charles Tilly (Princeton, 1978), 139.

Still the problem of younger children has, if only in one way, been exaggerated. There is a belief, not uncommonly to be encountered, that families before the twentieth century were very large. In landed history this belief translates into an undue emphasis upon the problem of younger children. Mere consideration of the arithmetic of compounding must put an end to such a belief. If we imagine an average family in which four children survive to breed, population will in little more than a century increase sixteen times over. Only the modern third world approaches anything like this. In its essence, the growth of European population may be said to lie in the change, about 1750, from an average family in which two children survived their parents to one in which three survived. Crude though this statement undoubtedly is, it gives some sense of the fundamentals of family numbers. That an average family of three is large and vastly different from an average family of two is an idea that environmentalists still have trouble getting across. So notable a historian as Georges Duby once took for fact the statement of the Anglo-Norman chronicler Orderic Vitalis that twelfth-century nobles usually had five, six, or seven sons reach maturity.[47] A significant work in women's history, speaking of portions for daughters in the early modern period, declares that "a moderate-sized family might easily have as many as five or six daughters."[48] More often, there is merely the unspoken assumption that there always was, or almost always was, a younger son or sons. Not only does this assumption fail to represent demographic facts at any time, but on this assumption, even if the common law as to female heirs is understood, female heirs are hardly worth historical consideration.

Younger children may be said to have always been a problem for aristocratic landowners, and one that grew larger. They were a problem that it is easy to exaggerate, however, and one that has undoubtedly been got out of proportion. Moreover, the problem of numbers for landowners in the eighteenth century was considerably countered by the increase in new opportunities for the employment of younger sons that then took place. As Edward Gibbon noted, the eighteenth century saw an increase in the civil and military establishments both at home and abroad that opened up many new paths to fortune for younger sons.[49] Thus the English aristocracy had not only the good luck to have the strict settlement in place as population began its climb, but it also had the good luck to have an increase in the means of providing for younger children as their numbers increased.

47. Georges Duby, *The Chivalrous Society* (Berkeley and Los Angeles, 1977), 117.
48. Julia O'Faolain and Lauro Martines, *Not in God's Image* (New York, 1973), 270.
49. H. H. Milman, *The Life of Edward Gibbon* (Paris, 1840), 9.

A summary of younger children's history in a comparative context would run as follows: Younger children were always a problem for aristocratic landowners, and they were one that grew larger as population increased. Nevertheless younger children were always relatively a small problem, much smaller by landowners' calculation than other problems they faced in determining inheritance matters.

4   The Pattern Considered

The land Salic is in Germany.

—*Shakespeare*, Henry V

Previous chapters have looked at the history of particular members of the family against particular common law rules. This chapter discusses the overall pattern that emerges from what has been a major shift in the angle of vision. Although looking at the history of the landed family against the common law rules of inheritance is not a wholly new method of proceeding, it is a method that has not hitherto been carried out with any consistency. Carrying it out with consistency has meant drawing attention particularly to a neglected figure, the heiress-at-law. Dropping her into the story has been rather like dropping the proverbial pebble into still water. Ripples have spread out that have come to touch all members of the family and to involve traditional concepts about the direction of female inheritance and about the rationale perceptible in much of the history of real property law. A new pattern of development has emerged that must disturb received ideas in many respects, from landowners' supposed devotion to perpetuities to the beneficial role that equity is supposed to have played in women's history.

1

When Chief Justice Popham protested in the sixteenth century against landowners' attempting to keep land always in the same sex, he evidently protested in vain. His words serve to point up what is the major development in landed inheritance. When the histories of the heiress, widow, and younger children are considered together, the most striking feature is the decline of women's rights over land. So long as the common law prevailed, women were important in landholding. So long as it prevailed, roughly 25 percent of land would have been inherited by females. Approximately another 15 percent would have been in the hands of widows as dower. All in all, despite a common law noted for sending estates from eldest son to eldest son, females would have had under its rules rights to 40 percent of English land. (The figure of 25 percent assumes a stationary population. If growth is assumed, that figure becomes 20 percent, and the total about one-third of English land.) By the eighteenth century among great landowners both female rights had been eliminated—the right of succession so far as was biologically possible and dower in practice completely.

This loss of female rights to land is explicable only in part. In the case of the heiress titles were undoubtedly an early factor making for her rejection. In the fourteenth century titles began to be created that descended only in tail male, in contrast to the earlier baronies in fee. The first dukedom was granted in 1337, the first marquisate in 1385, the barony by letters patent in 1387, and the viscountcy in 1440.[1] Thus gradually over the fourteenth century the common law inevitably became a problem for titled landowners. The dignity and influence of families who had won peerages could only be maintained if some substantial land accompanied the title rather than going to the common law heiress.

The rejection of the female heir was not limited, however, to peerage families. By the sixteenth century mere surnames had become important in the minds of landowners in determining the descent of their property. Even had we not the statistics on actual female inheritance that we now have, the postponement of heiresses by nonpeerage families can without much difficulty be observed in the successions to estates recorded in Burke's *Landed Gentry*. Examples of the postponement of heiresses are found among the Sneyds of Keele Hall, the Chandos-Poles of Radbourne, the Puseys of Pusey, the Brights of Badsworth, the Dymokes of Scrivelsby, the Meynells of Meynell Langley, the Mitfords of Mitford Castle, the Harcourts of Nuneham Park, the Bullers of Downes, the Bonds of Creech, the Hamblyns of Buckfastleigh, and among the Sitwells of Renishaw before they gained a baronetcy. Moreover, where a woman is recorded as succeeding, it can be because there was no collateral male close enough to be

1. Anthony Wagner, *Pedigree and Progress* (London, 1975), 121.

considered. Individual circumstances may account for any particular decision in the choice of heir, but the Cliftons of Clifton undoubtedly indicate
in their history the long-term trend. Having let an heiress succeed in 1512
although she had an uncle living, in 1694 they disherisoned an heiress in
favor of a nephew.

Very likely the practice of postponing heiresses did not spread to the
lowest level of the gentry, to the gray area where that class shaded off into
the class of small landowners. That the practice did not extend to this social
level might indeed be taken for granted; but we have evidence demonstrating that it did not spread to this level in the fact that a collection of settlements consisting of all the settlements extant in two county record offices
shows a somewhat greater willingness to allow the succession of females
than do the data on actual successions to substantial estates. Some small
landowners apparently used settlement to keep estates intact only against
the perils of younger children. But the significant point is that postponing
females was a practice that went far beyond families where a title in tail
male could explain it. Most of the landowners covered by the Stones' data
were untitled, though by far the greater part of them postponed heiresses.

Why surnames should have had quite the power they evidently had is
not easy to explain. "The Christian name belongs to the world of fancy,"
Philippe Ariès has said, "the surname to that of tradition."[2] There is an
obvious element of truth in this statement. Still the question why surnames
should have had a power akin to titles, a power to overcome the natural
flow of family sentiment, remains puzzling.

The coming of the Tudors may have much strengthened the tendency
to emphasize the patriline. At any rate it has been noticed that interest in
genealogy became conspicuous in Tudor England. The medieval English-
man had apparently taken little pride in his ancestry. His interest in his
family, it has been said, was horizontal rather than vertical.[3] He was anxious to associate himself with powerful living relations. It was in these that
he took pride, and from them that he took his status. The coming of the
Tudors, it has been suggested, changed this attitude because the Tudors
were new men. As new men, they felt an unusual necessity to prove their
credentials by demonstrating that they came of ancient and famous stock.[4]
An interest in ancestry in the presence of surnames inevitably means an-

2. Philippe Ariès, *Centuries of Childhood* (New York, 1962), 15.
3. G. D. Squibb, "The End of the Name and Arms Clause?," *Law Quarterly Review*
69 (1953): 219.
4. Ibid.

cestry in the male line, and perhaps such an interest cannot really develop in the absence of surnames. Following female lines is impracticable, exactly because of name changes. Many improbable genealogies were at first constructed to satisfy the Tudors' evident longing for distinguished ancestry, but by the seventeenth century serious genealogical research had begun. J. Smyth's *Lives of the Berkeleys*, published in 1618, was the first of a long line of works of the sort, the histories of Sir William Dugdale being by far the most notable. Inevitably these works are heavily patrilineal, histories by title or surname—the history of the Talbots, the Ogles, the Thynnes, the lords this or that—at one and the same time proof of a patrilineal trend and a strengthening of it.

However the trend is to be explained, it found its apotheosis in the eighteenth century in the invention of the name and arms clause. This was a clause by which the beneficiary of a will or settlement was required to change his name to that of the testator or settlor as a condition of receiving his estate. The name and arms clause has sometimes been held to be a benefit to women.[5] To be sure, it opened the possibility that a settlor could choose his daughter as heir, requiring her husband to take her name and thus preserving the family's name despite the succession of the female. Inherently, however, the name and arms clause must be evidence of the growth of the patrilineal ethos. It would not have been invented otherwise. In its essence it indicates the importance that names had come to have. In practice, the fact that women so seldom inherited indicates that name and arms clauses were used as a last resort, that is, when a female heir was inevitable, nature having failed to create a male in any reasonably close branch of the family, and when only a name and arms clause could maintain the family name. Thus such clauses can have had no notable effect in favoring female inheritance in gentry and aristocratic families. Occasionally a name and arms clause was used to revive artificially a patriline that had come to an end. When a family already well-endowed with land accumulated a further estate through marriage to an actual heiress, it sometimes hived off the supernumerary estate to a younger son with the requirement that he revive the patronymic of his mother's family. In practice, name and arms clauses were thus used to disguise the fact that a patriline was about to end or that it had actually ended—striking evidence of the growth of patrilineage.

Not all men, however, were willing to abandon their own surnames for

---

5. Lawrence Stone and Jeanne C. Fawtier Stone, *An Open Elite? England 1540–1880* (Oxford, 1984), 119.

their wife's, and certainly those who bore the more illustrious name of the two, or who bore a name of equal luster, would object to being required to do so. Thus the name and arms clause provided that the husband take his wife's name or, failing that, add his wife's name to his own. Thus there arose those double-barreled names among English landed families: for example, the Cavendish-Bentincks, Dukes of Portland; the Leveson-Gowers, Dukes of Sutherland; and the Montagu-Douglas-Scotts, Dukes of Buccleuch. While the double-barreled name makes very evident the demise of a patriline, it also keeps remembrance of it.

It is an irony worth passing notice that when in 1945 name and arms clauses were for the most part rendered null and void, the test case was brought by a married woman who objected to the requirement that she resume her birth name.[6] This was historically very unperceptive of her. It was the very change of a woman's name on marriage that had been a cause of the postponement of women as heirs. Who knows, perhaps some version of the name and arms clause is due for revival in a climate of opinion becoming favorable to keeping birth names: a name and arms clause to prevent change of name upon marriage in the first place.

Titles in tail male and change of name upon marriage can have had nothing to do, however, with the reduction of the widow's right. Viewed together, the movements become even harder to explain, unless in pure gender terms. It is hard to associate them with any of the major trends in the nation's history. No influence is obvious stemming from religion, for they began under the old religion and continued under the new. No influence is obvious stemming from the growth of capitalism, for both movements predated capitalism and were to be challenged when capitalism was in its heyday. Scholars who see capitalism as the source of women's oppression must be hard put to their thesis by the long history of inheritance in landed society. Moreover, the movement against female heirs took place while any explanation stemming from military tenures became ever less tenable, and it reached its peak when any such explanation had become quite impossible.

It seems clear that there can only have been a growth of antifemale sentiment, the growth of a belief that large-scale landowning belonged only to males. High social status, it is to be noted, attached to the holding of land. In the words of Sir Lewis Namier, "some well nigh mystic power"

6. The case is *Re Fry* [1945] Ch. 348. For discussion see Squibb, "The End of the Name and Arms Clause."

was felt in England to inhere in the ownership of broad acres.[7] Women were gradually excluded from that species of property to which power and prestige were attached.

A nineteenth-century political economist once delivered himself of the opinion that the injury to women when they were denied property was more apparent than real. Indeed he hinted that it would be better for women if they were excluded from property. They could then find husbands on the basis of their beauty and accomplishments.[8] Perhaps the less said of this ideal male world the better. But the suggestion may serve to raise a question that needs to be considered. Was there not after all something less harmful to women than might seem to be the case in the decline of the heiress, in view of the further rule of the common law that gave a woman's property to her husband for his life? Is the story of the heiress to be seen really as a contest between two males, husband and uncle, the outcome of which was of little consequence to females themselves?

On several grounds the answer must, I think, be no. General perceptions about women cannot but have been involved in the story, which must have affected to some degree women in general. To disherison heiresses in the topmost rank of society was to make a conspicuous public comment upon the worth and capacity of women. Moreover, the heiress decidedly had her interests, and they corresponded with those of her husband rather than with those of her uncle, and she cannot have been indifferent between the two. It was husband and wife who lived together, and it must not be imagined that wives have ever been without influence upon husbands. Under the common law the husband knew very well whose land he held, if for no other reason than that he could not deal with it as if it were his own. He could not sell it or mortgage it without his wife's agreement. Though he held it for his life, her entitlement was clear. Above all, as husband and wife they normally had children, that is, they had heirs in common, a powerful joint interest. The uncle, on the other hand, was the heiress's natural adversary. His interests were not hers. As he displaced her in the succession, he did not take the land only for his life but sent it to his heirs, and his heirs were not hers. "As the rules of inheritance became established," J. C. Holt has written, "so in romance did the wicked uncle emerge as the

7. Lewis Namier, *England in the Age of the American Revolution*, 2d ed. (London, 1966), 18.
8. J. R. McCulloch, *Treatise on Succession to Property Vacant by Death* (London, 1848), 21.

archetypal villain.'"⁹ Holt spoke of a less common inheritance matter involving uncles than the one being discussed here, but his words have a general applicability.¹⁰

It is amazing how the reduction of female property has gone virtually unrecognized. Although Maitland suggested that the story of women's property was not necessarily an upward one, his suggestion has not hitherto been followed up.¹¹ Among modern family historians only Ferdinand Mount entertains the idea that women's property may have diminished until the Victorian era, although he does not expand on the idea.¹² Yet there has always been highly suggestive evidence that the movement was downward. Any comparison of later instruments, either the entail or the strict settlement, with the common law would suggest the downward movement, even if there were no further empirical evidence as to succession.

The history of the widow has, to be sure, been perceived, but inadequately. In considering economic movements in the sixteenth and seventeenth centuries, historians have had eyes far more for the rise of daughters' portions than for the connected and much greater fall in widows' jointures. Rising provision for daughters has been the story always emphasized. Stone, who is the historian to whom we are indebted for tracing the movement of the jointure/portion ratio, has said of the widow only that her jointure had become "flexible," while speaking in dramatic terms of the rise of portions.¹³ Lloyd Bonfield, who has presented valuable evidence on the longevity of the aristocratic widow—evidence I have used above—

9. J. C. Holt, "The *Casus Regis*, the Law and Politics of Succession in the Plantagenet Dominions 1185–1247," in *Law in Mediaeval Life and Thought*, ed. Edward B. King and Susan J. Ridyard (Sewanee, Tenn., 1990), 27.

10. Holt was concerned with what is known as the question of representation. Who was the heir of a man who had had two (or more) sons, the eldest of whom had predeceased him leaving issue? Was it his younger son, or was it the issue of his deceased eldest son standing in that son's place? The two possible heirs stood in relationship one to the other, of course, as uncle to nephew or to niece. The question arose in the royal succession between King John, younger son in the case, and his nephew Arthur. John settled the question, at least in his time, by murdering Arthur. (That he did not bother to murder Arthur's sister Eleanor, but merely kept her an unmarried prisoner, presumably shows some contempt for the female heir.) By earlier, as by later, rules Arthur and then Eleanor was right heir, not John. Holt tells the story in fascinating detail, including the well-advised wafflings of the legal authorities of the time.

11. F. Pollock and F. W. Maitland, *The History of English Law before the Time of Edward I*, 2d ed. (Cambridge, 1898), 2:403.

12. Ferdinand Mount, *The Subversive Family* (London, 1982), 235.

13. Lawrence Stone, *The Crisis of Aristocracy, 1558–1641* (Oxford, 1965), 643, 638.

and who is aware of the 10 percent ratio of jointure to portion that came to be established, has nevertheless concluded that widows were a heavy charge on husbands' estates and has even discounted the idea that the substitution of jointure for dower meant a loss to the widow.[14] G. E. Mingay, who early recognized that the 10 percent ratio meant that widows had come to provide for their own jointure (or their fathers had), proceeded to ignore his own insight in his account of estate developments.[15] Historians have long had all the evidence necessary for an appreciation of the widow's story, but they have, for whatever reason, only fitfully taken notice of it.

Especially amazing is how the history of the heiress-at-law has gone unrecognized. It is not that historians have been unaware of landowners' preference for male heirs. They have often emphasized that preference, noting that daughters did not succeed and speaking of landowners' patrilineal principles. It is rather that the direction of movement has been got wrong. That the common law gave only a limited preference to males and that landowners had to develop patrilineal mechanisms has not been appreciated, and with very few exceptions historians have portrayed female inheritance as increasing. They have failed to see that the female heir suffered demotion and that she was demoted only through a long and important legal process.

The reasons for this failure of perception vary greatly. Sometimes it seems simply to have been taken for granted that women would not have had succession rights until recent times, almost as if that were a law of nature. Such a view blots out any adverse movement for women that might otherwise be perceived in the development of entails and settlements and inevitably gives an upward trend to female inheritance. Sometimes early rights of succession have been considered, but the common law has been misperceived, being seen as decidedly more male-oriented than it was. With this perception, the trend of female inheritance inevitably again goes upward, doing so as the common law is pushed into the background. Sometimes the common law has been understood, but nevertheless female inheritance is portrayed as rising because the final device, the strict settlement, appears on its face to be a more liberal, a less dynastic, device than an entail in tail male. There is in this case a dependence upon surface appearance. Put settlement into the historical context of uses and wills, and this judgment must change. Sometimes, so it would seem, the whole

14. Lloyd Bonfield, *Marriage Settlements, 1601–1740* (Cambridge, 1983), 117–18.

15. G. E. Mingay, *English Landed Society in the Eighteenth Century* (London, 1963), 35–36.

question of female succession has been viewed as of little significance until recent times, because of a demographic misperception that premodern families were so large that there were sons aplenty to inherit. For one period (Anglo-Norman England), the common law right of daughters has been well discussed, but because of the periodization of historical studies the findings were not considered in any long-term perspective. Only on the long-term view does the story become perceptible. Occasionally the story has actually been perceived, out of the corner of the eye as it were, only to be dismissed as quite to be expected, quite natural, as the historian gets on with what matters, the affairs of younger sons.[16] The reasons for the misperception about female inheritance are thus numerous; but for one reason or another, the long and legally central story of the putting down of the heiress-at-law has gone largely unrecognized.

Terminology has helped to blind historians to the movement against females as heirs, particularly the use of the word "patrimony" as a synonym for "family estate" or "landed estate." The desire to avoid the word "estate" is understandable, for it can mean actual land—fields and woods— or a legal entitlement to land not necessarily in possession, or even the sum of a person's property of all kinds. Many words have several meanings depending upon their context, however, and no real confusion exists around the word "estate"; where any might be possible, it can be avoided by the addition of the words "family" or "landed." Real confusion enters when a family estate is spoken of as a "patrimony." The implication of "patrimony" is that the estate passed down in the male line as of right. In its way, this is a begging of the question. If it does not quite assume in the premise what is to be proved, it assumes as legal right what had been established only through a lengthy legal process.

Ultimately perhaps the idea of declining female inheritance has simply been too at odds with an ingrained belief about English history for it to have been seriously considered. There is a strong belief, entertained by all but Marxists, and even by some of them, that things move ever in a liberal direction in English history. There may be temporary backslidings recognized, and in some formulations of the idea things move upward to free

16. K. B. McFarlane proceeds in this way, as noted in chapter 1. So does Randolph Trumbach, who finds that settlement was less generous than the common law to women, but because it was more generous than the common law to younger sons, makes it the basis of a theory that the eighteenth century saw the arrival of the egalitarian family—which is to have a questionable notion of equality. See his *Rise of the Egalitarian Family* (New York, 1978), 81, 88. For discussion of Trumbach's views see chapter 6.

enterprise, and in others upward to the welfare state, but they tend ever in a liberal direction. In the words of Tennyson, English history tells of "freedom slowly broadening down from precedent to precedent."

There has as well been a connected belief about English history that has helped to obscure the decline of female inheritance: the belief that England has always been more liberal than the Continent. Europe has been associated in English minds with Salic principles through the history of the French monarchy. There took place in the annals of the French royal house a conspicuous move against female heirs that was not paralleled in England; the French monarchy has since been regularly contrasted with its more liberal English counterpart.

The Salic law, we are told on good authority, had nothing to do with women's succession to thrones.[17] It was not a political constitution, and it concerned females and their succession to land. Unfortunately, nice considerations about the Salic law seem to have become irrelevant. The law has irretrievably become associated with events that took place in France when Louis X died in 1316, leaving a daughter and, in due course, a posthumous son. Louis's brother Philip was appointed regent for the infant king, but this hapless monarch was to live only four days. Philip—who may have had something to do with the brevity of his nephew's reign—was in good position as regent to seize the throne for himself, which he proceeded to do, thus cutting out his niece and declaring that no female could inherit the throne of France. The rule was subsequently invoked—with a certain natural justice, it may be thought—when Philip himself died leaving only daughters; and was invoked again when Philip's successor, another of Louis's brothers, also died leaving only daughters. Unlike England, France was never to have a queen regnant.

It has all been a French thing, this putting down of female heirs. Or as Shakespeare would have it, a German thing. At any rate, not English.[18]

2

The histories of the heiress and the widow, of course, do not make up the whole of the aristocratic family's history. Younger children are not to

17. See "Salic Law" in the *Encyclopedia Britannica*, 11th and later editions, by separate hands.

18. A. W. B. Simpson has argued that it was a Scottish thing, but not an English one. See his "Entails and Perpetuities," *Juridical Review* (1979): 1–20.

be ignored in discussing the overall pattern. But while the heiress and the widow fell spectacularly from a high when the common law prevailed to a low in the eighteenth century, no spectacular movement marked the history of younger children. Their portions fluctuated from time to time, but within a range that was limited compared to other movements of family property. It was not on younger children that landowners had their eyes fixed as they developed inheritance stratagems. But even the interests of younger children declined in the eighteenth century, those of younger sons especially. Younger sons seem to have done rather well in medieval times. No doubt one of the reasons why they could be cut off with less in the eighteenth century lay in the increased employment opportunities that came their way with the growth of the professions and the rise of the administrative state.

When developments are considered over the whole family and over the long run, the pattern evident may be summed up somewhat as follows: What landowners wanted, or had come to want, was some means of husbanding resources in the hands of the male head of the family, while not utterly disinheriting the family's subordinate members. Under the principles of English law what they wanted was not easily to be obtained. They had had first to dispose of rules that provided for female inheritance far more generously than they thought proper, and for younger children less generously. Having gained freedom of alienation, they lacked any positive restraining device, which only at length was the strict settlement to confer upon them.

When seen thus, which is to say when seen in the light of the family, landowners' history takes on a coherence—one might even say a simplicity—that it does not otherwise have. The progression that is to be traced in their history from the common law to wills (that is, to testamentary dispositions through uses) and then from wills to the strict settlement appears on the surface to be an incoherent journey, being a journey first towards and then away from freedom of alienation. Looked at against the common law rules, it becomes entirely coherent, the natural working out of aristocratic ideas of heirship against those embodied in the common law. In current terminology, what has seemed discontinuity in landowners' actions becomes in a fundamental way continuity.

This view of landowners' history, as has already been suggested, differs from the one traditional in doctrinal histories. The traditional view sees real property law as reflecting a long struggle between landowners determined on perpetuities and the common law judges determined on freedom of alienation. The two views fundamentally agree in that they recognize a movement towards freedom of alienation with uses and then away from it with the strict settlement. Moreover, it is true that many common law judges, Coke in particular, were adamant against perpetuities. Nevertheless the traditional view is difficult to sustain. Landowners themselves had chosen to bar entails and to make wills, and had thus themselves sought freedom of alienation. Uses were not forced on them by judges in support of freedom of alienation; and some of the judges, possibly most of them, voluntarily supported Henry VIII in his attack upon uses.[19] Moreover, to judge by Christopher St German's *Doctor and Student*, some legal authorities could even say a good word for entails.

Sometimes landowners' skepticism about entails would be recognized and a more complex psychology attributed to them. They are then seen as desiring freedom for themselves but determined to tie up their successors as far into the future as possible. Sir Francis Bacon spoke of "an excess of will in [their] minds, affecting to have assurances of their estates and possession to be revocable in their own times, and too irrevocable after their own times."[20] The idea is frequently met in modern sources as well. No doubt many landowners harbored such contradictory desires. The fact that they did so will not, however, explain movements in property law. Why should the one aim have predominated at one time and the other at another time? The development of real property law is not more explained by this attempt at greater psychological realism.

Accounts of legal developments built around perpetuities are obviously not without point, for landowners desired to preserve their estates. But neither do such accounts realistically reflect landowners' history, excluding family concerns that landowners must always have been grappling with.

3

The major finding is, then, that the history of real property law is significantly marked by a conflict between heirs male and heirs female. This conclusion has been reached largely by reinterpreting statistics on inheritance among large landowners in the light of common law rules. These statistics indicate clearly the existence of the conflict and its outcome. A different sort of evidence is also available. The court records of the sixteenth and seventeenth centuries testify to the conflict as it took place. This evi-

19. J. H. Baker, *Introduction to English Legal History*, 2d ed. (London, 1979), 215.
20. *The Works of Lord Bacon*, ed. J. Spedding (London, 1857), 7:409.

dence might profitably be looked at afresh, for while conflicts between heirs male and female are recognized to have taken place, they have been treated by historians in a variety of ways. They have been held to be a matter of interest only for peerage history. They have been seen in reverse, as protests by fathers of daughters against a common law supposed to have sent estates to collateral males. They have been seen as a sixteenth-century phenomenon, the result of the Statute of Uses, which allegedly brought immense confusion into landowners' legal arrangements.[21] It is clear that they are to be associated with the changing conception of heirship among large landowners, and that they vividly illustrate the family discords that were engendered. A brief review of some cases will set them firmly into their social context and will, as well, show them to have reached further into the courts than has been realized.

PEERAGE CASES

Cases are, of course, most readily to be found in the genealogical records of peerage and baronial families. While baronies in fee, baronies that descended to common law heirs and were inheritable by females, continued to exist, the fourteenth century had seen the rise of a higher peerage whose titles were virtually all inheritable only by males. As power to devise land arose, testators who were possessed of either form of honor were free to decide whether, or to what degree, land and honor were to be kept together. Whether the honor was in fee or in tail male, then, contests between the collateral male and direct female were likely to occur. They took place in two notable baronial families, the Fitzalans and the Berkeleys, before 1420. Both ended in compromise, but in the latter case conflict broke out anew in the next generation, though it failed to alter the terms of the agreement that had earlier been worked out. Later in the century Edward IV is known to have made a division between the quarreling heir general and the heir male in the Dacre family.[22]

Contests became much more frequent in the sixteenth century. Perhaps confusion following the Statute of Uses had something to do with the increase, but it was not the main cause. In the cases that have been described

21. B. Coward, "Disputed Inheritances: Some Difficulties of the Nobility in the Late Sixteenth and Early Seventeenth Centuries," *Bulletin of the Institute of Historical Research* 44 (1971): 194–215.

22. K. B. McFarlane, *The Nobility of Later Medieval England* (Oxford, 1973), 119; J. P. Cooper, "Patterns of Inheritance and Settlement by Great Landowners," in *Family and Inheritance,* ed. Jack Goody, Joan Thirsk, and E. P. Thompson (Cambridge, 1976), 211.

in any detail the argument centers not on the interpretation of an innovative legal instrument, new-fangled from the statute, but regularly on a simple question of fact: Had the land been entailed by an ancestor? The entail—regularly appealed to by the male heir but apparently often not produceable, or when produceable apparently insufficient to sustain the claim—is a feature of these cases, not conveyances more complicated. The increase in the number of contests is to be associated with the increase in the size of the peerage and with the growing emphasis upon the patriline, of which a peerage with titles in tail male was a manifestation.

In some of these contests of the sixteenth and seventeenth centuries, the heir female continued to be successful, as she was when a second conflict broke out in the Dacre family. When the fifth lord died in 1566, his widow shortly thereafter married the fourth Duke of Norfolk, who became guardian to Dacre's four young children: his son and heir, now sixth Lord Dacre, and his three daughters. The son died three years later, however, still a boy, leaving his sisters heirs general to the Dacre barony and, in the mind of their (not quite disinterested) guardian, heirs to the Dacre estates as well. The girls' uncle, Leonard Dacre, held otherwise, and he presumptuously assumed the honor of the barony and instituted proceedings against his nieces for the estates, claiming that his father, the fourth lord, had entailed them on the heirs male. Such an entail seems to have existed, for one of Norfolk's sons, Lord William Howard, who by then was married to one of the heiresses Dacre, spoke heatedly of an attempt that his wife's grandfather had made to disherison her. As Lord William put it, grandfather Dacre had been "seduced by devilish instigation . . . to crosse Almighty God in his omnipotent course" and had sought "to bar . . . his right heirs of their due . . . belonging unto them, by the laws of God, of nations, and of this realme."[23] (Whether this phalanx of legal authorities would have required the succession of a Howard heiress, Lord William forbore to say.) No entail of the Dacre estates was produced at the trial, however, and Lord William implied it had not been properly executed. In the event, the land went to the heirs general, and Leonard Dacre's claim to the honor of the barony was also denied. When the issue of the barony was later raised by a descendant, it was again denied the male line.[24]

The heir female also succeeded in the Ogle family. Again the Ogle barony was in fee, and the seventh lord settled his estates upon his elder daugh-

---

23. Cooper, "Patterns of Inheritance," 206.

24. Neville Williams, *Thomas Howard, Fourth Duke of Norfolk* (London, 1964), 117–19; 174.

ter. In choosing the elder of his daughters as heir, he kept his estates intact, without sending them to a male. This was the course sometimes adopted with regard to female heirs when the honor was in fee. Ogle's next male heir was his uncle, who had feared that his nephew would do exactly what he did do. Before Ogle's death he had appealed, piteously though fruitlessly, to the Privy Council in an effort to prevent it.[25] Since Ogle in settling his estates fundamentally followed peerage law relative to baronies in fee, the fact that his uncle felt aggrieved can only point up the growth of the patrilineal ethos.

In another case a Talbot heir general succeeded even though the family's honor, the earldom of Shrewsbury, was in tail male. Gilbert, the seventh earl, preferred his three daughters to his brother and at his death in 1616 willed the bulk of his estates to them, and only a relatively small part to his brother, upon whom the title descended. The brother, upon becoming eighth earl, immediately instituted legal proceedings against his nieces, claiming again that his father had entailed the land in tail male. In this case there was to be no decision by a court, because the eighth earl died within months of his succession.[26] The distant cousin who then inherited the title may not have come within the scope of the entail, presuming that it existed and that it covered substantial land, and he thus possibly could not have continued the suit even had he desired to do so. He is reported, moreover, to have been a Catholic priest, and this may have been the reason why the suit was not pursued. As a religious celibate he may have had little interest in the succession.

Seldom, however, was the heir female so completely successful; compromise was probably the normal result of contests between heirs general and heirs male. Compromise was the result in a well-known case in the Stanley family. Ferdinando, fifth Earl of Derby, like the seventh Earl of Shrewsbury, preferred his daughters to his brother and on his death in 1594 left his estates to the eldest of them. His brother, upon whom the title descended, began legal proceedings against his niece, claiming once again that the land was entailed, claiming that it had been entailed by the third earl, grandfather of Ferdinando and himself. This can hardly have been proved, or else the entail was found to encompass little land, or a disentailing could be alleged on the opposite side, for soon the earl was offering a financial inducement to his niece to forgo a legal contest. Only after elaborate negotiations, which involved the Crown's rights over the Stanley fief-

25. Cooper, "Patterns of Inheritance," 211.
26. For a fuller account of the Talbot case see Coward, "Disputed Inheritances," 201.

dom of the Isle of Man, was a final agreement arrived at.[27] Compromise was similarly the result of contests that took place when the third Lord Chandos died in 1594, leaving two daughters; and when the third Earl of Cumberland died in 1605, leaving a sole heiress.

It would seem that compromise was generally on the lines of the Statute of Wills, which required that one-third of land held by knight service go to the heir-at-law. The financial arrangements in the Cumberland case are of interest as evidence of this division, and for another reason as well. The portion of the heiress in the case, Anne Clifford (later Anne Herbert, Countess of Pembroke) has frequently been pointed to, an early seventeenth-century portion of £17,000 inviting historians' awed comment. It has been seen as proof of the extreme rise of portions in the seventeenth century, as proof, that is, of increasing generosity to daughters. It is actually proof of the decline of female inheritance, for Anne Clifford was not an ordinary portioned daughter but an heiress-at-law; and in her day, she felt aggrieved. She held that she had been virtually disinherited. For years she contended for her rights against her uncle, who had succeeded to the Clifford estates. In the end, through an arbitration decision, she received more than £17,000, probably about £35,000, as by the Statute of Wills she ought to have.[28] The Clifford estates had a gross income in the mid-seventeenth century between £5,000 and £6,000; that is, they had a capital value of more than £100,000.[29] History has treated Anne Clifford unkindly. She has appeared not as a woman struggling for her rights but as an uppity female, a thorn in the side of the Earl of Cumberland.

Compromise was also the result in two contests that are particularly important, those over the baronies of Abergavenny and De Ros, for these mounted general challenges to heirs female.[30] In both, novel principles were sought to be established by the heir male, principles that would have gone far to curtail, and even to eliminate, the right of females to succeed to baronies in fee. It was argued in the one case that the person who was in possession, by deed or will, of the land to which a barony in fee was attached was entitled to the honor even if he were not heir-at-law, thus abolishing the principle that the honor descended (essentially) according to common

27. For a fuller account of the Derby case see ibid., 204.

28. J. P. Cooper, "The Counting of Manors," *Economic History Review*, 2d ser. 8 (1955): 379–80.

29. Stone, *Crisis of Aristocracy*, 761.

30. J. H. Round, *Peerage and Pedigree: Studies in Peerage Law and Family History* (London, 1910), 1:75–89.

law. In the other case it was argued that where a family had gained a title in tail male any barony in fee that it possessed was, by a process of attraction, converted to tail male. Both arguments were rejected, but nevertheless the barony of Abergavenny has since descended in tail male, though as J. H. Round has observed, "it is not known why."[31] In the decisions at hand in the two families, the land was divided. And in a sense so were the titles, for the Crown, apparently in order to facilitate settlement, created a new barony in each family, thus seeing to it that there were baronies enough to satisfy all parties.

CASES AMONG UNTITLED LANDOWNERS

Genealogical records for untitled families are not nearly so complete or so reliable as those for titled families; but the struggle between heirs male and heirs female is nevertheless evident among the untitled. It is all the more important to be noticed among these families, for the fact that it extended beyond the peerage indicates that it was a broad-based phenomenon. The struggle is indeed particularly evident in historical records in the case of untitled families, for it shows up in leading law cases, although this aspect of case law has been all but ignored. Several important precedents that go to make up the history of real property law and that thus standardly appear in legal texts were established in cases that sprang out of conflicts between heirs male and female. *Sharington v. Strotton, Shelley's Case, Mildmay's Case,* and *Dormer v. Parkhurst,* all leading cases, arose in this way.[32] The social background of these cases stands particularly in need of notice.

The earliest of them, *Sharington v. Strotton* (1565), arose out of a covenant that Andrew Baynton had made with his brother Edward, by which Andrew was to stand seised to the use of himself for life, remainder to Edward in tail male. Andrew had no sons, but he evidently had a daughter who was excluded by the covenant. The question in the case was whether the covenant between the brothers constituted a valid contract, for contracts to be valid required the passing of some consideration. That is to say, they required something to be done on the one side and on the other, a mere promise having no legal meaning; and consideration was required to be

---

31. J. H. Round, *Studies in Peerage and Family History* (London, 1901), 466.

32. In the *English Reports* these cases are, respectively, Plowden 298; 1 Co. Rep. 88; 6 Co. Rep. 40; and 6 Brown P. C. 351. Abstracts are to be found in J. H. Baker and S. F. C. Milsom, *Sources of English Legal History: Private Law to 1750* (London, 1986).

something to be done presently or in the future. Here the consideration was Andrew's love for his brother and the desire that the land should remain in the blood and name of the Bayntons. Counsel on the one side argued that the continuance in the name of the Bayntons offered no benefit to Andrew and was "not a worthy cause to raise a use," and he further argued that an agreement based on the long-standing affection of two brothers lacked any present or future consideration. He drew a contrast between the agreement at issue, which was based on affection but in which nothing was to be done presently, and an agreement similarly based on affection but which was made in expectation of marriage. Marriage was a benefit that made the agreement a valid contract; it was a valuable consideration. On the other side, counsel argued that any consideration proceeding from nature was sufficient in law to raise a use, and particularly argued that continuance in the name and blood was a worthy consideration because it was sensible to exclude females from land. The case has gone down as establishing the principle that natural affection is sufficient ground for making a settlement; but unless the facts that led to the case are taken notice of, the social significance of the case is obscured. In the circumstances at issue the common law actually paid more heed to natural affection than the covenant approved. From the family historian's point of view the case demonstrates the growth of an order of succession not natural.

The notorious case of *Shelley* (1579), which was to persist as a hurdle for law students and a trap for testators right into the twentieth century, began in an intention to defeat a female heir. Doctrinally *Shelley* ranks as "one of the deeper mysteries of the common law," as one legal authority has well called it.[33] But however complicated the arguments in the case, and however complicated its subsequent history, the circumstances that gave rise to the case are quite simple and unmysterious.

Edward Shelley, whose legal arrangements led to the case, had had two sons, Henry and Richard. Henry, the elder, had died in the lifetime of his father, leaving a daughter Mary, who by common law was then heir presumptive to the estate; Henry had died leaving as well his wife, Anne, pregnant. Edward set about settling the land so as to cut Mary and her possible-to-be-born sister out of the succession. Within weeks, and before Anne gave birth, Edward himself suddenly and most inconveniently died. Whereupon Richard, the younger son, entered upon the land, claiming to be heir in accordance with the settlement. Shortly thereafter Anne gave birth to a son, a son who was right heir by common law, and right heir by

33. A. W. B. Simpson, *A History of the Land Laws*, 2d ed. (Oxford, 1986), 96.

Edward Shelley's intention as well, as a certain feature of the settlement attested,[34] but whose uncle claimed possession through having been right male heir at the time of Edward Shelley's death. A contest over possession thus erupted as soon as the nephew came of age. What had begun as a desire to cut out a female heir thus ended in a conflict between a posthumously born son and his uncle.

No doubt the desire to ensure the land to the right male heir, right by any standard, does not entirely account for the doctrine that was enunciated, for the doctrine had an ancient rationale.[35] The law has a logical rigor that is not readily deflected nor casually to be ignored. But the spectacle of a right male heir cut out of his inheritance was a horrid sight. Queen Elizabeth herself followed the legal brouhaha with keen interest. The desire to rescue the right male heir appears at least to have been a significant consideration, for the judges were well aware of Edward Shelley's real intention, through "various circumstances appearing in the record," as Coke delicately phrased it. And other reports of the case, those by Anderson and Dyer, suggest the primacy of the desire to effect the settlor's intentions.[36]

The result of *Shelley* was to be paradoxical, doubly so. While the court carried out Edward Shelley's manifest intention and saw to the succession of his posthumous grandson, in the process it set up an obstacle to settlements, or reestablished an old one. As a result *Shelley* was to go rattling down the centuries frustrating the intentions of unwary settlors who failed to take cognizance of the obstacle it posed to settlements. Nevertheless the simple way around the obstacle was pointed out at the very time *Shelley* was enunciated, and this hint fell upon ready ears among English landowners, whose desires for settlements were not to be frustrated. Thus while *Shelley* went rattling down the centuries hindering settlements in theory— and sometimes doing so in practice—it had little effect on the settlement habits of English landowners. (The later history of *Shelley* will be discussed in chapter 5.) At any rate we may well imagine that had Anne Shelley given birth to a second daughter a great cause of complexity in English law might have been avoided.

34. The settlement contained a trust whose duration suggested that Edward Shelley had in mind the possibility of a lengthy minority, as would be the case if he was thinking that Anne might give birth to a son. Richard, who claimed to be heir, was only a few years short of his majority.

35. For two discussions of *Shelley* see A. D. Hargreaves, "Shelley's Ghost," *Law Quarterly Review* 54 (1938): 70–77; and R. E. Megarry and H. W. R. Wade, *The Laws of Real Property*, 3d ed. (London, 1966), 61–63.

36. Baker and Milsom, *Sources of English Law*, 149.

Mildmay's Case (1605) arose, on the other hand, out of a desire that a female should succeed. Anthony Mildmay, whose father had been Chancellor of the Exchequer to Queen Elizabeth, was determined that his only daughter should succeed to his estate rather than his brother, despite the existence of an entail reinforced by a clause of perpetuity that excluded her. Clauses of perpetuity, as has been seen, were used by some settlors in an effort to revive entails, which had become barrable estates.[37] It was Mildmay who five years earlier had tested judicial sentiment on these clauses by bringing a fictitious case, *Corbett v. Corbett*. In all, he was to fight three cases in the interests of his daughter, and his consistent victories put an end to clauses of perpetuity. Although these were not officially buried until 1614, Mildmay had caused sentence to be passed by 1605 in both Common Pleas and King's Bench.

Dormer v. Parkhurst (1740) finally determined the nature of the estate held by the trustee to preserve contingent remainders, determining that that estate was not itself contingent. If it were contingent Bridgman's invention was of no avail, for the trustees had been invented to overcome the fact that contingent remainders were destructible.[38] In practice, Chancery had assumed from the beginning that the estate in the trustees was vested, that is, was not contingent; and Chief Justice Willes warned that were the court in 1740 to determine otherwise, a hundred thousand settlements would be overturned. *Dormer v. Parkhurst* thus sounded the coda, long delayed, for the development of the strict settlement.

The case arose when John Dormer, in a collateral branch of the Dormer family, contested a disentailing that had earlier taken place in the senior branch between his uncle Robert and Robert's son, Fleetwood. Both Robert and Fleetwood had died shortly thereafter, leaving Fleetwood's three sisters as heirs general, who accordingly took possession of the land. They enjoyed possession for a dozen years before they were dispossessed by the court's decision. The settlement is not in the standard form but contains an unusual term of ninety-nine years to Robert and to the trustees. It is to be suggested that the term was a conveyancing error. (While such a term would extend the life of the particular settlement, it would render settlement as a system of entail operating through regular resettlements impossible.) At any rate, according to standard settlement practice, there was nothing abnormal about the disentailing that had taken place between Robert and Fleetwood, except that, through the quick demise of both parties,

37. See chapter 1, section 6.
38. See chapter 1, section 6.

it had not been followed by a new deed favoring the family's collateral males over its females. The case turned upon the estate held by the trustees, the defendants claiming that it was itself contingent, in which event the females were right heirs. But it was too late for such a claim. "Common error makes right" is a legal maxim of some force. Since Chancery had for sixty years assumed the estate in the trustees to be vested and not contingent, *Dormer v. Parkhurst* is really of more interest for its gender background than for what it finally determined. We may be sure that had Fleetwood's heirs not been female the case would never have arisen. John Dormer would not likely have challenged a male in the senior branch of the family who was in possession.

Important matters of legal doctrine were settled in these cases. As the judges made their decisions, they made them on the immediate questions that came before them, the meaning of consideration, the validity of particular clauses in settlements, and so on. Nevertheless the cases all began in one problem, the conflict between heirs male and heirs female in landed families. That is the social problem they testify to, and recognizing it is essential if the development of real property law is to be seen in social perspective.

4

To see the history of inheritance among large landowners as primarily the story of the elimination of rights that females enjoyed at common law is willy-nilly to emphasize the common law's generosity to females. It has not, however, been normal to associate the common law with anything progressive in the family, and certainly not with anything good for women. Equity is the branch of law that is usually associated with women's property rights. The large question thus naturally arises as to the relative roles that equity and common law have played in women's history. It is a question, moreover, of some current interest, for equity has recently been much emphasized in women's history. Old preconceptions about the common law would seem to be reappearing in a new form.

In the nineteenth century the common law was frequently attacked as undemocratic in its principles and illiberal in its attitude to women. Among intellectuals and middle-class people it was viewed even with incredulity, a medieval horror that ought long since to have been got rid of. The common law, after all, sent landed property to the eldest son to the complete exclusion of his siblings; it postponed daughters to sons; and it gave husbands their wives' property, absolutely or for life depending on whether that property was personal or real.

An attack on the common law was central to John Stuart Mill's *The Subjection of Women*. Mill protested particularly the rules applicable to the property of the married woman. "The wife's position under the common law of England," he declared, was "worse than that of slaves in the laws of many countries." Under ancient Roman law a slave might have property that the law guaranteed him for his own use, and while Mill acknowledged that the higher classes in England often gave a similar right to their women through contractual arrangements, he emphasized that the majority of English women were without such protection. Most married women lived under the common law, and in common law the husband and wife were, as Mill put it, one person, "for the purpose of inferring that whatever is hers is his, but the parallel inference is never drawn that whatever is his is hers."[39]

The common law also came under attack in the nineteenth century as reformers sought time and again to have equal division among children substituted for primogeniture as the principle of inheritance applicable to real property. Equal division had always been the principle applicable to personal property. The first work Maitland published on the laws of England was an attack on the rules of inheritance, which he treated with unmitigated derision. "Our canons of inheritance," he began "have two capital follies—primogeniture and the postponement of women." Calling these principles worthless in themselves, he went on to show how they disordered the body of property law. On their account, England maintained two systems of property law, one for land and one for personal property, operating on different principles and rendering English law full of "gins and pitfalls for the unwary and unknowable by all save experts." One system had to go, and there could be no doubt which: "For, of course, it is the law of descent, the law applicable to real property, that is threatened, no one being so enamoured of the heir-at-law as to desire that he should take, not only all the land, but also all the goods. Of the law of descent we are therefore obliged to speak though it is certainly difficult to criticize it without insulting the intelligence of our readers."

"The whole civilized world is against us," Maitland went on. Here he referred to a recently published book by Eyre Lloyd, which contained a comparative analysis of inheritance laws. This had shown that in almost

39. John Stuart Mill, *The Subjection of Women*, MIT Press ed. (Cambridge, Mass., 1970), 31–32.

all the countries of Europe property was divided equally among children without regard to sex and whether the property was real or personal.[40] Maitland fell on the exceptions: "The only exceptions of any importance, are Great Britain, Russia and Servia. Have we not lately learned . . . that of all countries Russia is the most barbarous and backward, save perhaps of Servia? And yet it is to the despised Russia and the contemptible Servia . . . that we must look for a law at all resembling our own. But let us not be downhearted. Mr Lloyd has concerned himself only with Christian countries; should he at some future time turn to the heathen he may obtain valuable and gratifying results."[41]

These are damning attacks on the common law. They were, however, made as part of contemporary politics. They were part of an effort to change the law in a democratic direction. The questions being discussed were questions of the day: Should women in the enlightened nineteenth century be postponed at all to men? Should married women any longer be denied their property? These attacks on the common law, made in an effort to effect change, were not, nor were they intended to be, historical analyses of the role of common law and equity in women's history.

There seems to have followed from these nineteenth-century controversies, however, a tendency for historians to think that equity was in principle concerned to right the wrongs the common law inflicted on women. The word "equity" might suggest as much; and as a branch of law, equity has been defined as the one that operates on the principle of conscience rather than by cut and dried rules. St German in the sixteenth century spoke of equity as bringing the law of the state into accord with the law of God and the law of reason, which certainly puts it on the side of the angels. Not everyone agreed with him. In the seventeenth century Selden suspected that equity was law "according to the Conscience of him that is Chancellor." (Chancery was, of course, the court of equity.) And any reader of Dickens knows how Chancery appeared to litigants in the nineteenth century. In the history of the family, however, equity is routinely associated with virtue and progress.

There are some obvious practical grounds for this association. Equity moved in several ways to abate the rigor of the common law rules of coverture, that is, the body of laws applicable to married women. It brought

---

40. Eyre Lloyd, *Primogeniture as it Exists in England* (London, 1870).

41. F. W. Maitland, "The Law of Real Property," in *The Collected Papers of F. W. Maitland,* ed. H. A. L. Fisher (Cambridge, 1911), 162–201. The article first appeared under the title "The Heir-at-Law" in the *Westminster Review* for 1872.

into existence the settlement to the separate use of a married woman. It furthermore established the principle known as the equity to a settlement. Lord Chancellor King in the early eighteenth century is usually associated with this development, but he himself found the principle operative earlier.[42] This principle was of narrow applicability, protecting only the wife whose husband had to appeal to Chancery to gain control of property due to her, say to assert her right to a legacy due her from an estate under court administration.[43] In such cases Chancery compelled the husband to settle part of what he gained on his wife. To gain from equity a man must do equity, it was said (a statement which incidentally again assumes for equity moral virtue). Thus it may be said that Chancery not only supported settlements on married women but compelled them when it could.

Equity also developed in the late eighteenth century the restraint upon anticipation. Whether this was of much benefit to women is, however, to be doubted. It was intended to protect the wife from the possibility that her husband might manage to gain her separate property for himself. The fear was, as the phrase went, that he might "kiss or kick it" from her. A husband who was so disposed could not be prevented from kissing or kicking her income from her each quarter, but the restraint on anticipation could prevent him compelling her to borrow upon her capital and depriving herself of income for the future, or compelling her simply to transfer the capital to him. Based on a traditional perception of women as inherently weak-willed, the restraint upon anticipation no doubt protected some wives who were weak-willed, though not without inconvenience to those who were not, preventing reasonable transactions by normal husbands and wives. And it is to be noted that as women in the twentieth century moved towards equality, the imposition of the restraint has been forbidden as a burden on the married woman, preventing her using her capital.[44] There was, of course, a genuine social problem that played a part in the development of the restraint—the violent husband. As has since been recognized, such a man is best dealt with through the criminal law rather than by restricting his wife's property rights. Still the restraint upon anticipation must be counted as having been good in intention. That equity is the origin

42. C. S. Kenny, *The History of the Law of England as to the Effects of Marriage on Property and on the Wife's Legal Capacity* (London, 1879), 118.

43. For a discussion of the equity to a settlement see ibid., 118–27.

44. Statutes, 25 & 26 Geo. 5, c. 30 and 13 & 14 Geo. 6, c. 78. See A. C. H. Barlow, "Gifts and Other Transfers Inter Vivos and the Matrimonial Home," in *A Century of Family Law 1857–1957*, ed. R. H. Graveson and F. R. Crane (London, 1957), 201.

of the married woman's right to hold property is well remembered in the lawyer's maxim that Chancery's business was with infants, lunatics, and married women.

While tributes are justly to be made to equity for its support of the married woman's right to hold property, equity does not deserve to be associated with the cause of women as a matter of principle. A balanced view is necessary if the historical record is not to be distorted.

Unfortunately Mary Beard's seminal work, *Woman as Force in History*, misleads on the subject of equity, a work currently of more interest probably than when it was written. Written in the 1940s, it was in advance of its day, being one of the first scholarly works to insist upon the importance of women in history and to decry the way their contributions had been forgotten or belittled. Beard aimed to portray women as active in all historical movements, and she particularly rejected the view that women's history had been one solely of oppression. The objects of her scorn became John Stuart Mill and William Blackstone—an unlikely combination. What the pair had in common was the idea of woman as powerless, though the one protested the situation and the other took it as right and proper. In Beard's eyes they shared "the dogma of woman's complete historical subjection to men," which she rated "one of the most fantastic myths ever created by the human mind."[45] It had come to blind even women to the historical contributions of their sex.

Beard objected above all to Blackstone's famous dictum about the legal position of the married woman. Husband and wife were one person in law, Blackstone had declared: "the very existence of the woman is suspended during the coverture, or entirely merged and incorporated in that of the husband."[46] For Beard these words stripped married women of their personality. They were the very origin of the false impression that women were historically insignificant, and she denounced Blackstone as a biased exponent of the common law who had sought deliberately to minimize equity. In the preface to her work she declared that one of her intentions was to examine "the rise and growth of Equity for the reason that it almost paralleled the development of the Common Law in time and had thoroughly riddled common law doctrines on married women's property rights long before Blackstone published the first volume of his *Commentaries*." In practice, she found that equity had wrought a "revolution . . . in the domain of marital relations."[47]

45. Mary Beard, *Woman as Force in History* (New York, 1946), 144.
46. William Blackstone, *Commentaries on the Laws of England*, 2:433.
47. Beard, *Woman as Force*, v, 86.

Beard's general argument that women's history in her day suffered sadly from neglect is undeniable, but her legal argument that equity had long overcome the disadvantages of the common law and had assured women of substantial property is nevertheless an unhappy one. Through a misperception that has, it seems, escaped notice, Beard greatly exaggerated the extent of married women's property. She made no distinction between a strict settlement and a simple settlement on a married woman. Being an American, she was apparently unaware of the strict settlement, which had barely existed in America, if it had existed at all. She unwittingly depended, however, upon statistics that referred to it. In her zeal to show the power of women in the past and the extent of their property, she declared that half the property of England was held in trusts, implying that the trusts were commonly on behalf of married women.[48] It is her only evidence as to the extent of married women's property. No figures for the extent of trusts in England existed, and the figure Beard used can only be the well-known estimate that half the land of England was held under strict settlements. Strict settlements were certainly trusts designed to alter the common law—but fundamentally to alter it against women, not in their favor. Through not recognizing that trusts were designed against all manner of common law rules, Beard much overestimated the property enjoyed by women and perceived only a part of equity's historical role.

Tributes to equity's role in the history of women are again in the air, as a trend has set in in women's history whose representatives are anxious, as Beard was, to portray woman's stature and authority in the past rather than her everlasting subjection. The history of women's property in England certainly lies in the interaction of common law and equity, and the recent studies that would discuss women's history in these terms are on the right track. But it is obviously necessary to begin with a proper perception of what the common law was, and to proceed keeping that in mind. Here there has been trouble, understandably, in view of how little the common law has been recognized, or if recognized how little attended to, by previous historians.

In an article that follows on her considerably noticed doctoral thesis, Maria Cioni makes the general claim that Chancery was by tradition and philosophy devoted to the cause of women. Unfortunately the claim is based on a conception of the common law that can only be described as an assemblage of misunderstood principles. "Common law provided," Cioni declares, "that an estate in fee simple should be divided allowing one-third

48. Ibid., 202.

to the widow for her dower, one-third to the children, and the remainder to the Crown.''[49]

Several other articles have recently associated equity with women's rights.[50] In the most conspicuous of them, published in the *Economic History Review*, Amy Louise Erickson focuses on marriage settlements, arguing that these indicate equity's beneficent attitude to women. Unfortunately she runs into a problem similar to that of Beard. Although unlike Beard she recognizes the existence of the strict settlement, she nevertheless lumps together strict and ordinary marriage settlements, assuming that the aim of both was to escape the common law doctrine of coverture. "The *primary* purpose of a marriage settlement in early modern England," she declares, "was to preserve the wife's property rights" (emphasis in the original). Pointing to Gilbert Horsman's book of precedents, she emphasizes that "every single one of the sample forms involved the wife's property rights."[51]

All marriage settlements granted women property, a fact that should occasion no surprise. The property granted, however, needs to be judged against the rules of law that would be applicable if no settlement existed. This is a principle that Erickson recognizes, her article being entitled "Common Law versus Common Practice"; but she unhappily fails to proceed in accordance with it. Thus she judges that the jointure/portion ratio of 10 percent in strict settlements was to the benefit of women, calculating that since widows on average survived their husbands for more than ten years, they received more by jointure than they gave as portion.[52] This calculation—whether adequate or not—is irrelevant in the circumstances. Proper assessment here requires the jointure to be related not to the portion but to the common law right of dower. Dower would have given the widow not an annuity equal to 10 percent of what she had brought her husband,

49. Maria L. Cioni, "The Elizabethan Chancery and Women's Rights," in *Tudor Rule and Revolution*, ed. Delloyd J. Guth and John W. McKenna (Cambridge, 1982), 163. Her thesis, "Women and Law in Elizabethan England with Particular Reference to the Court of Chancery" (Cambridge University, 1974), has been published in the Garland Economic History series (New York, 1985).

50. See also Janelle Greenberg, "The Legal Status of the English Woman in Early Eighteenth-Century Common Law and Equity," *Studies in Eighteenth-Century Culture* 4 (1975):171–81.

51. Amy Louise Erickson, "Common Law versus Common Practice: The Use of Marriage Settlements in Early Modern England," *Economic History Review*, 2d ser. 43 (1990): 21–22, 27.

52. Ibid. 30–31.

but an annuity of one-third of his landed income, and would have granted it to her regardless of what she had brought her husband. Moreover, though Erickson is aware of the common law rules of succession to land, she uses Horsman's precedents, which lay out portions on two scales—one for daughters in case there should be no son, and one for younger children should there be an eldest son—but fails to notice that in the first case mere portions were being granted to daughters to whom the common law would have given the entire estate. And as has become almost obligatory, the large portion of Lady Anne Clifford appears among the evidence indicating the generosity of settlements to women.[53] That portion is not proof of generosity to women in relation to the common law, but the reverse, for Lady Anne Clifford was by common law entitled to succeed to the estate.

If equity is to be assessed in women's history, or if the development of real property law is to be seen in family perspective, the two forms of marriage settlement need to be clearly distinguished. While both set aside common law rules, it was different common law rules they had in mind to set aside. Erickson may well have considered that it was unnecessary to distinguish the two forms because of the common perception that the strict settlement increased women's property. It would thus seem worthwhile to attempt to lay out generally the differences between the two forms of settlement, even though some repetition cannot be avoided in the process.

The settlement to the use of a married woman was a simple deed merely setting up a trust fund to pay a wife an income independent of her husband's control. It created no entail and usually divided the capital sum at the woman's death upon her children equally. It had no other purpose than to protect a married woman from the disadvantages of coverture. For want of a single word, the nineteenth century knew it as the ordinary marriage settlement, implicitly distinguishing it from the strict settlement. The strict settlement, on the other hand, was a complex deed that made a comprehensive settlement of a landed estate in which the interests of all the members of the family for a generation were spelled out. Either form of settlement could be made at any time, but there are reasons to associate each with marriage. In the one case the aim was to avoid the disadvantages that marriage had upon the property rights of women; in the other case the deed usually took place on the marriage of the heir male. As this book has abundantly shown, the purpose of the strict settlement cannot be summed up as being to benefit women, being on the contrary to preserve property in the hands of the male head of the family. The two settlements

53. Ibid.

are thus fundamentally to be contrasted rather than associated. (Two examples of settlements to the use of married women are reproduced in Appendix B. The simplicity of these deeds is to be contrasted with the strict settlement in Appendix A.)

The two forms belonged, generally speaking, to different social classes and to different species of property. The strict settlement embodied the ideas of large landowners, ordinary settlements those of lesser folk, particularly those of the business and professional classes, where personal property was of particular significance and where the common law was especially severe upon the married woman, giving her property to her husband absolutely. Although ordinary marriage settlements can be found in gentry and aristocratic families, complex movements have to be balanced in discussing them in that milieu. They were always subordinate to the demands of primogeniture and patrilineage that found their expression in the strict settlement, which was the main and characteristic settlement of such families.

Ordinary marriage settlements were the only form of settlement common in professional and business families. Developments have to be balanced even in this class, for legal developments in regard to personal property were not straightforwardly in favor of women. About the same time that it became possible to settle property on married women, widows lost what had been their indefeasible right to one-third of their husband's property when that property was personal. These two developments were almost certainly connected, although the connection between them has not been traced. Since the wife's personal property by common law became the husband's absolutely, when the husband in the seventeenth century gained the power to devise his personal property as he chose, he gained the power to devise not only his own property but also that which had been his wife's, without the ancient restriction in the widow's favor. To take away the widow's claim on her husband's property while continuing to deny her her own property would have been grossly unjust. That is nevertheless what happened where no settlement of separate property was made, a fact that needs to be emphasized in discussing ordinary marriage settlements. While it would seem that in practice most middle-class husbands devised at least one-third of their property to their wives, there was no certainty that any particular husband would do so, and the possibility existed that out of an unhappy marriage a husband just might cut his wife off with nothing. Prudent fathers would have taken to making settlements on their daughters partly at least in reaction to what was an increase in husband's power. The circumstances in which settlements on married women developed suggest that these settlements are not simply to be seen as an autonomous up-welling of a desire to benefit women.

Equity's claim to have furthered the interests of women is, then, badly flawed. If equity riddled common law doctrines, to use Beard's phrase, it riddled those that were favorable to women quite as much as those that were unfavorable to them. Equity protected trusts, whatever their purpose, and not all trusts were in favor of women. If the Chancellor's early support of uses had allowed younger children to be provided for, so it had allowed the destruction of dower and thirds. If equity later supported settlement on married women, so it supported settlements designed to disherison heiresses efficiently. There were marriage settlements and marriage settlements, and they differed as night and day, and equity supported them both.

Moreover, it might be noticed in passing that while equity declared there was no dower out of a use and none out of trusts in general, it went on to declare nevertheless that there was curtesy out of trusts. That is to say, it held that a trust could defeat the widow's interest in her husband's land, but that it could not defeat the widower's interest in his wife's land. A small matter, to be sure, for women in families with substantial land. Since they became less likely to inherit land in the first place, the right of their widowers to curtesy became correspondingly moot.

Maitland has pointed out that curtesy—which was a much larger right than dower, being the right of the widower to the whole of his deceased wife's property for his life rather than to one-third of it—was an inequality in the common law that had once been valuable to the wife herself. It offered her children protection against the lord's right of wardship should they be under age at the time of her death. A medieval mother would naturally have felt that it was better that her land should remain in the hands of her husband, who would normally have been the father of her children, than that it should fall upon her death into the hands of the lord in ward-ship. The different treatment that equity accorded to dower and curtesy, and the difference in their scale, became hardly defensible, of course, after 1660, when feudal dues were abolished. Curtesy seems, however, to have become an issue taken up by women only in the United States, a fact suggestive of the more egalitarian leanings of that country, which were earlier and firmly demonstrated, of course, by the rejection of primogeniture and entail at the Revolution.

Equity made for flexibility in property dealings against the straitjacket of the common law. No one today would defend the principle that the law should mandatorily determine the destination of property upon the death of its owner, although we do recognize circumstances where some mandatory principles are proper. I would not be thought to be defending mandatory rules in general. This is not a prescriptive work arguing what the law ought to be for today's society, but a historical work concerned with the questions how and why equity was brought in from time to time in the past to set aside the common law. These are complex questions in the history of women. Movement was not simply upward towards equality, and what equitable developments meant in different periods and for different classes would seem to need reassessment. For the landed classes, there is no maintaining that the common law was a body of law hospitable to females—except for centuries in relation to landowners' actual practice.

5 The Strict Settlement

But of course, the logic of lawyers is not merely

wanton. Their astonishing structures reflect actual

desires.

—*S. F. C. Milsom*, Historical Foundations of the

Common Law

The strict settlement occupies a prominent place in the history of real property law. It does so because it was the culmination of land-owners' legal history, and because with its invention the structure of English property law was substantially complete and was to remain essentially unaltered until 1925, a structure in one way and another to be marveled at. One of the consequences of considering the history of real property law from the angle of vision adopted in the earlier chapters of this work is that various legal instruments appear rather differently than they have traditionally done. This is particularly true of the strict settlement. There are then two reasons for singling it out for further discussion: its significance in the corpus of real property law, and the difference between its actual and its perceived role in the family. In discussing it further, the focus will shift to doctrinal matters. If settlement's role in the family is to be seen in a new way, its doctrinal development might well be reexamined as well.

This means entering the domain of the sixteenth- and seventeenth-century conveyancer, a fearsome place that the social historian might be well advised to pass prudently by. The *Saturday Review* once wrote that even "the leaders of the Chancery Bar tremble in their wigs when their course lies through that valley of the shadow of death in which the pilgrim's narrow path is beset by springing uses, contingent remainders, terms which might be merged at any moment and the ghostly relics—still occasionally endowed with a sepulchral vitality—of fines and recoveries, base fees, and tenants to the *praecipe.*"[1] Still, doctrinal history and social history must accompany one another in the interests of historical understanding. The view of the social historian may prove of some use in charting a rather different path than has been traditional through what is a bewildering period in the history of law.

1

As it has appeared here, settlement was the means by which all the affairs of a generation yet to be born were determined at the marriage of its parents. It was the means by which landowners solved the problems of heirship that inhered for them in the common law. This is not the way that settlement has gone into the history of real property law. It has been treated, not against the background of the common law rules of succession, but against the background of perpetuities, and has gone into the history of real property law as a form of entail.[2] What has been emphasized is that through a system of making and remaking settlements each generation between father and son, a family estate might be made to descend generation after generation from one life tenant to another despite the rule against perpetuities.

The scenario runs thus: The legal situation between father and son, as the son came to marry, was that under a settlement that had been made a generation earlier on the father's marriage, the father was possessed of an estate for life and the son was possessed of an estate tail, that is, an entail. Or in other words, the one was tenant for life and the other tenant in tail.

---

1. *Saturday Review*, 3 October 1857.

2. See, for example, J. H. Baker, *An Introduction to English Legal History*, 2d ed. (London, 1979), 244–48; A. W. B. Simpson, *A History of the Land Law*, 2d ed. (Oxford, 1986), 233–41; S. F. C. Milsom, *Historical Foundations of the Common Law* (London, 1969), 140–63.

If the son were to succeed to the inheritance still possessed of the entail, he would be able to make himself owner in fee simple, entails being barrable. Before he succeeded, however, father and son acting together could bring the settlement to an end. Paradoxically, the fact that the old settlement could be brought to a premature end by father and son acting together was what made for settlement's aspect of entail. Were it not for this fact, every settlement must have shortly ended in an owner in fee, usually after one generation. The old settlement would be brought to an end, however, in circumstances that were likely to lead to a new one. The father, grown responsible with his years, would be anxious to ensure the inheritance for a further generation. The son would be in need of an income for himself and his wife during the years before he would succeed to the inheritance. Thus, in return for a present income, the son would agree to a new settlement in which his future interest would be cut down to a life tenancy after his father's and in which the inheritance would be entailed upon his as yet unborn son. That son would be expected someday to make a similar resettlement with his father. In this manner the estate would descend in the family generation after generation with never an absolute owner in possession.

Undoubtedly settlement often operated in this way. In the nineteenth century, critics of aristocracy, and especially those imbued with the free-trade principles of classical economics, frequently denounced it as a form of entail. Inherently settlement restricted sales of land, and it operated as well to hinder the improvement of land, obstructing leasing and mortgaging for commercial purposes. Adam Smith, Jeremy Bentham, and John Stuart Mill all denounced it as a restriction of the market in land, and throughout the latter half of the century settlement was a subject of much political controversy.[3]

Settlement's force of entail is starkly demonstrated in the story of the poet Shelley. A descendant of the family of sixteenth-century legal notoriety, Shelley was of their blood but not of their spirit. He refused on idealistic grounds to join his father in resettling the family estate, balking at passing it on to his unborn son, "one whom I know not—who might, instead of being the benefactor of mankind, be its bane, or use [the estate] for the worst purposes." Unable to make his father see matters in this unaristocratic light but in need of an income until he should inherit, Shelley

3. For a discussion of the nineteenth-century debate on settlement see Eileen Spring, "Landowners, Lawyers, and Land Law Reform in Nineteenth-Century England," *American Journal of Legal History* 21 (1977): 41–59.

set out to bar the entail so far as he could do so by himself, planning to borrow on his expectations. He was to discover what it was that made settlement work as entail. He soon found that his current legal interest was of very little value in the marketplace. The technical reasons for this economic fact need not be entered into here. They lie in the legal complexities that surrounded the "base fee," the interest that the son could create and offer as security to a lender when attempting to bar the entail by himself, complexities that rendered the security a risky one for the lender and correspondingly costly for the borrower. Borrowing on base fee was inherently foolish, and few base fees were ever created, although George Eliot has woven a good story around one in *Felix Holt*. Grudgingly Shelley came to the realization that the only reasonable way for him to gain an immediate income was to capitulate to his father and resettle the estate. "When I look back," he later wrote, "I do not see what else I could have done than submit. What is called firmness would have . . . left me in total poverty."[4]

Since settlement had an aspect of entail, clearly the traditional view of it and the different view advanced here are not mutually exclusive, but run alongside one another. It might well be said that the difference between the views is one of emphasis. Yet there are several reasons for thinking that the traditional view does not reach to essentials. On the one hand, if entailing land had been the essential aim, if keeping land permanently out of the hands of a tenant in tail had been the simple object landowners had in mind, they would surely have worked settlement more efficiently than they did. Resettlement normally took place on the marriage of the eldest son. The father could have insisted, however, that it take place as soon as the son was of age and capable of dealing with his expectations. In postponing resettlement to the son's marriage, the father took the risk that he himself would die before that time and that his son would accordingly succeed absolutely to the estate. The period of time between the son's coming of age and his marriage was not brief. In the late seventeenth century, average age of marriage of eldest sons was twenty-eight. At the same time, life expectancy was such that there was only a 50 percent chance that a father would be alive when his son reached that age.[5] Obviously many more fathers would have been alive to compel resettlements had these taken place, not at the son's marriage, but seven years earlier at his coming of

4. Shelley to Elizabeth Hitchener, 15 December 1811, in *The Letters of Percy Bysshe Shelley*, ed. Roger Ingpen (London, 1909), 1:196.

5. Lloyd Bonfield, "Marriage Settlements and the 'Rise of Great Estates': The Demographic Aspect," *Economic History Review*, 2d ser. 32 (1979): 490–91.

age. Since few settlements were in practice made at the son's coming of age, it would seem that preventing the son from succeeding absolutely was not quite the object historians have assumed it was. Aristocratic fathers apparently did not greatly fear the possibility that a young man in possession of a large fortune would waste it in gambling and riotous living. That possibility has figured far larger in the imagination of historians than it evidently did in the minds of landowners. That many landowners in practice let the chain of settlement and resettlement break when they need not have done so must cast some doubt upon the object they had primarily in mind in making settlements.

More important, the traditional view largely ignores the content of the individual deed. It emphasizes duration and pays at best cursory attention to content. It says nothing about the heiress, describing the object of settlement as being to send the estate from eldest son to eldest son, whereas the major point of a settlement was to send the estate to a male collateral when there was no son. If stressing son-to-son succession is intended to be a simplification of a difficult subject, which sometimes may be the case, it is a simplification that does away with the problem that gave rise to settlement. While by implication it conveys the idea that landowners desired successions in the male line, it skips over the problem that really faced them in attempting to ensure such successions. Nor does the traditional view say anything about the other members of the family beyond a regular nod to the effect that a settlement could provide for them, which is obviously correct but which is potentially misleading all the same. It may carry the implication—and has indeed done so—that family members were better provided for by settlement than they had been earlier.

That one settlement could, and often did, lead directly to another is an important historical fact. But it is a fact that has undoubtedly been emphasized at the cost of a more basic understanding of settlement. The objections that are to be made to treating settlement simply or primarily as a form of entail in effect turn attention to it as a single deed, a marriage settlement. As a marriage settlement its short-term duration comes to the fore and, with that, its content. Its disposition of property in the family becomes of the essence. Looking at settlement primarily as a marriage settlement is really only to treat it consistently in accordance with its common name, for it is regularly called the "marriage settlement" even as it is set into real property law as a form of entail. No one thinks it was a real entail; everyone recognizes that structurally it was but one marriage settlement set upon another. It was a marriage settlement, however, that had extensive consequences even if not part of an unbroken chain, as Lord Nottingham appreciated, consequences that he personally disapproved of. Attention might well then be shifted doctrinally from the strict settlement as a form of entail to the strict settlement as a marriage settlement, and its development traced in that way.

Treating settlement as a marriage settlement is to begin doctrinally at the bottom, with the basic building block. In traditional accounts the basic building block is in practice lost sight of. Typically, elaborate attempts at perpetuity are rehearsed, attempts by individual settlors to extend their power beyond the grave as long as possible. But the climax of the story comes abruptly and on a different principle. What suddenly appears is a short-term agreement made and remade between two men, father and son, generation after generation, an agreement whose origins and development have not been specifically discussed.

Fortunately, treating settlement as a marriage settlement makes for a simpler account of doctrinal developments than is traditional. While no account can be unqualifiedly simple, treating settlement as a marriage settlement may make for a doctrinal account that has some prospect of being generally intelligible. Fanciful conveyances decidedly aiming at perpetuity that were regularly struck down by the courts almost as soon as they appeared, leaving no mark on real property law—such as the perpetual freehold—can be ignored. In this class may be included entails reinforced by clauses designed to prevent barring, which as Coke declared in 1614 were perpetuities "born under some unfortunate constellation, for they . . . never had a judgment given for them, but many judgments given against them."[6] Coke was, of course, aware of one judgment in favor of such perpetuities that had been delivered forty years earlier, that in *Scholastica's Case*, and in his assessment he took care to notice it. Stressing the isolation of the judgment, he held that the case had been wrongly decided and that it was to be dismissed as an aberration.[7] Not only may fanciful conveyances soon struck down be ignored, but also much that was of little practical importance to landowners, particularly the mind-boggling intricacies of executory devises, instruments that bulk large in descriptions of the development of settlement when entail is emphasized. Luckily a marriage settlement is by definition not a devise. Contingent remainders, alas, are not to be escaped. But even these need not be discussed in their full complexity, but only in the form that was important to landowners. This process of limiting the field of discussion will not explain fully the development

6. *Mary Portington's Case*, 10 Co. Rep. 42b.
7. Ibid., 10 Co. Rep. 39b.

of the doctrine of future estates. But it will clear away underbrush and light up the development that socially mattered.

The following discussion will thus ignore many precedents normally considered important in accounts of real property law in the sixteenth and seventeenth centuries, deeming them not to belong to the socially important line of development; but those that will be discussed are the same that always appear in the textbooks. There will be no radical reinterpretation of these, no reinterpretation of them at all. They will stand as they always have stood. Nevertheless new insights will emerge from looking at them from a fresh point of view. The reason why the first change of judicial sentiment towards contingent remainders failed for long to have any practical effect will become clear once it is looked at in practical social terms. The major precedent about contingent remainders, *Colthirst v. Bejushin*, will have its meaning better brought out once females are taken into account. Again, remembering females will suggest why an early form of settlement sometimes pointed to as practically important could not really have been so. All in all, a story with sharper outlines will be told, one that accords more closely with settlement's social meaning.

While the strict settlement is to be associated with marriage, it needs to be noted that settlements could be made by will and that quite frequently they were made by will. They were naturally made by will by founders of families, few self-made men being ready to give up their power over their property while they lived. They might be made by will by men who for one reason or another came into possession of their estates as tenants in tail. The son who succeeded as tenant in tail because he did not marry in his father's lifetime was likely to resettle on his marriage all the same, but obviously if he never married he was likely to make a settlement by will. The collateral successor who came into possession as tenant in tail might resettle either on his marriage or by will. (The collateral successor who was nephew to his predecessor was likely to be a tenant in tail, a brother or uncle likely to be a tenant for life.) In concept and in general usage, however, the strict settlement was a marriage settlement.

It has been suggested that strict settlements are more to be associated with wills than with marriage settlements.[8] Settlements by will, the argument runs, were not uncommon and would have been more effective in entailing land than settlements made at marriage, because a settlement made by will could last a long time. It is true that a settlement made by

8. Barbara English and John Saville, *Strict Settlement: A Guide for Historians* (Hull, 1983), 101–3.

the will of an ancient patriarch could last a long time. A deed of settlement could reduce to life tenancy all members of the family who were in existence at the time it was drawn up. This was the utmost allowed by the rule against perpetuities, which in essence forbade that unborn persons be reduced to life tenancies. Under this rule an aged settlor might therefore reduce the members of his family through several generations to life tenancies, because several generations might have been born in his lifetime. In practice, however, the chance that a will would last a long time was slim. In the seventeenth and eighteenth centuries most men did not live even to the birth of their grandsons. In such circumstances a settlement by will usually lasted no longer than one made on marriage.

Settlements by will actually indicate that the scheme of settlement often failed when judged against the ideal. They represent men who lived and died in possession of their estates. As a historical phenomenon, of course, settlement has to be judged in a chronological framework, against an earlier age in which virtually all men had been in possession of their estates. It need not have been perfect to have significant social meaning.

2

Marriage settlements as a class go back into the mists of time, and within the class there were various kinds. Discrimination among them is necessary to set the background for the strict settlement and to find its particular roots. Early marriage settlements are indeed rather to be contrasted with strict settlements than associated with them. The maritagium and the strict settlement are both marriage settlements, yet they have almost nothing in common. The one was made on the marriage of a younger child; the other, normally, on the marriage of the eldest son. The one encompassed little land, leaving the bulk of the family estate to be transmitted by the common law. The other transmitted the bulk of the family estate, sidestepping both the common law and the will. The two differ so radically because their purposes differ. Early marriage settlements had what might be called a straightforward purpose. To use an illuminating word that C. S. Kenny applied to them, they were dispositive.[9] A father granted a portion of his land to a younger son or daughter on his or her marriage, his aim being simply to benefit the donee. Such settlements distributed land rather than

---

9. C. S. Kenny, *The History of the Law of England as to the Effects of Marriage on Property and on the Wife's Legal Capacity* (London, 1879), 123.

preserved it. The strict settlement is not to be traced to such settlements. Nor is it to be confused with settlements on married women, settlements that were designed to overcome the disadvantages of coverture and to give property to a wife independent of her husband's control. These were also dispositive, aiming simply to benefit the donee.

The germ of the strict settlement is to be found in the settlement whose purpose was to bar dower and to substitute for it a jointure of lesser value. Like the maritagium, the settlement in bar of dower was unambitious in that it did not encompass the whole or the major part of a family's landed property. Its purpose, however, was no longer dispositive. Quite the reverse. The widow in gentry and aristocratic families received less under such a settlement than she would have received had no settlement existed. Her jointure was not a genuine gift made to benefit the donee; and the designation of these settlements in positive terms as jointure settlements rather veils the fact. Jointures in such settlements fell into the class of gifts that, in Kenny's words, were "only nominal gifts made for the purpose of restraining some incident which would otherwise have attached to the donor estate."[10] With such settlements the marriage settlement took on a new function, that of protecting the family estate from the future claims of a subordinate member of the family; it became, in Kenny's terminology, restrictive. Certainly the jointure settlement restricted the widow's right, but from the point of view of the estate, the word "restrictive" is perhaps not the most telling one to use, for it gives no hint of the social purpose of the restriction. With the settlement in bar of dower, marriage settlements became, to characterize them by a more socially meaningful word, "preservative." They became preservative of family estates. It is to such settlements that the strict settlement is to be traced.

Settlements in bar of dower appeared with the development of uses, but it was the Statute of Uses that gave them free rein. Whatever other effect that statute may or may not have had, it made the settlement in bar of dower the normal accompaniment of aristocratic marriage. While the statute turned landowners' attention to marriage settlements as never before, it must particularly have turned attention to the settlement on the marriage of the eldest son. If the family estate were to reap the advantage that the statute offered and widows were to be barred from dower, then eldest sons who married in the lifetime of their fathers had to make settlements barring dower, not only landowners who married already in possession. Before the statute an eldest son who married in the lifetime of his father had been

10. Ibid.

unable to bar dower to any extent, because his wife gained dower right over any land he inherited after his marriage, and most of his inheritance came to him on his father's death.[11] The statute had made it possible to bar dower for the future no matter when inheritance took place, but barring had to be done before marriage to be effective. Thus the settlement made on the marriage of the eldest son took on a significance that it had not earlier possessed. Earlier a settlement on the marriage of an eldest son had been merely an agreement in which a father made interim provision for the son and his bride until the son should succeed to the estate. After the statute, a settlement made on the son's marriage could fix what jointure his widow was to take out of the estate. After the statute, fathers were thus regularly involved, when their eldest sons married, in a transaction designed to protect the family estates from widows.

The idea must naturally have suggested itself that determining other aspects of inheritance at that time would also be prudential. It would be more prudential than leaving them to be determined by the son's will, or even possibly by the law of intestate succession. If making premarital arrangements was so valuable in the case of the widow, why not extend the principle to other inheritance problems in the family? Looked at in this way, it would seem that landowners set out to develop the settlement in bar of dower into a generally preservative settlement, one limiting in advance the claims of all the subordinate members of the family. Admittedly this is a speculative reconstruction. We have only the instruments conveyancers designed to go on; but it would seem a more realistic speculation than that landowners were gung ho for entails. And it is powerfully supported by what almost immediately followed the Statute of Uses: attempts to make grants on unborn persons. Attempts to make grants on unborn persons appear in the circumstances to be attempts to determine family dispositions at marriage.

3

Though the idea is a short step conceptually, it is a long journey in law from the settlement in bar of dower to the strict settlement. If the course of development is looked at in some detail, it will be found to have taken place in three distinct stages. In each a fundamental legal problem had to be overcome, and until all of them were overcome there really was little of

---

11. The point has been discussed above in chapter 2, section 2.

substance gained. The three stages may be said to have been these: first, establishing the form of the strict settlement, that is, gaining acceptability in law for the interests it created; second, making the form secure, which happens to be a different matter; and, finally, making settlement practicable, that is, adapting it to the demands of family life.

ESTABLISHING THE FORM

If a landowner was to determine, at the marriage of his eldest son, inheritance matters for a generation to come, clearly grants to unborn persons had to be legal. This was sine qua non for the strict settlement. The deed the landowner would be aiming at would consist of two elements: a life estate to his son, thus precluding the son's will, followed by a remainder in tail to the son to be born of the marriage. Schematically the limitations of the desired settlement, in the terminology that would then be usual, would run: A (the settlor), to B (his eldest son) for life, remainder to the heirs male of the body of B. These limitations do not, of course, fully represent what most large landowners required in a settlement, who were not concerned only with sons, or even mainly with sons; but this simple form may serve to begin discussion, for there were obstacles in law even to it. If even this form was impossible to achieve, so was anything more complicated.

To begin with, the remainder in this simple settlement was necessarily contingent, for it went to the son to be born of the marriage, a person who did not exist and who might never come to exist. Moreover, even after the birth of a son to the tenant for life, the remainder was held to be contingent, on the ground that no living person could have an heir. Who the heir was could only be ascertained after the tenant for life was dead, being before that time merely speculative. The strict settlement is in its essence dependent upon a contingent remainder. The law, however, had long held that a remainder that was contingent was void. By definition it involved uncertainty; and it could end, pending the contingency, with what was unthinkable, an abeyance of seisin, that is, with no one in possession of the land. This point is most evident if we take a different example of a contingent remainder than the one landowners were after. Suppose a remainder to a person contingent upon his reaching the age of twenty-five, and suppose the tenant for life dies when the remainderman is only fifteen. Who then possesses the land? "In every weal-public," Serjeant Pollard declared in support of the established legal principle, "it is necessary and requisite that the conveyance of things should be certain, for certainty is the mother of repose, and incertainty the mother of contention, which our wise and provident law has ever guarded against and prevented all occasions thereof."[12]

As if the law's objection to contingent remainders were not conclusive against our settlor's plans, another problem loomed for him in the doctrine of merger, the doctrine emphasized in *Shelley's Case*. Our settlor also desired, for the support of his eldest son, to grant him a life estate. By the doctrine of merger, a grant to a living person for his life followed by a remainder to his heirs was considered to convey to the living person an estate in fee (either in fee simple or in fee tail) rather than to convey, as it ostensibly did, two separate estates, one to the living person and one to his heirs. Thus despite our settlor's obvious intention to create two estates, one in his son and one in his grandson, the two estates would merge upon his death, leaving his son in possession of the land. As H. W. Challis in his *Law of Real Property* put it, the principle of merger made such a settlement as our settlor desired "to a large extent nugatory in its inception."[13]

Until these legal barriers were surmounted, any approach to the strict settlement was obviously impossible. Between roughly 1550 and 1600, however, developments took place in regard both to contingent remainders and to the doctrine of merger that were favorable to our settlor's scheme.

Even before 1500, it seems that the court's hostility to contingent remainders had begun to abate. A contingent remainder to the heirs of a living person was sanctioned, provided that the living person died in the lifetime of the settlor. If we read back from words uttered by Serjeant Morgan in 1551 in hope of resisting further change, the argument for making this exception to the doctrine of contingent remainders is perceptible. The death of a living person was after all a certainty, while at the same time "the law presumes that [every person] shall have an heir, whom it will appoint to take the remainder *nolens volens*."[14] There was, that is to say, no real uncertainty about a remainder to the heirs of a living person, no possibility of an abeyance of seisin. Though no living man could have an heir, as soon as a man was dead his heir was evident. The legal change is important, but it is so only as a harbinger of things to come. Because of the proviso that accompanied it, it cannot have been of any practical significance in forwarding landowners' desires. The proviso required that the living person die in the lifetime of the settlor. In the case under discussion this would require that the son die in the lifetime of his father. It has been

---

12. *Colthirst v. Bejushin*, Plowden 25.
13. H. W. Challis, *Law of Real Property*, 3d ed. (London, 1911), 136.
14. *Colthirst v. Bejushin*, Plowden 28.

suggested that the court's early move relative to contingent remainders was of practical significance to landowners on the ground that many sons did die before their fathers in the sixteenth century. A father, it is reasoned, could thus ensure an entail in his grandson.[15] If his son died in his lifetime, a father could have secured an entail in his grandson anyway. A settlement that depends upon a son's predeceasing his father cannot ever be of any real use.

Not surprisingly, grants to unborn persons are not found until further developments had taken place. Joshua Williams, dean of real property law in the nineteenth century, could find no grant to an unborn person before 1557, a conclusion that Holdsworth has confirmed.[16] The date upon which such grants are first found suggests forcibly the importance of the Statute of Uses as catalyst. The statute had certainly made marriage settlements of new significance for landowners, and it would logically have suggested further ideas in regard to them. For lawyers and judges, the statute had put many new legal concepts in the air. It was in this atmosphere that the courts again took a look at contingent remainders.

The precedent is *Colthirst v. Bejushin* (1551), and it indicated that the court's attitude had altered radically. "Anyone who is the lawful owner of any land," said Chief Justice Mountague, "may give it to what person, in what manner, and in what time he pleases, so long as his gift is not contrary to law or repugnant."[17] ("Repugnant" means here simply unclear or self-contradictory.) The courts thereafter set out on a policy of controlling rather than prohibiting contingent remainders. Determined to prevent their being used to effect long-lasting settlements, they enforced a series of rules that meant that a settlor could not reach to a second generation unborn. After a grant to an unborn person, no grant could be made to a child of that unborn person. What mattered, though, was that the courts had come to countenance the grant to an unborn person of the first generation.

Discussions of *Colthirst* have canvassed the sorts of contingent remainders that settlors might wish to avail themselves of. Remainders contingent upon residence, place of education, religion, and the like have been noticed, as well as the remainder to an unborn person. The remainder to an unborn person, however, was the only one of importance to landowners, the only one of major social significance; and as Joshua Williams told law students

15. Lloyd Bonfield, *Marriage Settlements, 1601–1740* (Cambridge, 1983), 28.
16. W. S. Holdsworth, *A History of English Law* (London, 1922–66), 4:441n.
17. *Colthirst v. Bejushin*, Plowden 34.

in the nineteenth century, it was the one contingent remainder they would commonly meet in practice.[18]

There remained the second obstacle to our settlor's plans, that which lay in the rule of merger. Fully enunciated only in 1581 in *Shelley's Case*, the rule—to recapitulate—prevented a settlor from granting a legal estate to a living person and another to his heirs; or rather, it determined that if a settlor attempted to do so, the estates merged, leaving the living person owner in fee or in tail, as the case might be, thus leaving the settlor really no closer to his object than he had been. In its way the rule made sense. In long-established terminology, the grant of an estate in fee simple—in demonstration of the finality of the act on the part of the grantor—ran "to A and his heirs"; and the grant of an estate in fee tail—in demonstration of the long duration of the grant—ran "to A and the heirs of his body." If there was no mention of heirs, a grant was for life only and was not inheritable by the grantee's heirs. It made sense, then, to look upon a grant to a man followed by a remainder to his heirs as an unnecessarily fancy, or as an erroneously expressed, way of granting an estate of inheritance.[19]

It has been suggested that the decision in *Shelley* had a more immediate rationale, being connected with the Crown's defense of its feudal dues. Logically there is a connection of this kind. Even after the Statute of Wills the Crown maintained a fiscal interest in the succession of the heir-at-law, and it did so until 1660. Thus it had an interest in Shelley's right heir. But the case was too unusual to constitute any real threat to the Crown. No army of landowners was lying in wait ready to seize on a way of disinheriting right male heirs in favor of younger sons. Shelley had not designed to do that himself.

At all events, *Shelley* became a deeply held principle of English law. So far as it actually took effect, it encouraged alienability and it frustrated settlements.[20] But as was so often the case in the history of English real property law, theory and practice came to differ. Just as primogeniture remained the law, but younger children were not disinherited; just as daughters without brothers remained heirs, but did not inherit; just as entails existed, but were barrable, so it was to be with *Shelley*. The wishes of En-

18. Joshua Williams, *Principles of the Law of Real Property*, 16th ed. (London, 1887), 308.

19. For further discussion of the rationale for *Shelley* see A. D. Hargreaves, "Shelley's Ghost," *Law Quarterly Review* 54 (1938); and R. E. Megarry and H. W. R. Wade, *The Laws of Real Property*, 3d ed. (London, 1966).

20. Megarry and Wade, *Laws of Real Property*, 62.

glish landowners were not to be frustrated by legal niceties. *Shelley* was not read out of English law until 1925, but the rule and its evasion long lived together.

Coke himself, at the moment he enunciated the principle of merger, pointed to the means by which it could be evaded. The rule would not prevail, he said, "if the remainder was limited to the heir in the singular."[21] In other words, settlors need only avoid the traditional and reverberating word "heirs." "Heir in the singular," to quote Megarry and Wade, was not "an apt word of limitation for an estate of inheritance."[22] Coke pointed to no precedents, however. There was nothing to go on but his opinion. But the hint was not lost on landowners. Cases involving the heir in the singular soon appeared, and precedents satisfactory to landowners were established. This occurred first in *Archer's Case* (1595), where a limitation to "the right and next male heir" was accepted. Later, in *Lewis Bowles's Case* (1615), a limitation to "the first issue male" was held to be good.[23] These phrases were construed as descriptions of the person intended to take, and not as words intended to create an estate of inheritance, and thus they avoided merger.[24]

By the early seventeenth century, then, through the decision in *Colthirst* on the one hand and developments relative to *Shelley* on the other, a landowner on the marriage of his eldest son could make the settlement we began by imagining him to desire, provided he watched his words. He could make a settlement that ran: A (the settlor), to B (his eldest son) for life, remainder in tail to B's first issue male. This was a simplified form, however, of what the landowner actually wanted. All that this simple form would do would be to ensure the descent of the estate to the settlor's unborn grandson, and when settlement is treated as entail this is all that is taken notice of. The grandson, who was after all the settlor's heir-at-law, cannot generally have been in need of such protection. A great deal of trouble had been gone to if this was to be the sum achieved. What the landowner further required— what he really was aiming at—may now be considered. This was a second remainder, an alternate one to come into effect in case the eldest son died without issue male.

Here we must return to *Colthirst* for a closer look. It was exactly an

21. *Shelley's Case*, 1 Co. Rep. 104a.

22. Megarry and Wade, *Laws of Real Property*, 64.

23. *Archer's Case*, 1 Co. Rep. 66b; *Lewis Bowles's Case*, 11 Co. Rep. 104a.

24. For a discussion of wording that avoided the rule in *Shelley's Case* see Megarry and Wade, *Laws of Real Property*, 64–65.

alternate remainder on a younger son after the death of the elder that had been validated in that case. The particular remainder at issue hardly seems momentous on the surface. A settlement had been made to a husband and wife for their lives, then to the elder of their sons for his life, and then if the elder son should die in the lifetime of his parents to his younger brother. There is apparently nothing here about the son's issue male or about unborn children. And yet by implication there really is, for it was possible that the elder son would die leaving children. By the principle enunciated by the judges, an estate could be made to shift from an eldest son to a younger upon a specified condition. By the principle enunciated, then, a contingent remainder to a younger son in case an elder died without issue male had become allowable. Because *Colthirst* has been associated with the general validation of contingent remainders, it gave rise in its own day, and has done so since, to general discussion of the subject, and the particular remainder at issue in the case has been less discussed than it needs to be. Though *Colthirst* did not ostensibly originate around female heirs, that is who it principally affected.

Thus *Colthirst* is in practice to be added to that list of cases of the sixteenth and seventeenth centuries that involved female interests: *Sharington v. Strotton, Corbett v. Corbett, Mildmay's Case, Shelley's Case,* and *Dormer v. Parkhurst.* All in all, these were many of the most famous cases of the age, but historians have not treated them as a whole, as manifesting a struggle over heirship.

By the early seventeenth century, then, the expanded form of settlement that was the landowner's real desire had become sanctioned by the courts. Its effect is to be well noted, for when settlement is treated as entail it goes unnoticed. Upon the marriage of his eldest son a landowner could make a settlement in the following terms: A (the settlor), to B (his eldest son) for life, remainder in tail to B's first issue male; but if B should die without issue male then to C (B's younger brother, or his next male collateral) for life, remainder to C's issue male. The alternate remainder, "the remainder over," is not a peripheral extra, unimportant to be noticed. It is the heart of the deed. To B's son if he should have a son, but to his younger brother if he should not, is a limitation that cuts out in advance B's female heirs. Although it has never been put this way, it needs to be: Grants to unborn persons were really grants away from certain unborn persons.

Strict settlements in practice were more elaborate even than the above outline suggests, building up a series of remainders that provided for all possible successions in the family; but the above is the essence of the device. And nothing short of the above could have done. By the end of the sixteenth century, then, the first phase of the development of the strict settlement had been completed. On the marriage of his eldest son, a landowner could draw up a settlement, acceptable in law, that would both limit his son's widow and shift the estate automatically away from the son's female heirs should his marriage produce female heirs.

MAKING THE FORM SECURE

The form, however, was highly unreliable in practice. Whether contingent remainders were valid, and whether they were secure, are two different questions. All the courts of the sixteenth century had done was to allow that a settlement employing contingent remainders of the kind described was valid in the sense that on the death of the tenant for life they would direct the land to the remainderman indicated. They had refused to protect the remainderman before that time. So long as the remainder was contingent, it was only a potential estate in the land, not an actual one, and the courts declined to protect it from a tenant for life who chose to destroy it. Quite simply, the courts refused to bother themselves about estates until they had actually come into existence. Thus despite his nominal position, the tenant for life was not in fact in the position of a tenant for life.

This had paradoxically been emphasized in *Archer's Case*. While the judges in that case had protected the settlement from the rule in *Shelley's Case*, they had gone on to support the right of the tenant for life to destroy remainders while they were contingent. "The remainder to the right male heir . . . is good," the court had declared, adding, "although he cannot have a right male heir during his life." In other words, the remainder was valid, but it could be destroyed by the tenant for life. Given the principle that no living man could have an heir, the tenant for life had power to destroy the remainder at any time during his life. The judges in *Archer's Case* thus had given with the one hand and withheld with the other.

With some variation of wording a settlement could be devised that was subject to destruction by the tenant for life for a shorter time, subject to destruction only until the remainderman was born, that is, until the tenant for life had a son. The wording in *Lewis Bowles's Case* had been held to protect the remainders after the birth of the son. Despite appearances, however, settlements of this kind offered no real advantage to landowners. It was the man who never had a son—but who did have daughters—against whom the whole thing was designed, and that man could destroy either settlement. Before the invention of trustees to preserve contingent remainders, settlements containing remainders to unborn persons were in their essence "precarious," the word that is always attached to them.

Precarious though they were, settlements employing contingent remainders became fairly common in the early seventeenth century. The question must arise why they should have done so. One answer is that such settlements were not—could not be—more subject to destruction than the settlements they replaced, which instead of a life tenancy had granted the son an entail, which had become an alienable estate. There was simply no more secure estate settlement available. Moreover, such settlements may well have possessed some enhanced power of moral persuasion, because the son had clearly been intended by his father to be but a tenant for life. A son did nothing illegal if he destroyed contingent remainders, but for him to do so was nevertheless considered wrongful. The tenant for life who alienated land committed "a tortious feoffment." That is to say, he did wrong, only it was not a wrong the law would take cognizance of, his victim being unborn or unascertainable.

Such settlements may also have offered some protection to the families of men who became subject to the law of forfeiture for political crimes or misdemeanors. To take the extreme situation, should a man be attainted as a traitor his land upon his execution was forfeited to the Crown; but if he were only a life tenant he would technically have no land to lose, and thus his family was spared notionally at least financial loss. Tudor experience would have taught that the risk of attainder was not small for those who had political ambitions; and the looming of the Civil War under Charles I would have brought the general lesson home to the whole body of landowners, who willy-nilly found themselves having to take sides in a dangerous controversy. It may be, then—and the suggestion is not new— that the approach of the Civil War encouraged settlements of this sort as protection against political errors of judgment.

The conclusion is inescapable, however, that landowners generally remained as free, despite such settlements, as they had been before them. In sum, though the courts had taken cognizance of the form of the strict settlement, they had left the form without substance. Thus the second stage in the development of settlement was the devising of means to prevent the destruction of the settlement by the tenant for life. Only then would the unborn son be actually secure; or more to the point, only then would the collateral male be secure should there be no son.

About 1650 means were found in the invention of a special trust for the purpose. After the creation of the life estate, a limitation to trustees during the life of the tenant for life was inserted into deeds of settlement, trustees who were to stand as watchdogs ready to enter on the land to preserve the contingent remainders should the tenant for life attempt to destroy them.

The presence of these "trustees to preserve contingent remainders" is what defines a settlement as strict. Trustees were usually men who were either members of the family's extended kinship network, or neighboring landowners.

According to tradition this invention was the work of Orlando Bridgman and Geoffrey Palmer, both members of the royalist gentry who, as Blackstone laconically puts it, "betook themselves to conveyancing during the time of the civil war," presumably for want of the more distinguished employment they might otherwise have enjoyed. Recently doubt has been cast on the tradition that attributes the invention to these men, and particularly on attribution to Bridgman.[25] Even if the argument offered be accepted, it is not one on which anything of historical importance hangs. The chronology of the strict settlement is not altered by the argument, neither the time of its invention nor the pace of its spread. The idea of protecting the remainders would naturally have been in the air, especially after *Lewis Bowles's Case*, which had offered protection after the birth of issue to the tenant for life, and it may be that some obscure conveyancer who has been forgotten first hit on the means by which the remainders might be thoroughly protected.

The argument against Bridgman is, however, weak. It is of the negative kind, stressing a lack of firm evidence for the tradition but naming no alternative inventor. Much is made of the fact that Bridgman's *Conveyances* was not the first printed work to include strict settlements. A book of precedents by George Billinghurst shows familiarity with trustees to preserve contingent remainders, a book that was published in 1674, or eight years before Bridgman's more famous work appeared. Bridgman's precedents, however, were collected and published after his death, and among them is one containing trustees to preserve contingent remainders that bears on its face the date 1666, which is eight years before Billinghurst's work appeared.[26] Another of Bridgman's printed strict settlements has been traced from internal evidence to 1655.[27] No date has been established to show when Billinghurst actually employed the trustees. A settlement by an unknown conveyancer dated 1641 is pointed to that contains in an incipient form trustees to preserve contingent remainders.[28] One of Bridgman's pre-

25. Bonfield, *Marriage Settlements,* 60–66.

26. Orlando Bridgman, *Conveyances,* 2d ed. (London, 1689), 392.

27. H. J. Habakkuk, "Marriage Settlements in the Eighteenth Century," *Transactions of the Royal Historical Society,* 4th ser. 32 (1950): 18n.

28. Bonfield, *Marriage Settlements,* 69.

cedents, however, that also uses the trustees in a primitive way has been claimed by other scholars to be of the same year.[29] Bridgman's professional standing was of the highest in his own day, and that must be significant. Lord Nottingham in the *Duke of Norfolk's Case* went out of his way to note that the settlement at issue had been drawn by Bridgman. "These indentures," he said, "were sealed and delivered in the presence of Sir Orlando Bridgman and . . . his two clerks, who subscribed their names as witnesses, which is to me a demonstration that the deeds were drawn by Sir Orlando Bridgman himself."[30] There was no need for this observation but for the respect in which Bridgman was held in his own time.

While apparently it cannot be proved beyond possibility of doubt that Bridgman was the inventor of the strict settlement, it will nevertheless take more evidence than has been presented to dispose of the tradition that credits him with the invention—if credit is indeed what is owing for an invention that is the main cause of the complexity of English land law. One nineteenth-century political economist summed up Bridgman's work thus: "It was only then that that mosaic of legal antiquities—that thing of shreds and patches of dead law, or rather of fraudulent evasions of legal principle and legislative enactment—which is called a marriage settlement, received its full completion."[31]

MAKING THE FORM PRACTICABLE

Although by about 1650 the form of the strict settlement had been recognized in law and that form had been made secure by the invention of the trust to preserve contingent remainders, there would still have been no viable form of settlement had Bridgman not taken a further step. The device that had been invented thus far had the natural fault of the unbarrable entail: It contained no means of providing for the heiresses whom it postponed, nor means of providing for younger children. It could at best have been used on parts of estates. The work of medieval scholars has time and again gone to show that landowners have not been willing to leave children unprovided for. A workable settlement, one with comprehensive capability, required the inclusion of trusts to pay portions. Trusts to pay portions made settlement humanly acceptable while at the same time they limited in ad-

---

29. English and Saville, *Strict Settlement*, 16.

30. *Lord Nottingham's Chancery Cases*, ed. D. E. C. Yale, Selden Society, vol. 79 (London, 1961), 905).

31. Charles Neate, *The History and Uses of the Law of Entail and Settlement* (London, 1865), 14.

vance the rights of children by taking it out of the hands of their father to determine their rights by deed or will as he chose. Trusts could be inserted in strict settlements, as had not been possible either with the entail or with the marriage settlement that had preceded the strict. In the case of the entail, trusts could not be inserted because the entail was a gift in fee that could not be derogated from. In the second case, the insertion of trusts to pay portions would have been pointless, or would have been an expression of a hope rather than a command, for the settlement was so easily destructible by the tenant for life.

The main trust needed, and almost immediately inserted, was naturally one to pay portions to the heiresses who were postponed. These portions belong, it may loosely but not inappropriately be said, to the class of gifts which Kenny described as "gifts made for the purpose of restraining some incident which would otherwise have attached to the donor estate." Thus there appear in Bridgman's precedents those "portions for daughters," the misunderstanding of which has helped to turn the history of female inheritance in landed society upside down.

For some decades settlements gave portions only to daughters who were heiresses-at-law. Few of Bridgman's precedents provide portions for younger children. Until younger children were similarly provided for, however, land had to be kept free for them, and settlement could not be comprehensively used, or even very effectively used against heiresses. The final step of including younger children followed naturally, and by about 1700 settlements in practice regularly provided portions for younger children.

The final form of providing for children who were not to inherit the family estate is exemplified in the precedents of Gilbert Horsman. Horsman printed many fully developed eighteenth-century marriage settlements, and in them portions are laid out on two scales, one for younger children, and another, normally somewhat higher, for heiresses-at-law. To take an example, one of Horsman's settlements provides £10,000 for one younger child, and £18,000 for four or more younger children; for daughters "if no son survives" (that is, for heiresses-at-law) it provides £16,000 for one such daughter, and £24,000 for three or more of them.[32] (Another example of a Horsman precedent is reproduced in Appendix C.)

Thus through the cobbling together of various elements—the entail, the life estate, trustees to preserve contingent remainders, and trusts to pay

32. Gilbert Horsman, *Precedents in Conveyancing*, 2d ed. (London, 1757), marriage settlement no. 12.

portions—there had eventually appeared a settlement by which all the affairs of a generation unborn were determinable by a deed made at the marriage of the heir male. And from one male heir to the next.

4

What, in sum, is to be said of the strict settlement?

Above all, it is to be recognized as having established a family constitution, the character of which is summed up in three words: patrilineal, primogenitive, and patriarchal. The words need stressing, for casual judgments have been made about the family meaning of the strict settlement on the basis of superficial characteristics. We should not be impressed by the fact that settlements provided for all members of the family. Families have always been provided for by some means or other. There was nothing new in the eighteenth century about a man's caring for his family. The realistic question for historical discussion is whether the various members of the family did better or worse as legal changes took place. Nor should we be impressed because the father under settlement found himself limited in his power over the estate. This limitation of the father's power was not realistically a limitation of patriarchy. The father was limited in his capacity to provide for his immediate family, being so limited in the interests of the patriline. The father, it might really be said, was limited in the interests of patriarchy writ large.

To be sure, limiting the power of the father over the estate was of advantage to the family of a feckless and irresponsible man, for such a man was prevented from utterly destroying the basis of the family's wealth. This was one of the reasons, no doubt, why the father of the bride was so accommodating to the father of the groom in marriage negotiations. But while this aspect of settlement is to be recognized, it needs also to be kept in perspective. It does not justify the view that the strict settlement was generally advantageous to women. How many men were liable to destroy their ancestral estates leaving their families penniless? The idea that landowners were always on the verge of gambling away their land or recklessly treating it must be one of the greatest of misperceptions about them. The English aristocracy was among the world's most successful and long-lived ruling classes, and it cannot have been generally improvident and disorderly. Nor does the idea that landowners were ever wantonly liable to destroy their estates cohere with the other idea commonly held of them, that they were ever intent upon increasing their estates and raising their families in the hierarchy, even at the cost of abusing their children. (These stereotypes agree only in holding that landowners were not emotionally like other men.) Thus while a few wives with their children must have been preserved from ruin by the limitation imposed upon their husbands by settlement, this is to be seen rather as a side effect of settlement, the silver lining in the cloud that settlement was for women, but not its explanation. Settlement needs to be construed in the more normal family setting. The normal cause of the disintegration of estates lay in the family itself. Preserving estates can only mean limiting the shares of all but the head of the family. The analogy of the limited warranty again comes to mind. Though the limited warranty guarantees consumers certain rights, it is fundamentally designed to reduce rights they would in other ways enjoy.

A second thing to be said about the strict settlement is that merely as a marriage settlement, as a device for predetermining heirs and distributing property, it preserved estates. The real sources of disintegration were controlled by such advance planning, for the real sources of estate disintegration lay less in extravagant young bachelors than in unrestrained paternal affection. Accordingly, so long as estates were settled on or before marriage, it little mattered whether there was an unbroken chain of settlement and resettlement. So long as settling at marriage was the social norm, expected by father-in-law as well as by father, not to mention by uncle and brother, settlement preserved estates. T. E. Cliffe Leslie, a supporter of the land law reform movement in the nineteenth century and a professor of law and political economy, emphasized the importance that the timing of settlements at marriage had. A young man settling his estate at that time necessarily acted, Leslie observed, "before he has any experience of his property, or what is best to do, or what he can do in regard to it; before the exigencies of the future or his own real position are known to him; before the character, number, and wants of his children are learned, or the claims of parental affection and duty can make themselves felt."[33] If one settlement led without a break to another, so much the better for estates, of course; but the regular limiting of provision for the family in a series even of disconnected marriage settlements went far to preserve estates.

Settlement sprang, of course, from a society already patrilineal and primogenitive in its beliefs, and it could only work amid such beliefs. Its effects should thus not be exaggerated, but there can be no doubt that in giving the aristocratic ethos a legal vehicle, settlement went far to strengthen it.

33. T. E. Cliffe Leslie, *Land Systems and Industrial Economy of Ireland, England, and the Continent* (London, 1870), 200.

What George Brodrick said of the law of primogeniture is applicable to the strict settlement: "Its indirect effect on the minds of testators and settlors cannot be measured by any definite test, but reason and analogy would certainly lead us to believe that it has been a most powerful agent in moulding the sentiment of the [landed] class."[34] Quite precise rules about what was right and proper to be done about estates and families became widely disseminated through the ritual of the marriage settlement and generally were followed. This is evident in the common knowledge of what the proper relation of jointure to portion was. It is evident too in the ease with which English conveyancers were able to suggest to the Committee on Scottish Entails what it was proper for younger children to receive. Settlement thus did more than make planning possible for the individual family, it went far to establish class norms.

A contrast with wills is to be drawn. Wills are individual deeds, marked by secrecy, and they are naturally and directly subject to personal feelings and even to a certain waywardness. Marriage settlements, on the other hand, are negotiated deeds that involve two families. They would inherently have been more standardized in their dispositions, more closely representative of the aristocratic ethos than wills. In addition, marriage settlements were to some degree naturally and immediately public. This was particularly true of the marriage settlement that was the strict settlement, for this was an immensely complicated deed. It led to the development of a large profession of conveyancers, far larger than in any continental country. English landowners were peculiarly dependent upon lawyers, and lawyers in turn formed a large network among whom very detailed estate and family information passed and repassed. Sir Frederick Pollock emphasized that the English landowner was "a good deal in the hands of experts," and he likened the role the solicitor played in the landed family to that which the prime minister played in the state. It was the family solicitor who was "the real possessor of the secrets of the estate, the real familiar spirit at whose bidding the magical powers of the settlement [were] called forth, and without whose aid nothing of weight [could] be undertaken."[35] James Loch did not hesitate to give his opinion to Lord Egerton on the portions in a proposed family settlement: "It strikes me that the sum is enough to charge your eldest son with as between him and your other children."[36] (The sum was considerably less than two years' estate

34. George Brodrick, *English Land and English Landlords* (London, 1881), 96.

35. Frederick Pollock, *The Land Laws*, 3d ed. (London, 1896), 10, 119–20.

36. James Loch to Lord Francis Egerton, 28 January 1843, Ellesmere Manuscripts, Northamptonshire Record Office, 35A no. 193.

income.) As vehicles of inheritance, the will did not have the potentiality for establishing class norms that the strict settlement had, which was a legally complex deed in which two heads of families and various other family interests were all involved.

Finally, settlement was the culmination of a long legal history. If arrangements in the landed family were not altogether different after its invention from what they had been before it, that is because the story was a long-running one. In this long-term sense, settlement stands as an undoubted landmark in the aristocratic family's history. Its development forms the last chapter in the long story of landowners' grappling with a common law that gave more rights to women than landowners thought proper. In the strict settlement they found the legal device that was better for their purposes than the common law, which was lineal rather than patrilineal in its principles; better than the entail, which was either impracticable or inadequate depending on which way it was applied; and better than the unlimited power to devise that uses had conferred.

6 Theories of the Family

Most people marry upon mingled motives, between

convenience and inclination.

—*Dr Johnson*, Life of Sir Thomas Browne

In the process of discussing heirship and the division of property, the previous chapters have given some insight into the spirit of the landed family, some conception of its emotional character. The long effort of landowners to overcome rules of common law that they held to be too favorable to females obviously indicates there was a growing dominance of males in the family, a growing emphasis upon descent in the patriline, which is to be associated with titles and surnames and the preservation of estates. At the same time, it is clear that landowners were always concerned for the various members of their nuclear families. It was concern for the lesser members of the family that made for the maritagium, for the original entail, and for the use. It was concern for the lesser members of the family that made entails on eldest sons unsatisfactory and that required portions to be laid out in settlements for children who were not to inherit the estate. There is no way of putting legal developments into a coherent framework except through the assumption that landowners cared for all the members of their families and were determined to provide for them, although certainly not equally. Landowners were, then, involved from early times in balancing natural family sentiment and a growing patrilineal ideology. What their attitude to marriage was is not completely clear in the sense that the emotional relationship between bride and groom has not come into view in earlier chapters. Nevertheless something about marriage is to be inferred. In discussing economic movements in the family there has been no necessity to take account of interfamily concerns. These movements are fully accountable in terms of changing social conceptions that equally affected all families of the class. There follows from this perception a discounting of the idea that marriage in the gentry and aristocracy was a relentless struggle between families for economic advantage.

This view of the emotional constitution and history of the landed family is considerably at odds with thinking on the subject. The landed family has been the center of much investigation, and we have a series of notable works that have put forward theories about its development. The series may be said to have begun with H. J. Habakkuk's path-breaking article on marriage settlements in the eighteenth century, and it contains Lawrence Stone's monumental work and significant works by Randolph Trumbach and Lloyd Bonfield. None of these works finds in the succession of legal instruments a long history of fatherly concern for the nuclear family. All of them find aristocratic marriage to have been most of the time a struggle for dynastic aggrandizement. None sees the strict settlement as the culmination of a historical movement, but all instead find in it evidence of radical change in the emotional life of the family. There are different ideas as to what change it implied, and two conflicting theories run strongly through the literature. The theory that has become dominant postulates through settlement the arrival of the nuclear, loving family in the eighteenth century. Settlement is associated with a change in habits of marriage, and with growing equality between the sexes. This is the conception that has gone to form historians' perceptions of the history of the family in general.

This chapter will review what are, then, different theories of family development than the one that has emerged in these pages. The basic construction of each of the theories will be analyzed, and the ideas about marriage that run through them will also be considered. The chapter will end with an overall discussion of aristocratic family principles and their implications for family history in general.

1

As a historian of English landownership Habakkuk did not set out with the intention of discussing the history of the family, or even that of the aristocratic family. He was led to conclusions on the subject through seeking an answer to an economic problem, being anxious to account for the growth of large estates that he held took place in the eighteenth century. Drawing attention to the arrival of the strict settlement, he showed that this form of marriage settlement preserved estates as the immediately preceding forms had not. At the same time, taking note of Blackstone's statement that the purpose of the strict settlement was "to secure in family settlements a provision for the future children of an intended marriage, who before were usually left at the mercy of the particular tenant for life," he argued that settlement would have increased portions for younger children.[1] He began, then, with the idea that settlement preserved estates, and also that it increased portions.

Whether settlement did more than preserve estates was the question that naturally followed. Had it "contributed positively to the accumulation of estates?" Here the argument turned upon the portions of daughters. Several demographic reasons were adduced for thinking that in the seventeenth century there must have been increasing competition among women for husbands (such as the death of men in war) and thus for thinking that daughters' portions would have risen. The proof offered that daughters' portions actually rose was the movement of the jointure/portion ratio in Orlando Bridgman's precedents. The falling of the ratio showed that the terms of marriage were moving against women. On the one hand, eldest sons were promising less to their brides should they become widows, and on the other hand, they were demanding that their brides bring more into marriage. Marriage had been an important method of accumulating property in all ages, Habakkuk noted, but these movements showed that it was being more systematically used for this purpose than hitherto. Since in an increasingly competitive marriage market the heirs to great estates naturally held the advantage, they married the women with the largest portions. Thus the growth of large estates was to be traced to "the spread of the arrangements associated with the strict settlement."

While Habakkuk had begun with an economic question about estates, he ended with a theory that attitudes to love and marriage in the landed family had changed. His argument for the growth of large estates involved the conception that female property became of increasing size and importance as landowners increasingly sought dynastic advantage through marriage.

Habakkuk was the first to recognize that female inheritance was even important in estate history, and to draw the attention of historians to it.

---

1. H. J. Habakkuk, "Marriage Settlements in the Eighteenth Century," *Transactions of the Royal Historical Society,* 4th ser. 32 (1950): 15–30.

His critic ultimately stands on his shoulders. There must arise, however, a question about the reality of this family scenario. Is it likely that land-owners, who had taken to the strict settlement in the desire to preserve their estates, would at the same time have increased their outgoings on daughters? Aside from the likelihood of this scenario, there are troubles now evident in the legal arguments used. Orlando Bridgman was not concerned with daughters as a class, but only with daughters who were heiresses, and his precedents did not raise daughters' portions, but instead limited heiresses-at-law to mere portions. The significant trends were a decline in both female inheritance and in jointure. Nor are Blackstone's words to be taken at their face value. When analyzed in their context, they dissociate rising portions and the strict settlement. Habakkuk was an economic historian courageously venturing into a legal field. Unfortunately the legal tradition itself may be said to have failed him. Legal scholars had neither pointed to the main object of Bridgman's work, nor scrutinized Blackstone's words, being interested in the duration rather than in the content of landed family deeds.

While Habakkuk's ideas were intended to apply only to the English aristocracy, Lawrence Stone's *Family, Sex and Marriage* presents a general theory of family development, Stone intending it to describe how and when the modern Western form of family took shape. A work on a grand scale, the book covers centuries and is full of insightful observations on all sorts of family matters, from forms of address to domestic architecture. Its social focus is, however, on "the wealthy professional and landed classes." Stone naturally did not hold that these classes consisted of typical English families. Rather, as he explained, he found that these classes formed the "lead sector" in society making for change. It was among them that "the most significant changes took place earliest and with widest impact."[2] Stone had previously, of course, written extensively upon the aristocracy and the rising gentry of Tudor time. In *Family, Sex and Marriage*, then, we have a general theory of family development that is based very largely upon the gentry and aristocracy.

Stone's thesis is that the family underwent great emotional change in the eighteenth century, although in the opposite direction to that of Habakkuk. In earlier centuries the family had been ruled authoritatively by the father and held together by considerations of property and lineage. Marriages were arranged; marriage as an institution was for the begetting

2. Lawrence Stone, *The Family, Sex and Marriage in England, 1500–1800* (New York, 1977), 394.

of children and the transmission of property, and it was not expected to confer personal happiness. In such a society the majority of people "found it very difficult to establish close emotional ties to any other person. Children were neglected, brutally treated, and even killed; adults treated each other with suspicion and hostility; affect was low, and hard to find."[3] Against this early family of cool, not to say cold-blooded, relationships, the eighteenth-century family was intimate, nuclear, and bound together by love. People married for love, they cared for their children, and there was an increase in equality between men and women, as women's property rights increased. The patriarchal family had given way to what has come to be known, following Stone's terminology, as the "affective family."

Judging of emotional relationships in the past is inherently difficult. The family is the most private of institutions, its inner feelings walled off from the public world. When these feelings are found expressed in diaries or letters or novels, historians are confronted by questions of typicality, a question as to the typicality of the writer, and another as to the typicality of the events that he or she deemed worthy to record. They are also confronted by changes in literary style and in conventions about what is proper to be talked of. Styles and conventions may change without marking any change of heart. Hard evidence was necessary if a theory was to be credible that posited vast and general emotional change in the family—evidence that could not be dismissed as impressionistic or insubstantial. Stone sought hard evidence naturally enough in law, and especially in inheritance law, which became the basis for his outline of family history.

In this outline there are three stages in the family's history, depending on the facilities for entailing land. The first stage, the "open lineage family," is associated with the unbarrable entail. Here the family estate was the asset of the lineage, tied up to be passed on from eldest son to eldest son. Younger children were at the mercy of their father or their elder brother, dependent upon one or the other to provide for them out of income. The second stage in the history of the family, "reinforcement of patriarchy," appeared as entails became barrable. With entails barrable, landowners possessed power to dispose of family property as they wished, and this age is associated with the use of marriage to increase dynastic power. Fathers could bribe or threaten their children by granting or withholding property in order to control their choice of spouse. The third stage

3. Ibid., 99.

in the history of the family, that of the affective family, is associated with the strict settlement.[4]

Several questions arise about the two early parts of this outline. Despite the fact that entails and freedom of alienation are legally at opposite poles, the move from the one to the other is treated as linear progression, indicating a strengthening of patriarchy. There is no recognition that the entail could be used to provide for younger children, and that as a legal form it began that way. The assumption is that entails were used to tie up estates upon a series of eldest sons. Historians have, to be sure, seldom clearly appreciated that the entail was an ambiguous instrument. While the same may be said of the later instrument, the use, in this case medieval historians have stressed that it represented the desire to provide for younger children. Stone, however, sees the freedom of alienation that the use conferred as just as bad for children as entails on eldest sons, or even worse. The father's freedom to dispose of property by will allowed him to manipulate marriage in the interests of the lineage. The family motives at work in these instruments have not been well considered by historians in general, but as the earlier chapters of this work show, they are more complex than Stone allows.

What matters most in Stone's theory, however, is the last part of the scheme, where the strict settlement provides proof of the change from patriarchy, of whatever stripe, to the affective family. This is where the emphasis falls. This "third set of family property arrangements" proves "the new reality of a decline of patriarchy within the family."[5] Here is the "key" development in the history of the family.[6] The strict settlement is thus associated with greater equality in the family between males and females, and especially with marriage for love, for these are the main features that are celebrated in the new family.

The words with which Stone introduces the strict settlement as an egalitarian and affective device show some hesitation. Settlement, he declares, was the "reaffirmation of the principle of primogeniture to preserve in perpetuity the family estates," and "at first sight" it would seem to run contrary to the theory of increasing equality in the family.[7] By an argument

4. For the laying out of the family scheme according to facilities for entailing land see ibid., 87, 156, 243.

5. Ibid., 243.

6. Lawrence Stone, "Family History in the 1980's: Past Achievements and Future Trends," *Journal of Interdisciplinary History* 12 (1981): 84.

7. Stone, *Family, Sex and Marriage*, 244.

about disinheritance, however, the problem is resolved. Under settlement a father could no longer "deprive any of his children of their arranged inheritances." His arbitrary control over property was reduced, and with it his power to force his will upon his children "over such critical issues as marriage."[8] After this cautious beginning there follows a discussion emphasizing the rise of women's property.

The first question for analysis is, then, to what degree the basic argument about disinheritance is valid. There is certainly one thing to be said in its favor. Under settlement a father could not disinherit his eldest son. It may well be wondered, however, how often fathers ever had disinherited their eldest sons. Eldest sons were virtually secure anyway, and settlement's action in making them absolutely secure would have had little practical meaning for them. In any case, it was simply a situation where landowners could not have their cake and eat it too. Making eldest sons secure was but the inescapable concomitant of ensuring male succession. Male succession had to be fixed in order that no female might break in upon it. "To eldest son, and then to his eldest son if he should have a son, but to his younger brother if he should not"—the principle of settlement—could not be fulfilled if eldest son was free to do as he wished should he turn out to have daughters only as children. Guaranteeing eldest sons and then a rump of collateral males certainly prevented the disinheritance of the heir male, but this was but the converse of the keeping out of the heir female.

Moreover, though eldest sons were made secure, younger children as a rule were not. Settlements soon came to give the father a power of appointment over portions. That is to say, they soon came to give him the power to divide the total sum allowed for portions among his children in any way he thought fitting. Thus a younger child could, as the phrase goes, be cut off with a shilling, if the father thought that appropriate. One legal scholar, who once argued that settlement made disinheritance impossible, has since found that half of early strict settlements contained a power of appointment over portions.[9] That was decidedly the direction in which practice was moving. Joshua Williams in the nineteenth century spoke of the power of appointment over portions being normal in settlements of the

8. Ibid., 243.

9. Lloyd Bonfield, "Marriage, Property and the 'Affective Family'" *Law and History Review* 1 (1983): 302; idem, "Affective Families, Open Elites and Strict Family Settlements in Early Modern England," *Economic History Review*, 2d ser. 32 (1986): 351.

day.[10] (An example of the normal trust to pay portions is given here in Appendix C.)

Viewing the whole, it would seem that the power of disinheritance was forgone only so far as was necessary to guarantee male succession. This is hardly ground for casting the strict settlement in an affective and egalitarian role.

It may, perhaps, be wondered whether great importance should ever be given to the power of disinheritance in family history, meaning by disinheritance the utter cutting out of a child from the family's property. How often did fathers ever act thus? The whole history of landowners' interaction with the law shows rather that they were determined to provide for their children. This work has had a good deal to say about the cutting out of heiresses from the succession to land, but it has also emphasized that they were not totally disinherited. The history of landowners' interaction with the law in this case shows that the strict settlement reduced portions and more efficiently reduced heiresses exactly because it precluded fathers' determining family matters by their wills. The power to do or not to do what there is little tendency ever to do is hardly of major social significance. Fathers may threaten to disinherit their children, perhaps with some frequency, but threats that are not seen to be frequently carried out are threats perceived to be idle. Some children were disinherited, of course; even the odd disinherited eldest son can be pointed to. Edward Wortley Montagu disinherited his only son, who seems to have been incorrigible, not to say mentally unbalanced. And admittedly Montagu had been able to effect the disinheritance exactly because his estate had not been settled at his marriage, he and his wife, the well-known Lady Mary, having eloped.[11] But it is to be doubted that enough children were ever disinherited for the power of disinheritance to be of general importance in family history. Again I would stress that the power of disinheritance in the context in which Stone has raised it means the utter cutting off of a child from the family's property, a different question than the cutting out of females from the succession to land.

It is even to be suggested that the power of appointment over younger children's portions was developed less to maintain the father's power to disinherit particular of his younger children than to allow him to make

10. Joshua Williams, *The Settlement of Real Estates* (London, 1879), 220.

11. Robert Halsband, *The Life of Lady Mary Wortley Montagu* (Oxford, 1957), passim.

some adjustment of portions to the needs of different younger children, for their needs would have varied according to whom they married. If a landowner could not disinherit his eldest son, why anyway should he have concerned himself to maintain his power to disinherit his younger children, who did not much count? The history of the father's power over portions is probably not best seen in terms of disinheritance. Probably conveyancers, developing a complex instrument in which younger children played a small part, had originally paid little attention the father's power over portions. When the advantages of some flexibility in the provision for younger children became evident, they provided it.

Historians have emphasized the importance of the power of disinheritance because they have reasoned that it provided the means by which landowners had been able before the eighteenth century to control marriage. Whether landowners *had* controlled marriage is thus a question with bearing upon the alleged importance of the power to disinherit children. Later sections of this chapter question the evidence that has been used to show that landowners had controlled marriage.

Stone's second line of argument is that in the eighteenth century a series of legal changes occurred that increased, or better secured, the rights of women. These, he declares, offer "the hardest of hard evidence" for change in the relations between the sexes.[12] Unfortunately the discussion that follows lacks balance. Thus Stone declares that "the property of heiresses was now more carefully safeguarded against seizure and exploitation by the future husband." This is clearly an inadequate treatment of the fate of heiresses, giving no hint of their decline. Much the same is said about the property of widows, which is declared to have been better protected against second husbands. This is again an inadequate treatment of the fate of widows—whose fate at the hands of their first husbands is surely the major matter—and Stone himself in an earlier work had shown what that fate was.[13] He also notes that portions for daughters rose in the seventeenth century, but he does not put the rise into relation with the fall in jointure, though again in his earlier work he had indicated the fall. He is quite right to point to pin money and settlements to the separate use of the married woman, but their significance cannot be weighed when all contrary movements are ignored.

Stone's treatment of portions shows in acute form the problem of trying to maintain that the strict settlement was the legal foundation of a more

12. Stone, *Family, Sex and Marriage*, 330.
13. Lawrence Stone, *The Crisis of Aristocracy, 1558–1681* (Oxford, 1965), 644–65.

egalitarian family while also declaring that it represented "the iron law of primogeniture."[14] In accordance with the former view, daughters' portions are described as rising all through the eighteenth century. Indeed daughters' portions are said to have risen so high that some landowners could not afford to marry their daughters off.[15] In accordance with the latter view, however, portions for younger sons are described as falling through the century. Indeed these portions are said to have fallen so low that an "economic crisis" ensued for sons, as they often became too poor to marry.[16] In neither case is any empirical evidence supplied as to the movement of portions in the eighteenth century, and the question why they should have moved differently for one sex and the other is not raised.

In these seminal works by Habakkuk and Stone we have, then, statements that acknowledge the primogenitive nature of the strict settlement mingled with arguments that turn it to the advantage of younger children, especially daughters. In the one case the increase of daughters' portions is held to prove that the family was becoming increasingly commercial, and in the other that it was becoming increasingly loving and egalitarian. Whichever theory any later historian chose to adopt, he emphasized the rising of daughters' portions, which has no doubt contributed to the fact that the incompatibility of the theories has gone largely unnoticed.

Randolph Trumbach's theory of family development is very similar in its general thrust to Stone's, as the title of his book, *The Rise of the Egalitarian Family*, suggests. His book and Stone's are independent works, however, that happen to have been published almost simultaneously. Trumbach focuses upon the top section of landed society, the peerage, but he argues that "domesticity" grew in peerage families in the eighteenth century, "domesticity" being his term for Stone's "affective family." Trumbach proceeds upon a rather different path, however, and uses a rather different terminology, one that owes much to anthropology.

He begins with the idea that landowners were involved in a balancing of family principles. In the terms he uses, the history of the landed family exhibits constant tension between patrilineal and kindred principles, the latter being alternatively called "cognatic principles."[17] Kindred or cognatic principles are ambilateral, stressing the equality of the female side of the family with that of the male. They are principles associated with equality

14. Ibid., 652.
15. Stone, *Family, Sex and Marriage*, 381.
16. Ibid., 377–78.
17. Randolph Trumbach, *The Rise of the Egalitarian Family* (New York, 1978), 16.

among family members, and with a relatively high position for women. They were the principles observed in peasant and lower-class families.[18] They were principles recognized even among aristocratic families, for society at all levels observed rules of mourning and sexual taboos that treated the male and female sides of the family equally. Landowners, like others, mourned for their relatives on the female side of their families as for those on the male side. And like others, they were bound by ecclesiastical prohibitions upon contracting marriage with relatives which placed affines (relatives by marriage) on virtually the same footing as blood relatives.[19] From about the tenth century onward, however, landowners across Europe adopted a patrilineal ideology on top of their underlying cognatic one.[20]

Rather as I have done in this work, Trumbach thus views landowners as perpetually engaged in attempting to balance contradictory family imperatives. But where I have presented them as balancing the demands of their immediate families against their increasingly patrilineal desires, Trumbach presents them as balancing two principles, the patrilineal and the cognatic or kindred. The words are different, but the concept is the same. Since Trumbach is alive to the common law and to the fact that its principle was not patrilineal, it would seem that we should reach a similar conclusion. Out of the long-term conflict in the family between natural sentiment and ideology, the strict settlement should appear as the legal means for guaranteeing the patriline. This is not what happens, however, for Trumbach goes on to dismiss patrilineage and female interests in discussing the strict settlement.

Landowners manifested their patrilineal ideology, Trumbach declares, in their attitude to succession to land and to titles.[21] "As far as land went," he declares, "the common law was more generous to a woman than was settlement practice." He further declares that "aristocratic families were determined that once a family estate had been increased by marriage the vagaries of demography should not take it away."[22] After these brief statements his attention shifts away from land, though land was surely the essence of the matter in a society based on that species of property. Landowners were "more generous with money." Daughters received pin money

18. Ibid., 1–2.
19. Ibid., 18–40.
20. Ibid., 1.
21. Ibid., 17.
22. Ibid., 81.

and portions settled even to their own use.[23] The conclusion is thus reached that, after all, "patrilineage was a minor concern of the settlement."[24]

Settlement's real concern, in Trumbach's terminology, was "sibling solidarity." That is to say, settlement's real aim was to increase equality between eldest son and younger children and, in Trumbach's view, particularly to increase equality between eldest son and younger sons. Portions for younger children are thus again held to rise, and settlement again serves as the foundation for a theory of equality.

Trumbach's argument is a new one, however. It depends upon contrasting strict settlements made before 1690 with those made later. After 1690 settlements always provided for younger children. "This was a great change," Trumbach argues, "from the seventeenth century when family settlements had guaranteed the inheritance of younger children only in the case of a marriage that produced daughters but no sons."[25] Two settlements in the Cavendish family are pointed to. The first, made in 1688, contained no provision for younger children; the second, made in 1711, contained such provision.[26] This contrast is assumed to mark real increase in the provision for younger children, especially for younger sons, upon whom Trumbach's prime interest falls. Younger sons were no longer being cut off—in the memorable words of Sir Thomas Wilson, which have echoed and reechoed through the literature—"with that which the cat left on the malt heap."[27]

In Trumbach's case the conclusion that the eighteenth-century peerage family moved in an egalitarian direction is again based upon a misperception of the course of development of the strict settlement. Younger sons (and ordinary daughters) were ignored in early settlements, not because they were ignored in family arrangements at the time, but because they were not the first object of concern in the development of settlement. Bridgman had put first things first. That younger children appeared only in the fully developed form of settlement is not proof of increasing equality in the family, but proof that patrilineage, which Trumbach had first em-

---

23. Ibid., 81, 83.

24. Ibid., 70.

25. Ibid., 89.

26. Ibid.

27. Thomas Wilson, *The State of England in 1600*, an early seventeenth-century work published by the Royal Historical Society in the Camden Miscellanies, series 16 (London, 1936), 24.

phasized only to dismiss at the crucial point, was indeed settlement's first concern.

Lloyd Bonfield is a legal historian rather than a family historian, but law has been much appealed to by family historians, and Bonfield has been drawn into family history. Coming down firmly on the side of the affective family, he also holds that settlement increased equality in the family. He has indeed taken a more extreme position than any of the authors considered above. There is no waffling on the subject; he denies unequivocally that settlement was primogenitive: "It spread wealth rather than concentrated it."[28] His arguments appear in his book *Marriage Settlements* and at rather greater length in two subsequent articles.

The first thing to be noted in reviewing the corpus of Bonfield's work is that the idea of increasing family equality emerges in telling surroundings. It emerges in *Marriage Settlements* from a discussion of portions between 1660 and 1700, which shows that at the first date settlements provided only for daughters, and only for them when "a marriage produced no surviving male child," but that by the second date settlements provided for all children.[29] The legal reason why only some daughters were of concern in early settlements is never raised throughout what is a lengthy discussion, and indeed can hardly be raised, when from explicit statements made earlier in the book it is evident Bonfield has an imperfect conception of the common law.[30] Inevitably, then, movement seems to be in the direction of equality. There apparently grew among landowners a concern first for their daughters and then for all their children. Here are combined two misperceptions about settlement. There is the common failure to perceive the rules of succession as to daughters, and as well the misperception noted in discussing Trumbach's work, the assumption that because younger children were not encompassed in early settlements the movement of their interests was upward.

In the articles that followed *Marriage Settlements* Bonfield elaborates the theme of rising portions by discussing settlement against the legal background of the sixteenth century. Arguments problematic in various new ways appear. The first article argues that settlement was affective and egalitarian in its thrust, on the ground that it followed an age of freedom of alienation. The Elizabethan landowner had been seised of an entail, which had become an alienable estate, and he had therefore been able "to dispose

28. Bonfield, "Affective Families," 347.
29. Lloyd Bonfield, *Marriage Settlements, 1601–1740* (Cambridge, 1983), 103–20.
30. See the discussion above in chapter 1, section 5.

of land for his own purposes." He had the power to cut off his children with nothing at all if he so desired, having "absolute discretion with regard to the amount of provision or indeed whether there would be any at all."[31] With the coming of settlement and its portions for children, "a more rational and secure system of wealth distribution" had been substituted for "an arbitrary and capricious one based upon patriarchy."[32]

Underlying this argument is an unconvincing view of human nature. It assumes that a father provides better for his children by a settlement made at his marriage than he would do by his will. It is assumed that men provide better for hypothetical children than they do for children who stand before them, known and loved beings.

Having apparently reconsidered, Bonfield argues quite differently in his second article. While still arguing that settlement's thrust was in the direction of equality for family members, he does a complete volte face as to its legal background: The sixteenth century was not an age in which landowners enjoyed freedom of alienation. "Quite the contrary." It was an age of perpetuities. Landowners had no freedom until 1614.[33] To change the background of settlement is, of course, to change its thrust. Against a background of perpetuities settlement is bound to appear a move towards equality in the family.

As this second view involves upsetting well-established ideas as to the legal character of the age before the strict settlement, one looks for the grounds for it. Bonfield, however, gives no grounds other than a general reference to his *Marriage Settlements*.[34] This is puzzling, doubly so. *Marriage Settlements* was published before either article, and was much referred to in the first, which portrayed the sixteenth century as an age of freedom for landowners. Moreover, what *Marriage Settlements* says about the age before the strict settlement is clear in its opening chapter. To establish the background for the strict settlement, it begins with an analysis of all the settlements noted in the law reports from before the Statute of Uses until 1601. It concludes that landowners "were destined to come into possession of their estates as tenants in tail with powers of [disposition]."[35] For the period between 1600 and 1614 Bonfield depends for evidence upon

31. Bonfield, "Marriage, Property," 300, 302.
32. Ibid., 304.
33. Bonfield, "Affective Families," 349.
34. Ibid., 349 n. 39.
35. Bonfield, *Marriage Settlements*, 8–9. Moreover, Bonfield several times declares that the extent of perpetuities has never been demonstrated (14, 39, 44); and several times suggests that historians have exaggerated landowners' desire for entails (18, 53).

a collection of actual settlements. Not one of these settlements, he has else-where declared, contains a clause of perpetuity.[36]

Marriage Settlements contains new and valuable data. It demonstrates the form of the sixteenth-century marriage settlement; it traces the spread of the strict settlement; it shows when settlements came to encompass younger children; and it gives information on the longevity of aristocratic widows. But these data have not been consistently or appropriately fitted into their social background.

If the theories discussed above are considered together, a clear pattern is evident. Their authors all base their theories on one legal instrument, the strict settlement. And all of them argue that with settlement the property of younger children increased, especially that of daughters. There are ob-vious difficulties in associating a primogenitive device with increased pro-vision for the subordinate members of the family. While Bonfield, with a certain consistency in this case, holds that settlement was not primogeni-tive, his attempt to maintain this belief ends only in a series of other con-tradictions. The causes for the confusion that generally persists about the strict settlement are various. Blackstone's words have been taken out of context; Orlando Bridgman's object in so conspicuously providing "por-tions for daughters" has not been grasped; the reason why younger chil-dren were not provided for in prior forms of settlement and in early examples of strict settlements has been misunderstood; and the loss of the power to disinherit children has been exaggerated, the fact unperceived that it went only so far as was necessary for the putting down of the female heir.

Historians have appealed to legal evidence in discussing the family be-cause they recognize that other evidence, that which is found in letters, in literature, and in sermons, is very subject to varying and impressionistic interpretation. (Compare, for example, the different impressions Lawrence Stone and Alan Macfarlane have of the diary of Ralph Josselin.)[37] The de-vice that historians have fallen upon for hard evidence on which to con-struct their theories of family development was an important device, but it did not indicate a revolution in the landed family's principles, or even a new beginning. On the contrary, settlement reinforced ideological princi-

36. Lloyd Bonfield, "Marriage Settlements, 1660–1740: The Adoption of the Strict Settlement in Kent and Northamptonshire," in *Marriage and Society: Studies in the Social History of Marriage*, ed. R. B. Outhwaite (London, 1981), 105 n. 15.

37. Stone, *Family, Sex and Marriage*, 113, 215; Alan Macfarlane, *Marriage and Love in England, 1300–1840* (Oxford, 1986), 52.

ples that had long been developing by giving them a legal vehicle. Historiographically, however, it has been given great significance in the wrong direction.

2

Marriage has obviously been a major theme in all the theories discussed above, as it must be, of course, in any discussion of family history. Habakkuk's theory is essentially about the principles on which marriage was made. Stone's theory encompasses many aspects of family life, being a general theory of family development; but the arrival of what, following his terminology, has come to be known as the "companionate marriage" is prominent in it. "The many legal, political and educational changes that took place in the late seventeenth and eighteenth centuries," he writes, "were largely consequences of changes in ideas about the nature of marital relations."[38] The arrival of marriage for love is a major theme in Trumbach's work, and the idea finds its place, though less conspicuously, in Bonfield's thinking.

The question focused on has been whether from time to time marriage was motivated by romantic love or by economic calculation. While all the authors agree as to the direction of female inheritance, not all see the same change in habits of marriage. Habakkuk, whose ideas were first in the field, held that the rise of portions indicated that marriage was becoming more commercial, not less so. He offered proof for this theory beyond the legal one already discussed, pointing directly to a pattern of marriages between eldest sons of peers and heiresses in the late seventeenth and early eighteenth centuries. In many families, the eldest son in two successive generations had married an heiress; and in some families eldest sons had married heiresses in three or four generations in a row.[39] The pattern alone was evidence that the landed family had become grasping and commercial in its attitude. Habakkuk's theory could thus be held independently of any legal argument about the strict settlement. It might be seen as essentially about the pursuit of heiresses, and an early critique of it has been entitled *The Pursuit of the Heiress.*[40]

In this form the heiress was to enter into historians' consciousness—not

38. Stone, *Family, Sex and Marriage,* 325.
39. Habakkuk, "Marriage Settlements," 28.
40. A. P. W. Malcomson, *Pursuit of the Heiress* (Antrim, 1982).

as a person with her own history, but as an object of pursuit. And accordingly the historiography of the heiress was to assume a strange form. While the heiress herself was largely ignored, neither her legal right nor her history appreciated, she became greatly important in an oblique way. Unseen directly, she nevertheless became of intense historical interest. It might perhaps be said that the heiress has been to historians rather as certain celestial objects are to astronomers, bodies unseen themselves but perceptible by disturbances they cause around them.

The history of landed estates came largely to revolve around marriage to heiresses, and not only in the eighteenth century and not only in England. In some accounts the eldest son pursues heiresses of his own volition; in others it is the father who is the pursuer, tyrannically requiring his son to marry for the profit of the estate regardless of his inclinations. One way or the other, the history of estates became largely the story of the effort to augment them through marriage. The determined search for heiresses appeared as a major theme in Lawrence Stone's *Crisis of Aristocracy*, which covered the sixteenth and seventeenth centuries, and Stone applied Habakkuk's idea with the vigor for which he is noted. The pursuit of heiresses became a stock theme in European history, in French and in Venetian history particularly, and from medieval times through the eighteenth century. The idea reached perhaps its peak in Georges Duby's study of French medieval society. Here bands of young men are portrayed as roaming the countryside in search of heiresses. "All *juvenes* were on the lookout for an heiress. If they came across one, they tried to reserve her before she was nubile. Sometimes they took the child with them on their journey, and were prepared to restore her to her father if they should find a more desirable match on the way or if another 'youth' should come to claim her too insistently."[41] A fanciful story, to be punctured by the question how a female who was yet a child and whose father was alive could be known to be an heiress. But the story is indicative of the immense sway the theory came to exercise.

Statistical analyses of marriages were undertaken to show what a scramble for heiresses aristocratic marriage was. Stone undertook the first in his *Crisis of Aristocracy*. Finding that one out of every three peers in the mid-seventeenth century had married an heiress and that the rate had been increasing, he concluded that financial profit had become the most important single consideration in marriage.[42] David Thomas undertook a much

41. Georges Duby, *The Chivalrous Society* (Berkeley and Los Angeles, 1977), 119.
42. Stone, *Crisis of Aristocracy*, 618, 789.

larger study, which analyzed the marriages of peers' sons from the late seventeenth century to the end of the nineteenth. He found an even higher rate of marriage to heiresses, finding that about the end of the seventeenth century 42 percent of peers' sons had married heiresses, and he naturally emphasized the extent of heiress-seeking.[43] Although Thomas also showed that marriages to heiresses declined in the eighteenth century, he explained that his data took no account of portions. Under the strict settlement the young man's fancy—or his father's—would have turned to the large-portioned daughter, and as a consequence the data for the eighteenth century underestimated the extent of heiress-seeking.[44] What stood out from both studies was the extremely high proportion of marriages to heiresses at the end of the seventeenth century, proof that financial gain had become the overriding object in aristocratic marriage.

That marriage in the gentry and aristocracy was a determined pursuit of heiresses was thus the historical background when in his next major work Stone ventured on his history of the family. In this he found great change in the family in the eighteenth century, and it was represented above all by the arrival of the companionate marriage. The strict settlement, in granting children secure portions, had made them able to marry as they chose.

This new conception of aristocratic marriage was again bolstered by empirical evidence as to the pattern of marriages. Stone now took note of what Thomas in his statistical analysis of peerage marriages had minimized, the decline of marriages to heiresses in the eighteenth century. Thomas had found that 42 percent of the marriages of peers' sons about 1700 had been to heiresses, but he had also somewhat disconcertingly found a great decline in such marriages as the eighteenth century progressed. By the end of the century only 11 percent of peers' sons had married heiresses.[45] Thomas had explained away this unexpected finding by pointing out that his data, in ignoring portions, underestimated the proportion of marriages that were made for financial profit after the development of settlement. Apparently rejecting this explanation, Stone took Thomas's evidence at its face value. While persistent heiress-seeking had earlier marked the family, a fact he himself had underlined in his *Crisis of Aristocracy*, the eighteenth century had clearly seen its decline. "It was believed at one time that the pursuit

43. David Thomas, "The Social Origins of Marriage Partners of the British Peerage in the Eighteenth and Nineteenth Centuries," *Population Studies* 26 (1972): table 7.

44. Ibid., 105 n. 15.

45. Ibid., table 7.

of heiresses was intensifying," he noted. "It is now clear, however, that it was declining rapidly throughout the eighteenth century."[46] Thomas's data, which had been in table form, were converted into a dramatic graph in *Family, Sex and Marriage*, visual evidence of the arrival of marriage for love.[47]

Lawrence and Jeanne Stone together undertook a further analysis of marriage to heiresses. In *An Open Elite?* they produced a table, converting it into another dramatic graph, that shows that marriages between eldest sons and heiresses rose before 1700, reached a peak about that date, and thereafter notably fell.[48] For the eighteenth century, the Stones' graph and Thomas's are virtually identical, and the Stones stressed this fact. The only significant difference in the two graphs is that the Stones' extends back into the sixteenth and seventeenth centuries, where it shows a rising line as did *Crisis of Aristocracy*. The Stones' discussion of the graphs indicates that they were intent largely upon showing that Habakkuk had been right about there having been an age when the pursuit of heiresses had been on the rise. Habakkuk had, of course, put that age in the eighteenth century.

Taken all together, the evidence seemed to indicate that a high proportion of landowners had married heiresses about 1700, in the range of 36 to 42 percent, and that the proportion fell notably thereafter. Extensive statistical evidence thus seemed to point to a change in habits of marriage having taken place about the beginning of the eighteenth century. While aristocratic marriage had earlier been for financial profit, and had then apparently been increasingly so, in the eighteenth century it became for love.

Now that the earlier chapters of this book have outlined the history of the heiress, the question comes readily enough: Who were the heiresses being counted in these various graphs and tables? Were they actual heiresses, or were they heiresses-at-law? Obviously it would have made a great difference to the property at issue whether they were the one or the other. And obviously too the chance of marrying an actual heiress was very different from the chance of marrying an heiress-at-law. The numbers of the former were primarily determined by legal deeds, the numbers of the latter by biology. The meaning of all this statistical evidence then depends on the answer to this question.

Thomas made clear that he drew his data from genealogies, particularly

46. Stone, *Family, Sex and Marriage*, 718 n. 72.

47. Ibid., 319.

48. Lawrence Stone and Jeanne C. Fawtier Stone, *An Open Elite? England 1540–1880* (Oxford, 1984), 122–23.

from Burke's *Peerage*.[49] Peerage guides, of course, trace the descent of titles. While titles normally descend in tail male, sometimes they descend in tail general, going then to females by rules essentially those of the common law. The legal status of wives can thus in some cases have consequences for the inheritance of titles. Whether for this reason, or for some conception of the superior status that a daughter without brothers would have in her father's eyes, and presumably in the division of his property, peerage guides divide wives into their two classes as by common law, denominating them heiresses if they had no brother, otherwise simply daughters. There is no implication that family estates went with these heiresses, or even that land accompanied them.

Obviously it is essential to exemplify this genealogical usage, and particularly from Burke. To take what is a particularly telling example, Burke indicates that the second Viscount Portman married "the daughter and heiress of Viscount Milton." Viscount Milton, eldest son of the fifth Earl Fitzwilliam, never himself inherited, however, dying in the lifetime of his father, and the Fitzwilliam estates went to his younger brother and not to his daughter. The daughter then was heiress-at-law, and not actual heiress. In another example Burke indicates that the fifth Earl of Huntingdon married one of the coheiresses of the fifth Earl of Derby. But the sixth Earl of Derby was brother to the fifth, and the bulk of the estate went to him, not to the coheiresses. Similarly, the first Earl of Leicester is said to have married the coheiress of the sixth Earl of Thanet, but the estates went to the collateral male and not to the coheiresses. Leicester's eldest son married Lady Mary Campbell, described by Burke as coheiress of the Duke of Argyle, but the land of the Campbells certainly did not come with Lady Mary. The first Earl of Bradford and the first Earl of Burlington are respectively declared to have married the coheiress of the fourth Viscount Torrington and the heiress of the seventh Earl of Northampton, but in each case the estate went not to the heiress but to her uncle.

Sometimes of course the heiress-at-law was actual inheritor. When the third Earl Fitzwilliam married the coheiress of the second Marquis of Rockingham, he really married an heiress. The patriline of the marquisate was at an end, and through this marriage the Fitzwilliams came into possession of the great Wentworth Woodhouse estate. Likewise, when the sixth Duke of Somerset married the heiress of the eleventh Earl of Northumberland, he married a real heiress, gaining with her the ancient Percy inheritance, which was shortly to go to Sir Hugh Smithson through an-

49. Thomas, "Social Origins," 99.

other real heiress. So too the second Earl of Godolphin married a real heiress in Henrietta, daughter of the first Duke of Marlborough.

Burke's heiresses are then heiresses-at-law. Occasionally he slips up, which is to be expected in so vast a genealogical undertaking. Thus he declares that the seventh Earl of Carlisle married the coheiress of the fifth Duke of Devonshire, but the first Earl Granville, who married her sister, is said to have married only the duke's daughter. (Neither was real heiress. The Cavendish estates went not to the fifth duke's daughters but to his great-nephew.) But the principle in Burke's *Peerage* is clear, and it is to use the word "heiress" in its meaning of heir-at-law. Thomas's evidence, then, dependent as it is upon Burke, deals in heiresses-at-law, who sometimes inherited but usually did not.

The evidence presented by Stone in his *Crisis of Aristocracy* also deals with heiresses-at-law. There the heiresses are described as "heiresses of partial failure of the male line and of total failure."[50] The phrasing is cumbrous; and the meaning could be uncertain. Partial failure obviously refers to the situation where a man had a daughter or daughters but where he also had a collateral male relation. But were all daughters in that event counted heiresses, or only those who actually inherited? The meaning is made clear by the fact that Stone further notes that where there was a partial failure of the male line the heiress was likely to take what is called a large part of the estate, being as much as one-third of it. Obviously, then, all daughters of men who had no sons are included.[51] Thus the legal meaning is indisputable. The heiresses are all the daughters of men who had no sons, together with collaterally inheriting females in families where there were no males direct or indirect: heiresses-at-law.

The evidence in *An Open Elite?* about marriage to heiresses is also about heiresses-at-law. In discussing heiresses and this book, however, an important distinction needs to be made if confusion is to be avoided. As a rule, the heiresses in *An Open Elite?* are real heiresses. That the book as a rule deals with real heiresses is what makes it so important a contribution to inheritance studies. It provides information on actual successions by females in three English counties. And I am a beneficiary of the information on successions that it provides, having used it in chapter 1. But the evidence about marriage to heiresses in the book is another matter, and cannot but be another matter.[52]

---

50. Stone, *Crisis of Aristocracy*, 170–71, appendix 14, 769.
51. Ibid., 170.
52. There has been confused discussion on this subject. In a debate between Stone

The evidence on marriage to heiresses is based on the marriages of the male inheritors in the three counties.[53] These men would not have conveniently chosen their brides from the counties in which they lived. For much the greater part, the brides of these men would have come from families outside the three counties, and thus would have been from families outside the Stones' purview. (There were forty counties in England.) Genealogies would seem to have offered the only feasible way to determine the status of the brides. And genealogies mislead on the subject of heiresses.

Moreover, it is statistically impossible for the brides in the Stones' table on marriage to have been real heiresses. The table shows that at the crucial peak about 1700 more than one-third of eldest sons married "heiresses." Eldest sons being then 60 percent of the male population (for population was then stationary, a point that the Stones make at length), more than one-third of them could not have married heiresses who were real, not even if absolutely every real heiress had fallen to an eldest son. As other information provided by the Stones shows, actual heiresses made up only about 8 percent of the female population.[54] Finally, the virtual identity of the data on marriage presented by the Stones and by Thomas—an identity that the Stones emphasize—is hardly possible unless both sets of data were based on heiresses-at-law, not to mention the coherence of the set in *Crisis of Aristocracy* with that in *An Open Elite?* All the data we have, then, about marriage to heiresses is about marriage to heiresses-at-law, who sometimes inherited but usually did not.

Heiresses-at-law were, of course, common, and it is not surprising that many marriages were to heiresses so defined. In a stationary society one-third of daughters would have been directly heirs of their father, and when collateral inheritance is added to direct inheritance, about 40 percent of women would have been heiresses-at-law. There was nothing remarkable, then, in several generations of eldest sons in a row marrying "heiresses." And none of the evidence that has universally been assumed to indicate a

---

and myself on *An Open Elite?* I argued that the heiresses in the table on marriage were not real, but were heiresses-at law. Stone replied that the heiresses in the book were real. He misunderstood my point. I did not doubt that the heiresses in the book were as a rule real. I was concerned only with those in one table, that on marriage to heiresses (and its graph). Since I had been severely limited for space in which to reply in that debate, this confusion has not until now been cleared up. For the debate see *Albion* 17 (1985): 149–80, 393–96.

53. Stone and Stone, *An Open Elite?*, 123, table 4.3.

54. Ibid., table 4.2.

high degree of heiress-seeking around the eighteenth century actually does so, or even indicates heiress-seeking at all. About 1700 population was stationary, and the apparently dramatic peak about that date for marriages to "heiresses" that appears in all the various studies actually indicates that landowners were marrying women who were heiresses-at-law almost exactly in proportion to their numbers in the population.

The falling line of the graphs for the eighteenth century represents demographic movement, as does the rising line for the late seventeenth century. As population rose in the eighteenth century, the number of heiresses in the population fell, and with it obviously the chance any man had of marrying one. Contrariwise for the preceding period, a period when population fell somewhat below replacement level.

The fall in the eighteenth century also represents another factor that may well be mentioned in passing in order to avoid possible puzzlement, for the rate of marriage to heiresses falls ultimately to levels that are too low to be accounted for by rising population. The explanation lies again in legal terminology. The word "heiress," like the word "heir," strictly speaking belongs only to real property. There is no heir to personal property, which is divided at common law among children or other relatives as the case might be. As landowners came to marry the daughters of men who had no pretensions to be landed—businessmen and professionals who had not inherited land and who had not, or had not yet, purchased land—they came to marry women who could not be denominated heiresses even when they were daughters who had no brothers. But this is by the way.

What the evidence does not show is a change of attitude to marriage, though that is what it has been accepted as showing. The theory that marriage had increasingly been a matter of pursuing heiresses in the eighteenth century, or that it had been such a matter in the seventeenth century and had ceased to be in the eighteenth—whichever—has thus not been proved by these demographic investigations. The would-be proof has collapsed in the recognition that there has been confusion in the use of the word "heiress."

Both Stone and Habakkuk have been pioneers, the one in the history of landed estates, the other in the history of the family. If the maps they have drawn have turned out to be imperfect guides to navigation, that is often true of the maps of pioneers. But pioneers point to new worlds for investigation that would otherwise remain unexplored. Habakkuk raised questions about the history of landed estates and the problem of family indebtedness. Stone has helped open a major new field in history, the history of the family, and has attempted to show when the family took the form known in the West today. The questions that historians have since been investigating are those that Habakkuk and Stone raised, and all historians owe them a debt of gratitude.

Nevertheless, considering together the theories that have been constructed about inheritance, and the evidence that has been offered about the pattern of marriage, it must be concluded that historians have failed to see a drama around females that did take place, while they have created one that on the evidence offered did not. Both the drama missed—the loss of female property—and the drama created—great change in marriage habits—are curiously connected. Both arise from misperception about the heiress, from seeing her indirectly as an object of pursuit while neglecting to look at her directly as a person.

3

Although the data examined above do not prove what they have been held to prove, they are valuable if looked at in a new way. Do they actually go to show that marriage in the aristocracy has been essentially misunderstood? Do they show that it was not as a rule directed to financial profit? An answer to this question would flesh out the portrait of the aristocratic family that I have given in this work, which has not said anything directly about the ground on which marriages were made, although it has by implication discounted the importance of interfamily competition in determining the division of property. Even the strict settlement, which has been emphasized to be a marriage settlement, has been seen as essentially an agreement between father and son that predetermined inheritance matters within the family, thus avoiding the will of a single person. Marriage has been seen as the necessary occasion of the deed within the family. The question whether marriage was for love or profit might well be pursued further.

Perhaps only evidence about the marriages of women who had actually inherited and of those whose succession could be perceived to be certain at the time of their marriage could really indicate whether aristocratic marriage was for profit. Then again such evidence might mislead, for the women concerned would be so small a part of the population. An initially good case can be made, on the data that have been supplied in the theories discussed above, that marriage was not generally for profit. Heiresses-at-law often had larger portions than other daughters, and marriage to them may thus after all be an index to marriage for profit. In this case the fact that eldest sons married heiresses-at-law only in proportion to their numbers in the population at the critical peak of the data seems evidence itself that marriage was not subordinated in landed society to the augmentation of estates.

But quite so simple a proof may not carry much conviction. Most heiresses-at-law would end up postponed, and a question as to their value must have arisen for the aristocratic young man tempted to seek profit in marriage. Did the postponed heiress, which was likely to be what he ended up with, bring enough more than the ordinary daughter to be worth pursuing? A more convincing argument might paradoxically lie in the smallness of the post-poned heiress's provision despite the fact that it was larger than that of the ordinary daughter. One could risk too much for too little, in other words.

Some perspective on the difference between the portions of the two sorts of daughters, at least under settlement, is to be gained from Gilbert Horsman's precedents. Not all Horsman's precedents allow comparison to be made. Like all compilers of precedent books, Horsman intended to illustrate for the benefit of juniors in the profession the forms through which they might meet the legal needs of a variety of clients. Some of his marriage settlements are thus agreements for second marriages; some are in tail general; some are complicated by unusual considerations; some involve both land and personal property. Eight are clearly settlements made by owners of substantial land and are in tail male, and these allow comparison, for they set out portions for the two sorts of daughters: for postponed heiresses on the one hand, and for younger children on the other hand, among whom ordinary daughters fell.

Comparison has to be made in two ways. Settlements laid out portions on sliding scales, both for younger children and for postponed heiresses (for daughters if no son survived, as the wording runs). In both cases a top limit was set for a generation of children, but in the case of postponed heiresses a sole child received an unusually large portion. The scales have to be compared, then, as to their top limits, and as to the portions for an only heiress and for an only ordinary daughter. When the top limits in Horsman's precedents are compared, little difference is apparent. In five out of the eight precedents the limit for a generation that consisted of daughters only is the same as the limit for a generation of younger children. In two the limit increases by 50 percent, and in one by 33 percent. For an only heiress, however, the difference is more substantial. One precedent grants a lone heiress double the portion of a lone ordinary daughter. All but one grant her over 50 percent more than a lone ordinary daughter, and that one grants her almost 50 percent more.[55]

55. Gilbert Horsman, *Precedents in Conveyancing*, 2d ed. (London, 1757). The marriage settlements analyzed are those numbered 1, 2, 3, 4, 8, 9, 12, and 21.

Given what we have learned about the low level of younger children's portions in relation to estate value, these portions for sole heiresses, though they involve an increase, may well have been insufficient to trigger heiress-seeking on the scale that has been portrayed. It must be allowed, however, that a lone heiress might attract attention if her father's estate was great, and thus her portion was large relative to the run of estates. Coheiresses, if they numbered three or more, would seem often to have been reduced to the same portions as ordinary daughters. Thus the smallness of most heiresses' portions rather than the fact that they were larger than those of other daughters might be held proof that marriage was not directed to profit.

A. P. W. Malcomson early speculated that aristocratic marriage in the eighteenth century had been misunderstood on the ground that the scale of women's property had been exaggerated. He drew the conclusion in large part from a consideration of terminology. He recognized "inexact use of the word 'heiress,'" and although he did not notice the common law and thus missed the full implications of what lay behind the confused usage, he pointed to a resulting inflation of ideas about the extent of women's property. Women called heiresses often brought no land with them. He also pointed to the use in the seventeenth and eighteenth centuries of the word "fortune" as a synonym for the word "portion." "Fortune," he noted, "has an inflationary ring about it."[56] Again, it tends to encourage exaggerated ideas of the importance of women's property. Settlements, Malcomson foresightfully concluded, gave little scope for dynastic advancement, and aristocratic husbands, recognizing this, sensibly opted for the marriage for love.[57]

The evidence from the period before the strict settlement offers even stronger proof of landowners' marriage principles. Before the strict settlement heiresses, though postponed, stood out more conspicuously from ordinary daughters than they later did. Fathers could control the distribution of their estates, and husbands could have much larger effect upon the property that was to come their wives' way. That peers before the coming of settlement married heiresses only in proportion to their number in the population is rather convincing evidence that seeking profit was not the main object in marriage.

The work of Alan Macfarlane gives further reason to believe that this was so, and his work deserves more than passing consideration here. (Alan Macfarlane is not to be confused, of course, with K. B. McFarlane, who has

56. Malcomson, *Pursuit of the Heiress*, 4.
57. Ibid., 49.

also appeared in these pages.) Macfarlane, like Stone, has provided a great general history of the English family, although the two histories differ fundamentally. Since Macfarlane declared at the outset an intention to concentrate on the lower classes, it might be thought that nothing could be said of his work here. Whatever his intention, however, not only does the upper class figure prominently in his book, but also the theory he advances has general applicability.

Macfarlane drew his inspiration from the work of demographers, and discussion of it must begin with the important discovery made by John Hajnal. In 1965 Hajnal drew attention to the peculiar pattern of marriage that prevailed in northwestern Europe, a pattern he found to be "unique for all large populations for which data exist or for which reasonable surmises can be made."[58] Ever since the sixteenth century, people in northwestern Europe had married at an unusually late age, and a considerable number had never married. In all other societies, women were married off shortly after they reached puberty, and marriage was virtually universal.

Hajnal's discovery has sent sparks flying in several directions. It forms the basis of the work of Peter Laslett, E. A. Wrigley, and the school of demographers centered upon Cambridge, who have worked it up into a theory of economic development. Delayed marriage and low nuptiality meant comparatively low fertility and a favorable balance between population and resources. In a society with such a marriage pattern wealth could accumulate, and the spirit of innovation could be unleashed. Societies where young marriage was the norm lived from hand to mouth, and their history was a recurrent cycle of explosive population growth followed by famine and disease. This new perception about the historical pattern of marriage has entailed the abandonment of traditional thinking about economic growth, and particularly about the causes of the Industrial Revolution. Traditionally it had been held that the decline of the death rate, brought about by improved medicine in the eighteenth century, had allowed population to grow, and the resulting expansion of the market had caused the Industrial Revolution. Things are now reversed. Low fertility, which was apparently especially low in England, allowed for the accumulation of capital, and thus for the Industrial Revolution, which then permitted sustained population growth.[59] The English family has thus been given crucial historical significance.

58. John Hajnal, "European Marriage Patterns in Perspective," in *Population in History*, ed. D. V. Glass and D. E.C. Eversley (London, 1965), 101–43.

59. E. A. Wrigley, *Continuity, Chance and Change* (Cambridge, 1988).

Macfarlane formulated his theory in the light of this thinking, adding to it the insights of an anthropologist with wide experience of different societies. He emphasizes two things. First, late marriage is almost by definition marriage by choice. Mature children cannot be married off at their parents' behest, as children little beyond puberty may be. The companionate marriage is thus not an invention of the eighteenth century but is far older. Macfarlane believes that it goes back beyond the thirteenth century in England. As parish registers, the source of the statistics as to age of marriage, do not exist before the sixteenth century, this belief is speculative. Macfarlane also emphasizes that late marriage indicates a loving and responsible attitude to the family. He believes indeed that a high age of marriage develops only in legal systems based on private property, for such systems, unlike tribal or peasant communal systems of property, force prudence in the founding of families. People must have property of their own before they can marry. They thus undertake marriage only when they can provide an acceptable standard of living for a family; and having postponed gratification, they expect to find in marriage companionship and love. Macfarlane thus argues that the accumulative ethic and romantic love developed hand in hand. In his account, English family life has long been much as we know it, based on affection between husbands and wives and between parents and children. The contrast with Stone's account, which stresses change from age to age, is obvious.

If the aristocracy married late, its family life should more or less follow the pattern Macfarlane has laid out. The idea is a general one: late marriage has emotional implications for the life of the family. The idea is about the effect that maturation has upon the spirit of independence of children. While there may be debate about certain aspects of Macfarlane's theory, the significance of age of marriage can scarcely be doubted.

We have some figures for age of marriage for different classes in England. In the early seventeenth century mean age of marriage for the population as a whole was twenty-seven for men and twenty-four for women. For the gentry, it was twenty-seven for men and twenty-three for women; and for the peerage, about twenty-five for men and twenty for women.[60] While the figures for the gentry and peerage are somewhat lower than those for the general population, they are hardly so low that children could have been readily married off at their parents' command, particularly not sons, who were in their mid-twenties, and who are the children often portrayed as compelled to marry against their wishes in dynastic interests.

Macfarlane never mentions age of marriage for the aristocracy, and it is

60. Peter Laslett, *The World We Have Lost*, 2d ed. (New York, 1971), 86.

obvious that he hesitates to include the class in his theory. Among the reasons he gives for his intention to emphasize the lower classes is that marriages in the gentry and aristocracy were not made out of affection between bride and groom, but were "more like alliances, arranged between kin groups."[61] He begins, then, with the accepted interpretation of aristocratic marriage, at least with what is the interpretation accepted of the period before the eighteenth century. Nevertheless much of his evidence comes from the upper classes; and this can hardly be avoided, for upper-class families are the only ones to have left substantial records. Time and again Macfarlane has to acknowledge his dependence upon evidence from the upper classes. Quoting affectionate letters written between husbands and wives in the seventeenth century, he notes that "almost all" were written by members of the gentry.[62] Pointing to family affection exhibited in diaries and autobiographies, he acknowledges that these sources are rare for the lower levels of society and nonexistent before the seventeenth century.[63] Even his discussion of family economics begins with the use of aristocratic portions as a measuring stick.[64] Pointing to the themes of love in English drama and poetry, he notes that almost the whole of English literature was written by members of the upper classes.[65] Quotations frequently are from upper-class persons—the Duchess of Newcastle, Lady Mary Wortley Montagu, Lord Burghley, Viscount and Viscountess Lisle, Lady Brilliana Harvey, the Pastons, and the Verneys.

There is in Macfarlane's theory, then, almost in spite of himself, added reason to think that marriage in the gentry and aristocracy has been much misperceived and that it was generally based on affection and was deter-

61. Alan Macfarlane, *Marriage and Love in England, 1300–1840* (Oxford, 1986), 46.

62. Ibid., 192.

63. Ibid., 143.

64. Ibid., 264. To compare portions in the aristocracy with "marriage portions" in the lower classes is to compare apples and oranges. In the first case, while a portion was paid upon a child's marriage, it generally represented the child's inheritance, its small fraction of the family's property; in the second case, the portion was merely a gift upon marriage. The real portion of a child in the middle class was an equitable share of the family's property (unless father aspired to have his family join the gentry). Middle-class children could not receive their share of the family property at marriage—not unless their fathers were dead or were prepared to commit the folly of King Lear. It is therefore hard to see what the point of comparing "marriage portions" in the different classes is; and Macfarlane seems concerned only to show that people required property from some source before undertaking marriage in a system of law based on private property.

65. Ibid., 189.

mined upon by the partners themselves. It may, of course, be true that aristocratic marriages were once alliances arranged by the kin, but all the data we have would suggest that, if so, this must have been prior to the sixteenth century.

There have, to be sure, been some dramatic cases of the exploitation of children's marriages for family or paternal advancement. That great lawyer and unpleasant man, Sir Edward Coke, gained part of his reputation for harshness through his exploitation of his daughter's marriage. Having been dismissed as Lord Chief Justice, he sought to regain royal favor by forcing the unwilling girl, then aged fourteen, to marry the brother of the Duke of Buckingham, King James's special favorite.[66] (Christopher Hill gives a wonderful vignette of the man Coke.)[67] Or there is the extraordinary pattern of marriages in the family of the fourth Duke of Norfolk. That Norfolk's three sons married his three stepdaughters, who had become coheirs to the Dacre estates with the death of their young brother, can hardly be credited to romantic love. But these cases were doubtfully typical. They would seem rather to have been commented on in their own day, and remembered since, because they were abnormal.

All in all, there would seem to be good reason to think that the profit motive in aristocratic marriage has, at least, been greatly exaggerated. Any portion in five figures has often enough been taken to prove that the marriage revolved around it, and words like "huge," "staggering," and "extravagant" sprinkle discussions of aristocratic portions without the portions' being assessed against estate value. Straight-faced references to "the marriage market" are common, and R. B. Outhwaite has explicitly compared aristocratic marriage to a business operation. Showing, from Hollingsworth's data on the peerage, that there was in the sixteenth and seventeenth centuries a shortage of males in the population, he puts this together with the then rise of daughters' portions, deeming shortage and rise simple cause and effect. With a shortage of possible husbands women had to be better endowed if they were not to end old maids. Aristocratic marriage had the essential character of any business, being a matter of supply and demand, and with a shortage of husbands their price had risen.[68]

66. S. R. Gardiner, *Prince Charles and the Spanish Marriage 1617–1623* (London, 1869), 1:93–109; Catherine Drinker Bowen, *The Lion and the Throne: The Life and Times of Sir Edward Coke* (Boston, 1956), 398–411.

67. Christopher Hill, *Intellectual Origins of the English Revolution* (Oxford, 1965), 225–27.

68. R. B. Outhwaite, "Marriage as Business," in *Business Life and Public Policy*, ed. Neil McKendrick and R. B. Outhwaite (Cambridge, 1986), 21–37.

Outhwaite attempts to convert what is certainly a chronological correlation into a causal one by adducing a few quotations about the nature of aristocratic marriage. Leaving aside the adequacy of this procedure, the real objection to his line of reasoning is one that by now it is almost tedious to mention. Once again there is a failure to separate the two classes of women. Outhwaite reasons that female property had to rise as women competed for husbands in a demographic situation where there was a shortage of males. The property of those women who were heiresses-at-law, however, fell. These women were no small part of the population, and their property had been falling over the long term, and through what must have been various demographic fluctuations. Inheritance in the aristocracy was not determined mechanically by these fluctuations, but by landowners' evolving social ideas and by the development of legal means for better effecting those ideas.

It is true, of course, that marriage to actual heiresses has had much to do with the success of those families who have conspicuously grown over the centuries. Estate histories cannot fail to notice the importance of inheritances gained through females in greatly successful families: the Russells, the Fitzwilliams, the Cavendish-Bentincks, and the Spencers, to mention a few. Most notable of the lot were the Grosvenors, who became among the richest families in the world through a marriage in the seventeenth century to Mary Davies, heiress actually to no extensive lands but to the manor of Ebury, five hundred acres on the then outskirts of London on which Mayfair was to rise. Given the uncertainty of life until recent times, however, as well as the difficulty a man would have had in knowing who would turn out to be an actual heiress in a society intent on reducing heiresses as far as possible, it cannot be assumed that the results were ordinarily anything but demographic good luck.

To conclude that aristocratic marriage was not generally a grasping for dynastic advancement by no means implies that landowners had not dynastic ends to be served. That they had has been the burden of this book. The conclusion actually highlights the way in which they found their dynastic interests best served. This was in a more certain and straightforward way than by trying to control marriage. They found their dynastic interests best served by securing the patriline and seeing that as little property as humanely possible was put at risk in marriage. That was the rational way to preserve estates, and names, and titles.

Within reason marriage might be left to take care of itself. Keeping marriage within reason does not require draconian measures. As sociologists tell us, marriage tends naturally to be endogamous. Historians may discuss whether marriage in the peerage was endogamous, and find that it was not. But this is because peerage and gentry were always one intermarrying group, having in common the landowning way of life. Or historians may notice the widening of the circle within which marriage became acceptable for landowners, and find that ultimately landed families ceased to be an endogamous group. But this is merely to point to the blurring of the distinction between landed and commercial wealth that grew to be acceptable on both sides. The point is that marriage is always endogamous if the word is used to mean that marriage is normally confined within the bounds of class ideas of the day. The heir to a landed estate was not about to marry the publican's daughter, nor his sister to marry the village shoemaker. Education and manners ensured that such marriages would be few and far between. No doubt parents sought to keep an eye on their children's associates—when do they not?—and no doubt they made clear that this or that person was not suitable. The misalliance was always deprecated, but it was hardly a threat that required parents to control their children's choice of spouse in the manner that has been imagined.

4

As the landed family's history has become clearer, a final question must arise, a really fundamental one: What implications does the history of this family have for the history of the English family in general? Or does it have any? Historians have heavily depended upon this family in forming their judgments, because it is the only one about which we have much detailed or intimate knowledge, as Macfarlane's difficulties in trying to reach to the lower classes go to show. Though it was not the typical English family, we must, under the circumstances, hope that its history has some general meaning. And I would submit that it has.

Two simple points may be made, but they are in different ways crucial. First, the long-term history of landowners' interaction with the common law would suggest that they have always been concerned for their families. It is family concerns that made for the gamut of legal inventions. There was no desire for perpetuities at all costs; nor was there any consistent desire for freedom of alienation; nor, above all, was there any discovery of the family with the strict settlement. There is no way of making a coherent story of English real property law unless through the family. To be sure, there are two aspects to this family story, but one is a constant affective concern that all members of the nuclear family be provided for. Even so patriarchal a family as that of the gentry and aristocracy was not devoid of love. Its history demonstrates this over centuries and in the hard evidence of legal developments.

The nuclear, loving family, then, is not a development of the eighteenth century but is of long standing, even in the aristocracy.

But if this form of family is to be recognized as nuclear and loving, it cannot be seen as egalitarian, or to the historiographical point, it cannot even be seen as moving in the direction of equality between males and females—not in the eighteenth century, and not in earlier centuries. Many of the very families whose affectionate words are quoted by Macfarlane were busy cutting down heiresses and destroying dower. Macfarlane does not recognize this development any more than other family theorists have done. Though he differs fundamentally from his predecessors on the subject of affection in the family, on the subject of inheritance by females he follows them. Thus he too points to rising portions in the eighteenth century, and once again Lady Anne Clifford does her inappropriate turn upon the stage.[69] The attempt to make love and property in gentry and aristocratic families run in step with one another is fraught with difficulties.

And this inegalitarian movement also has its general meaning. It goes beyond the confines of the gentry and aristocracy, for when a middle-class family became wealthy, it often bought land and promoted itself into the gentry. Significantly, a common phrase was that "it made an eldest son." The result was that gentry rules, primogenitive and patrilineal rules, tended in effect to be the ones applicable to large accumulations of property.

It might even be suggested—perhaps a bit cynically—that what a society thinks about equality between males and females is best observed in the division of property it makes in families where there is property surplus to the standard of living considered necessary to allow for marriage and the formation of new families. On this conception, the more egalitarian division of property that marked ordinary English families would to a considerable extent represent socially conceived necessity rather than any deep belief in the equality of men and women.

Be this line of reasoning as it may, middle-class principles in practice often did not outlast a family's rise to wealth. The persistent migration of wealthy professional men and, later, businessmen into the landed gentry indicates the second rule of English family life. If the first was that the nuclear family would be cared for, the second was that large property belonged to males.

69. Macfarlane, *Marriage and Love*, 281, 269, 289.

7   Conclusion

    This study began with the heiress-at-law as inheritor, and it has ended with her as matrimonial object. In the course of discussion many aspects of real property law and of the family life of large landowners have come under review. Extensive reappraisals of accepted ideas would seem in one way and another to have become necessary. This final chapter brings together the major conclusions that have been reached in the course of the discussion, and as well briefly notes some implications that lie in them but have not been discussed.

The conclusions that have been reached in this work all derive from a way of treating real property law in which a driving force for change is seen as lying in family concerns. While this way of treating real property law is not entirely new, it has not hitherto been carried out with consistency. Finding the heiress-at-law to be a neglected subject, this work began with her, which meant by definition considering her history against the common law rule of descent applicable to her. The idea naturally followed that other family members, widows and younger children, should be considered against the common law rules applicable to them. Not only was the family thus placed in the center of landowners' legal history, but the signal fact became evident that England maintained rules of succession to real property that no class of landowner could have thought satisfactory and that all sought in varying degrees to escape. Down to 1925—for eight hundred years—England maintained rules of inheritance that never had any real constituency in the community, apart from the Crown. And by 1660 they had lost even that. The realistic way of treating landowners' legal history, it became clear, was to treat it as the working out of objections to the common law rules of inheritance.

All landowners, whether their estates were large or small, objected to the utter disinheritance of their younger children, and all of them took to uses, seeking thereby freedom to will property as they chose. The ultimate appearance of the Statute of Wills, which allowed younger children to be openly provided for by will, no doubt largely removed the objections of small landowners to the rules of succession. If English law came early to embody the concept of property freely alienable, it was in large part because the common law, unlike feudal law on the Continent, had in the first place paid no heed to the simplest of family needs. Maitland made the connection between the strictness of English primogeniture and freedom of alienation, perceiving that the latter must come in the wake of the former; and he noted that England and France differed both as to strictness of primogeniture and as to freedom of alienation.

This perception, it may be noted in passing, has implications for Alan Macfarlane's theory of the origins of English individualism. In his book on that subject Macfarlane regularly stresses the early existence of freedom of alienation in England as proof that England had a more individualistic spirit than other nations, that from an early time its people were devoted to commerce and free enterprise. Given Macfarlane's theory of family history, it is curious that he should so fail to recognize why freedom of alienation came early to England. While freedom of alienation is no doubt essential to the development of commerce and capitalism, given the family reasons English landowners had for desiring it, its mere existence hardly supports the weight Macfarlane has placed upon it.[1]

The history of large landowners is more complex than that of small landowners. It has also been less perceived, despite having been far more discussed. Large landowners have been the focus of legal texts, and they are the class upon whom theories of the family have been based. Appreciating their history has thus dual significance, important in itself and even more so in its ramifications. Large landowners had, or came to have with the development of surnames and titles in tail male, further objections to the common law. The succession of females meant that land wandered from name and title—in landowners' eyes, "went out of the family." Heiresses

1. Alan Macfarlane, *The Origins of English Individualism* (Oxford, 1978). Macfarlane recognizes that large landowners were not commercially oriented, that they were not interested in buying and selling but desired instead to preserve their estates. He specifically limits his theory to landowners owning fewer than fifty acres (110n.). Yet large landowners had also sought freedom of alienation against the common law—a fact that itself suggests that the demand for it had little to do with the spirit of free enterprise.

were biologically common, and as the law of succession allowed females to succeed where there was no son, estates often fell at law to women. The history of real property law has been much influenced by the desire of large landowners to ensure the patrilineal, rather than lineal, inheritance of estates. It has been the common failure among historians to recognize that patrilineal principles were not embodied in the law of succession, but had to be achieved, that has led to the trend of female inheritance being got wrong.

Accordingly, the first and major conclusion of this work is that female inheritance declined. Even if it should come to be emphasized that large landowners were but a fraction of the landed population, and if it should be found that female successions did not decline among small landowners—which is quite likely—the trend of female inheritance would even then not be upward, though that the trend was upward has been a virtually constant belief. In other words, no distinction between large and small landowners will make female successions actually rise, nor make historians' perceptions correct.

Second, putting the family in the center of real property law has not only made clear what landowners' inheritance principles were, but has also brought a fuller understanding of various legal instruments. The entail particularly has been shown to have had dual aspects about it that made its employment problematic for landowners, and has made it problematic for historians' discussions as well. The use too has been shown to have dual aspects, not being simply a means of providing for younger children. Above all, it has been made clear that Bridgman in the strict settlement found a practical means of ensuring the patriline. The strict settlement has thus been put into estate and family history in a coherent way, demonstrated to be a patrilineal and primogenitive device that preserved estates by limiting charges for subordinate members of the family.

This fuller understanding of the strict settlement has implications for a question that has been the center of much historical debate: Did settlement do more than preserve estates? Did it make for the growth of large estates? "Large" in this context, it is to be emphasized, means large relative to the run of gentry and aristocratic estates. The question involves a division within the class of large landowners. It was a desire to account for a growth of large estates, believed to have taken place in the eighteenth century, that provided the inspiration for Habakkuk's seminal thinking about aristocratic marriage and legal change. The question whether large estates—large in this intraclass sense—grew in the eighteenth century has not, however, been discussed in this work, which has been concerned with the class as a whole, aiming to gets its general history straight before all else. Nevertheless, important things can be said about the growth of large estates in the intraclass sense as a result of this work.

Such estates could certainly not have grown in the manner that has been alleged. Allegedly women were better portioned under settlement; and in a competitive marriage market large landowners were at an advantage and, to the increase of their estates, married up the women who had the largest portions. The concept is of increasing female inheritance with the strict settlement.

In stressing the growth of patrilineal principles, however, this work has theoretically opened up a different way in which large estates may have grown. If large landowners took to patrilineal principles earlier than their lesser brethren within what was an intermarrying class, they protected themselves (so far as biologically possible) against the loss or disintegration of their estates through heiresses, while absorbing through marriage the estates of those who had not protected themselves. Since some landowners, certainly peers, would have taken to patrilineal principles earlier than others, such a differential may well for some time have existed in practice.

This is to propose a completely different family scenario, however, than that which has occupied historical thinking, and the difference needs to be well recognized. Indeed the two scenarios require to be contrasted. There is no increase of female inheritance in the now proposed one, but a differential rate of decline in female inheritance; nor is there any necessity in it for the psychological overtones that have, one suspects, made the earlier scenario so popular, where women are virtually bought and sold. Moreover, the growth of large estates that would have taken place in the now proposed scenario would not be associable with the eighteenth century and the strict settlement but, as logic would require, with earlier times and with the absence of the strict settlement. It would seem that under settlement only the lowest ranks of the gentry continued to allow heiresses to succeed. In earlier centuries, before patrilineal principles were firmly and generally established, the existence of a greater differential with greater consequences for land transfer is to be entertained. The point is that if large estates are postulated to have grown by the operation of a differential practice of patrilineage—an idea I throw out for discussion—the theory must be contrasted with the one involving increase of female inheritance that has run through the historiography of estates and families to much general confusion. Other than the fact that both center on female inheritance, there is no connection between the two.

A third conclusion of this work concerns the role of equity in women's history, which cannot be seen as a simple supporter of women's rights. Equity set aside common law rules; but as the objections to the common law had been of various kinds, so equity's interventions had various meanings, by no means all of them favorable to women. While the Chancellor's support of uses had early made possible provision for children by will, it had also made possible the destruction of dower and thirds. While equity later made possible settlements to the use of married women, thus setting aside the common law rules that a wife's personal property, and the use of her landed property, went to her husband, it also supported strict settlements that more efficiently disherisoned heiresses. The conspicuous nineteenth-century struggle over married women's property has obscured earlier developments and caused equity to be more associated with women's rights than is warranted. It is even likely that settlements to the use of a married woman were originally made necessary by the destruction of thirds. Although this last is but a speculation, there is no doubt that equity played a two-sided role in women's history. When equity's effects on widows and married women are balanced, it is doubtful that the eighteenth century saw legal advance for women, even for those in small landed families or in families who owned only personal property, let alone those in the families of large landowners.

Finally, looking at the development of real property law in family terms has provided certain insights into the family's emotional history, and especially into the history of the companionate marriage. It is clear that great landowners always had concern for the members of their nuclear families, and that their children and wives were as a rule never casually or indifferently treated. Perhaps this ought always to have been taken for granted, but since it has not been, it is worthy of remark. It would also seem that so far back as the fifteenth century marriage in landed society was not primarily determined by dynastic and financial aims. Data that have been held to prove a change in habits of marriage about the beginning of the eighteenth century have upon analysis collapsed, being based on confusion about the word "heiress." Actual inheritance by an "heiress" cannot be assumed to have taken place upon the wording of genealogies. Changes in the proportion of marriages to "heiresses" that have so impressed historians, first in one direction and then in the opposite, actually mirror demographic movements. Moreover, the data suggest on further analysis that continuity of attitude is what is displayed, a continuity that conflicts with long-held notions about landowners' marital principles. Not that equality ever entered the minds of large landowners. Marriage could be left to young couples themselves because the reliable way to preserve names and titles and estates was to limit the amount of property at risk of transfer through marriage.

The family story that becomes apparent thus had contradictory strands woven into it. Two very general principles significant for women's history are to be drawn from it. On the one hand, even great landowners with patrilineal principles always had concern for the members of their nuclear families. On the other hand, of growing importance was the principle that where property was large, where property entailed social consequence, it should go to male heirs.

All in all, whether one considers the history of the family, or the development of legal principles, or the economy of landed estates, a good many received ideas must change when female interests are taken proper account of in the history of real property.

Appendixes

Abstract of a Strict Settlement by Orlando Bridgman

Abbreviated and annotated by the present author from Bridgman's *Conveyances*, 2d ed. (London, 1689), 195–211:

THIS INDENTURE made between W.P. of the one part and H.S. and F.S., Son and Heir apparent of the said H.S., of the other part; [is made because] a Marriage is to be shortly hereafter solemnized between the said W.P. and S.S. Daughter of the said H.S.	The parties and the occasion
NOW THIS INDENTURE WITNESSETH, that in Consideration of the said Marriage and of the Sum of 3000£ to the said W.P. in hand paid by the said H.S. for the Marriage-portion of the said S.S. his Daughter [the said W.P. settles his Manors, Lands, Hereditaments, etc., excepting a part to be held by himself in fee, as follows:]	In consideration of the marriage and of the portion of £3,000, W.P. settles his land, exempting a part, as follows:
To the use and behoof of the said W.P. for and during the Term of his Natural Life, then	To W.P. for life
To the use and behoof [of a named person] upon Trust only, for preserving the contingent Uses and Estates herein after limited, and to make Entries for the same, if it shall be needful	Trust to preserve contingent remainders
And from and immediately after the death of the said W.P. to the intent and purpose that the said S.S. shall and may have for and during all the Term of her natural life, for and in	Jointure of £400 in lieu of dower

the Name of her Joynture, and in full re-
compence, lieu, and satisfaction of all the
Dower which she may, or otherwise might
claim, have, or challenge in all or any the
Manors, Lands, Hereditaments, [etc.] of the
said W.P., her intended Husband, one Annuity or yearly Rent-charge of 400£ [a trust is
accordingly established]

Then from and immediately after the Decease
of him the said W.P. *To the use* and behoof
of the first Son of the said W.P. on the Body
of the said S.S. to be begotten, and the Heirs
males of the Body of such first Son lawfully
to be begotten; and for default of such Issue,
To the use and behoof of the second Son of
the said W.P. on the Body of the said S.S. to
be begotten, and the Heirs males of the Body
of such second Son lawfully to be begotten;
[and so forth to the third, fourth, tenth and
all other Sons]

After the death of W.P. to
the first son of the marriage
in tail, and to the other sons
in order

And for default of such Issue, *To the use* of
[named trustees] for 99 years upon such
Trusts as are herein after to be mentioned

In default of sons, a trust
for 99 years, its purpose set
out below

Then to the use of the Heirs male of the body
of the said W.P. lawfully to be begotten

Then to W.P's issue male
by any other marriage

And for default of such Issue, *To the use* and
behoof of E.P. Brother of the said W.P. for
and during the Term of the natural life of
him, the said E.P.

If W.P. should have no issue male, then to E.P., his
brother, for life

And from and after his Decease, *To the use*
and behoof of the first Son of the said E.P.
lawfully begotten, and of the Heirs males of
the Body of such first Son lawfully to be begotten; and for default of such Issue, To the

After the death of E.P. to
his first son in tail, and so
to the others in order

use and behoof of the second Son of the said
E.P. lawfully to be begotten, and of the Heirs
males of the Body of such second Son; [and
so forth to the third, fourth, tenth, and all
other sons of E.P.]

And it is hereby declared that the said Term
aforesaid limited unto trustees for 99 years is
upon this special Trust and Confidence that in
case the said W.P. shall have any one or
more Daughter or Daughters, begotten on the
Body of the said S.S. then [the trustees] shall
by such means as to them shall seem meet,
levy and raise Monies for the Portion or Portions of such daughters as herein after mentioned (that is to say) *In case* there shall be
one such Daughter and no more, then the
Sum of 4,000£ shall be levied and raised for
the Portion of such one Daughter; And in
case there shall be two such Daughters, and
no more, then the Sum of 5,000£ shall be levied and raised for the Portions of such two
Daughters to be equally divided between
them; And if there shall be three or more
such Daughters, then the Sum of 6,000£ shall
be levied or raised for the Portions of such
three or more Daughters, to be equally divided amongst all such Daughters, Which said
Portion or Portions shall be paid unto such
Daughter or Daughters, at the day or days of
her or their respective Marriage or Marriages,
or at her or their respective Age or Ages of
21 years, whichsoever shall happen first.

The purpose of the 99-year
trust set out. It is to provide
portions for the daughters
of the marriage between
W.P. and S.S., but not for
all such daughters, since the
trust arises only in "default
of sons." The portions are
for the daughters, heiresses-
at-law, who are postponed
by the grant to W.P.'s
brother and his issue male.
(Portions would also be
payable to the daughters of
S.S. should W.P. have a
son by a later wife, al-
though such daughters
would not be heiresses-at-
law to W.P.)

APPENDIX B

Two Examples of Settlements to the

Separate Use of a Married Woman

An eighteenth-century deed in which a father gives an annuity charged on land. From Gilbert Horsman, *Precedents in Conveyancing*, 2d ed. (London, 1757), 1:23:

> [Land is conveyed to trustees upon trust that they shall] from and after the Decease of the said [father], by and out of the Rents, Issues and Profits of the said Capital Messuage, Lands, Hereditaments and Premises, pay and cause to be paid for and during the natural Life of [daughter] one Annuity, yearly Rent or Sum of 40£ of like Money, by four quarterly payments unto such Person or Persons and for such Uses and Purposes . . . as [daughter], notwithstanding her Coverture, and whether she shall be sole or married, shall by any Writing or Writings under her Hand from Time to Time shall direct or appoint, to the Intent that the same may not be at the Disposal of, or subject or liable to the Control, Debts or Engagements of [husband] but only at her own sole and separate Dispose.

A nineteenth-century deed in which personal property is settled. From Charles Davidson, *Common Forms in Conveyancing* (London, 1846), 131:

> [Personal property is conveyed to trustees upon trust that they] shall pay the interest, dividends, and annual proceeds of the said trust monies, stocks, funds, and securities, during the joint lives of the said [husband] and [wife] to the said [wife] for her sole and separate use, independently and exclusively of the said [husband], and his debts, control, interference, and engagements, and so that her receipt alone shall be discharge for the same, and that she shall not have power to deprive herself of the benefit thereof by sale, mortgage, charge or otherwise in the way of anticipation.

The Trust for Raising Portions: An Example of the Form Usual

in Eighteenth-Century and Nineteenth-Century Settlements

From Gilbert Horsman, *Precedents in Conveyancing*, 2d ed. (London, 1757), 1:549–52:

> For and concerning the said Term of four hundred Years herein before limited to [named trustees] it is hereby declared and agreed, that the same is limited to them upon such Trusts, and to and for such Intents and Purposes . . . as are herein after mentioned, that is to say, That in Case there shall be one or more Child or Children of the body of the said Andrew Ashton on the Body of the said Joan Boot his intended Wife begotton (besides an eldest or only Son) then upon Trust that they shall . . . raise and levy such Sum and Sums of Money for the Portion and Portions of all and every such Child or Children (not being an eldest or only Son as aforesaid) as are herein after mentioned; that is to say, If but one such Child, the Sum of 15,000£ . . . for the Portion of such only Child; and if two or more such Children, then the Sum of 30,000£ to be shared and divided between or amongst them, in such Parts and Proportions as the said Andrew Ashton, by any Writing or Writings under his Hand and Seal . . . or by his last Will and Testament in Writing . . . shall direct or appoint . . . And in Default of such Direction and Appointment, then the said Sum of 30,000£ to be equally divided amongst them, Share and Share alike . . .
>
> And in case the said Andrew Ashton shall happen to die without Issue Male of his Body on the Body of the said Joan Boot his intended Wife to be begotten, or that the Issue Male between them begotten shall happen to die without Issue Male of his or their Body or Bodies, and that there be Issue one or more Daughter or Daughters of the Body of the said Andrew Ashton on the Body of the said Joan Boot begotten . . . then upon Trust that they . . . shall raise and levy . . . the Sum of 30,000£ for the Portion and Portions of all and every such Daughter and Daughters, the same to be paid in the Manner following: that is to say, If but one such Daughter, then the said whole Sum of 30,000£ to be paid to such only Daugher; and if two or more such Daughters, then the said Sum of 30,000£ to be paid to and to be equally divided amonst them, Share and Share alike . . .
>
> And so also, that in case all the said Daughters shall happen to die

before any of them shall attain the Age of seventeen Years or be married, then, the said Sum or Sums of Money appointed to be raised for their Portions as aforesaid, or so much thereof as shall not be then raised, shall not be raised, but shall cease for the Benefit of such Person or Persons to whom the next and Immediate Reversion or Remainder . . . shall belong.

Index